SELECTED SPEECHES
AND
WRITINGS
OF
THEODORE ROOSEVELT

INTRODUCED AND EDITED BY GORDON HUTNER

Gordon Hutner, editor, is a professor of English at the University of Illinois Urbana-Champaign. He founded in 1989 and is the editor of the journal *American Literary History*, and is considered "one of the most influential editors of his generation." He is the author of *What America Read: Taste, Class, and the Novel, 1920–1960*. He also edited *Immigrant Voices: Twenty-Four Narratives on Becoming an American* and *American Literature, American Culture*.

SELECTED SPEECHES
AND
WRITINGS
OF
THEODORE ROOSEVELT

Selected Speeches

and

Writings

of

Theodore Roosevelt

———————◆◆◆———————

Theodore Roosevelt

Edited and with an Introduction
by Gordon Hutner

VINTAGE BOOKS
A Division of Random House LLC
New York

A VINTAGE BOOKS ORIGINAL, JANUARY 2014

Copyright © 2013 by Gordon Hutner

All rights reserved. Published in the United States by Vintage Books, a division of Random House LLC, New York, and in Canada by Random House of Canada Limited, Toronto, Penguin Random House companies.

Vintage and colophon are registered trademarks of Random House LLC.

Library of Congress Cataloging-in-Publication Data
Roosevelt, Theodore, 1858–1919.
[Works. Selections 2014]
Selected speeches and writings of Theodore Roosevelt / Theodore Roosevelt ; edited and with an introduction by Gordon Hutner.
pages cm
Includes bibliographical references and index.
1. United States—Politics and government—1865–1933—Sources.
2. Presidents—United States—Biography.
3. Roosevelt, Theodore, 1858–1919. I. Hutner, Gordon. II. Title.
E660.R72 2014   973.91'1092—dc23   2013033547

Vintage Trade Paperback ISBN: 978-0-345-80611-6
eBook ISBN: 978-0-345-80612-3

Book design by Joy O'Meara Wispe

www.vintagebooks.com

Printed in the United States of America
10 9 8 7 6 5 4 3 2 1

Contents

Theodore Roosevelt:
The Man in the Arena as Man of Letters

The most prolific author among U.S. presidents, Theodore Roosevelt (1858–1919) wrote about a startling number of topics in nearly forty years, an energetic pace of publication that included more than forty books, numerous book reviews, hundreds of speeches, and thousands of letters. Other presidents such as Washington, Adams, Madison, and Monroe wrote eloquently, and Jefferson was a redoubtable precursor in pursuing so many various interests, from his influential political writings to the comprehensive vision of *Notes on the State of Virginia*. Roosevelt wrote a vigorous, often vivid prose, but he was never the accomplished stylist that Lincoln was. John F. Kennedy and Barack Obama published critically acclaimed, best-selling books before entering office, and several others, since Ulysses S. Grant set the precedent, have penned memoirs of their careers or political treatises, or both, after their retirement from public life, like Dwight Eisenhower, Richard Nixon, and Jimmy Carter, who also wrote a novel. Among autobiographies, Roosevelt's is second only to Bill Clinton's in the number of pages needed to tell their stories. But no other president sustained his career as a professional writer or continued to write as copiously as Roosevelt did, while also pursuing political office.

His brimming intellectual curiosity took him so many places—into the West, foreign countries, and the past—and writing became the ineluctable expression of those abounding passions, whether it concerned nature and travel, a biography, history, politics, society, or culture. Roosevelt also published several books that compiled many of his countless articles and speeches about domestic as well as international politics and policy. He deliberated about what values historians should strive for in their historiography and tried his hand at literary criticism too, including a review of one of the first histories of American literature. Dozens of other subjects, like college football or the purposes of a university in the West, came to his expansive notice. He regularly corresponded with many of the era's most accomplished scientists, thinkers, and novelists, including Owen Wister and Edith Wharton (whose First World War charity he supported). He invited to the White House cultural luminaries as disparate as Booker T. Washington and Henry James (whom he disdained and who despised Roosevelt on principle, but who found the president engaging in person). Jacob Riis, the author of *How the Other Half Lives*, was a friend and confidant who wrote a biography of him.

Although Roosevelt chose to be the kind of doer he celebrated as the "man in the arena" rather than a mere critic—as described in his 1910 lecture, "Citizenship in the Republic"—he never fully gave up his life in letters. Even if he often disparaged what he thought of as the genteel, even effeminate character of being a "liter'ry feller," he found gratification there, not to mention sustenance. His biographers agree that for all of Roosevelt's rambunctiousness and for all his commitment to the strenuous life, a significant part of him was most at home in his study, finding comfort in his lifelong habit of reading (a book a day!) and fulfillment in the act of writing (later dictating). However a matter of temperament this emotional and psychological reward may have been, it was also a matter of money, too, since under his watch his family lost much of its fortune, and he squandered away a good deal more in bad investments over the years, most notably a disastrous ranching venture in North Dakota. Roosevelt surely felt the urgency to write, insofar as his ebullient personality and searching mind enjoyed an unceasing appetite for expression, but he also needed to write for pay since his various city, state, and federal salaries did not suffice to keep his family in the style to which he had been born and to which he had no interest in becoming unaccustomed.

When Roosevelt was a young man and casting about for a career, his father let him have no illusions that, because he came from money, he could simply abjure the world of affairs and follow his early interests in natural philosophy and settle comfortably into a professorship. In the end, Roosevelt forswore academe since neither the laboratory nor the lecture hall were arenas as exciting as the outdoors, where he might collect specimens. During a college summer, he followed his avocation as an ornithologist and coauthored a well-thought-of chapbook (about birds) before he began a short, desultory stay at Columbia Law School. His dissatisfaction there led Roosevelt, newly married, to contemplate a career as a writer. He set himself the formidable task of completing a project he had begun as an undergraduate at Harvard—an authoritative history of the U.S. Navy during the War of 1812. That volume reads today as a meticulous account whose lively battle narratives are weighed down by crushing detail. Yet its research and conclusions were so exact and so influential at the time that it became part of the curriculum at the U.S. Naval Academy for decades. Later, the book helped to secure his position as assistant secretary to the Navy, which he used to estimable effect, improving the country's defenses and launching him into national prominence. The year before the publication of *The Naval War of 1812* Roosevelt was recruited by Republican pols to stand for election as a state assemblyman from New York City, a position that exhilarated him. During his time in the legislature, he at last seemed to have found his calling, although politics was understood as an inappropriately grimy career for a young man of his station and looked down upon as a profession by men of his class.

So deep and abiding was his fascination with the world of the arena that he would thereafter be only a part-time author. Yet an author he certainly remained. Through the 1880s, as he continued to serve in Albany and experienced political ups and downs, he published two books about his adventures as a western outdoorsman, *Hunting Trips of a Ranchman, Parts 1 & 2* (1885) and, three years later, *Ranch Life and the Hunting Trail*. Later in the decade, he published two biographies of American statesmen, one devoted to the Missouri senator Thomas Hart Benton, who played an integral role in defeating John C. Calhoun during the Nullification Crisis, and another the following year on Gouverneur Morris, the least known of American founding fathers. Whereas the hunting and ranch books are filled with exciting personal details and observations, with Roosevelt articulating his responses to the weather, the fauna and flora, and the colorful, outsized personalities he encountered on his trips to North Dakota and beyond, the political biographies did not offer much that was not already known. But they did disclose Roosevelt's vaunted powers of perception and appreciation. We see these political actors and historical figures in the light in which they may have most wished to be seen: as men of political affairs acting for the public good, in circumstances in which it was often neither expedient nor rewarding to do so. In between these well-told narratives, Roosevelt also published his first collection of policy writings, *Essays on Practical Politics* (1888), which brought together two subjects he had begun to know a great deal about and that elicited his characteristic brio: "Phases of Albany Legislation," which lays bare the intricacies and frustrations of making laws at the state level; and "Machine Politics of New York City," which reads like the work of a gentleman with a muckrake.

Roosevelt closed the 1880s with the first book of his magisterial six-volume history, *The Winning of the West* (1889), an extraordinarily researched endeavor that ultimately took him another five years to complete. The first volume covered the "Spread of the English-Speaking Peoples" (excerpted here) and the movement westward, culminating in the story of Daniel Boone and the opening up of Kentucky. Over the next few years, Roosevelt completed his sweeping archival research in subsequent volumes on the Indian wars as well as one on Louisiana and Aaron Burr. He also published more of his recollections and travel sketches of his hunting expeditions, including *The Wilderness Hunter* (1893) and *Some American Game* (1897), along with three books with a collaborator, George Bird Grinnell, *American Big Game* (1893), *Hunting in Many Lands* (1895), and *Trail and Campfire* (1897). Roosevelt also collaborated, with his dear friend Henry Cabot Lodge, on *Hero Tales of American History* (1895), comprising profiles of several famous American military men and statesmen, along with Lodge's homage to historian Francis Parkman and Roosevelt's tribute to flag-bearers in battle. Three other volumes from that decade suggest more of Roosevelt's diverse interests: a short history of his native city, *New York* (1891); a collection of essays about U.S. culture, *American Ideals* (1897); and a book that is part memoir and part history, which capitalized on his celebrated campaign in the Spanish-American War, *The Rough Riders* (1899). One wonders how Roosevelt also found the time to serve, first as a federal official investigating abuses of the patronage system, then later as a member of the New York City Police Commission, and Assistant Secretary of the U.S. Navy, all of which he pursued zealously. By 1900 Roosevelt would become his party's nominee for vice president, but since that campaign was in the autumn, he had time, during his very brief stint as governor of New York, to publish another biography, *Oliver Cromwell*, along with another collection of his essays dedicated to his vision of right living and cultural well-being, *The Strenuous Life*.

One might suppose that when Roosevelt became president upon the death of William McKinley in September 1901, he would put aside his writing projects, and he largely did, though he still found the opportunity to express his thoughts on nonpolitical subjects, in such books as *The Deer Family* (1902), with T. S. Van Dyke, D. G. Elliot, and A. J. Stone; followed by *Outdoor Pastimes of an American Hunter* (1905); and *Good Hunting* (1907). After the election of 1904, he also published his *Addresses and Messages* (1905) from his first term, which included thirty-nine lectures, many drawn from an exhausting lecture tour of the West in 1903, which took Roosevelt from Chicago to the Pacific. The other two-thirds of the collection are made up of two hundred pages of his presidential letters and even more than that in messages to Congress, cabinet officials, and various members of his administration.

Retirement from public office in 1909 increased Roosevelt's desire to travel as well as his determination to remain a man of the arena. Indeed, he was only fifty years old. Before he embarked for Africa, he did collect some editorials he had written for an opinion magazine for which he served as associate editor, *The Outlook*. These included position papers on domestic and foreign policy, along with a meditation on the Russian novelist and social thinker Leo Tolstoy. The African safari resulted in a compendious study of the animals and vegetation he encountered, *African Game Trails* (1910), and a volume titled *African and European Addresses* (1910), which collected his various opinions about international politics (including his long-deferred Nobel Prize speech) and his impressions of the places he had visited. That same year, Roosevelt also published a collection of social writing, *American Problems*, and another comprised of political analyses and cultural reflections, *The New Nationalism*—articles that summarized his new Progressive faith. And, in 1910, he oversaw the publication of another collection, an ambitious eight-volume project, *Presidential Addresses and State Papers*. In 1912, Roosevelt added two more pamphlets on society, *The Conservation of Womanhood and Childhood* and *Realizable Ideals*, a series of lectures for the Pacific Theological Seminary on the place of religion in American politics and society, which Roosevelt thought of as an exercise in "applied ethics."

Roosevelt's retirement was—like a lot of vibrant individuals'—ungratifyingly short. He may well have come to regret his bold announcement, upon being elected to a second term, that he would not seek a third, even though he easily could have, since no limit, beyond Washington's forceful precedent, actually existed. So when the possibility emerged that Roosevelt might contend for the Republican nomination in 1912, he threw his hat in the ring (and coined the phrase). After the party bosses— outrageously, he held—had denied him his fair chance at the Republican nominating convention (described in a speech collected here), Roosevelt became a viable third-party candidate as the Progressive, or "Bull Moose," nominee. His final campaign caused only a momentary lapse in his writing career: over the following six years, he published no fewer than twelve books.

Before the advent of the Great War in 1914, Roosevelt busied himself first with his autobiography, a book short on revelation or dramatic personal narrative, though long on details about whom he met and when. According to the conventions of autobiography at the time, such memoirs were supposed to be reserved, though Roosevelt's seems reticent to a serious fault. He also collected a variety of cultural essays and reviews, using an address he made to the American Historical Association as the title essay, "History as Literature," but also as the impetus for his thoughts about the place of history and culture in the Republic and how history should be written. He includes such articles as his study of history and "biological analogies"—an essay rather too beholden to pseudoscientific application of premises to nonscientific questions—along with literary pieces, such as his reading of ancient Irish sagas, his meditation on Dante's willingness to write about the most concrete of human circumstances, even the squalid life encountered in the Bowery were he a modern poet, and a review of a recent modern art exhibit in which Roosevelt fulminates against Cubists, Futurists, and "Near Impressionists," among other movements he saw as the "lunatic fringe" (again, his own coinage).

Roosevelt assembled several papers on a general theme of policy, *Progressive Principles* (1913), before he embarked for an adventure in Brazil. On that Amazon journey, he suffered serious illness and almost lost his life, even as he also explored a river, which was renamed in his honor, an undertaking described in *Through the Brazilian Wilderness* (1914). He followed up this book that same year with more foreign travel notes, *African Game Animals*, coauthored with Edmund Heller. Later came *A Book-Lover's Holidays in the Open* (1916), containing articles on hunting cougars at the Grand Canyon, hiking in the bird reserves near the mouth of the Mississippi, observing a Hopi snake dance, stalking lions and elephants in

Africa, and attending a South American rodeo (included in this volume). Not to mention compiling a list of recommended reading for leisure hours during his expeditions, including painstaking distinctions within the oeuvres of favorite novelists, poets, and philosophers (*Macbeth* and *Othello*, yes; *Lear* and *Hamlet*, no.)

What preoccupied Roosevelt during this decade, however, was the war in Europe, as he was alarmed by the country's lack of "preparedness," the cause he championed while Navy assistant secretary. In a series of books collecting speeches and articles—*America and the World War* (1915), *Fear God and Take Your Own Part* (1916), *The Foes of Our Own Household* (1917), *Social Justice and Popular Rule* (1917), and *National Strength and International Duty* (1917), a pamphlet bringing together two articles—Roosevelt excoriated as a failure of leadership Woodrow Wilson's reticence concerning German barbarism, especially in "The Belgian Tragedy." These analyses were often combined with more general attacks on the failure of American society to live up to what Roosevelt saw as its best principles and how the nation might recover its standing, prior to the United States' belated entrance into the hostilities. In *The Great Adventure* (1918) Roosevelt ponders American values and the country's international responsibilities, a book he completed just two months before his death. His final work, published posthumously, was a collection, *Theodore Roosevelt's Letters to His Children* (1919), a book that traces his attentions to them in their youth ("A Presidential Rescue of a Kitten") and as they grew over twenty years. In fact, Roosevelt's most voluminous form of writing was his prodigious correspondence more than 100,000 letters.

This collection of Theodore Roosevelt's writings begins with the conviction that previous anthologies have done justice only to a limited sample of his work and are mainly drawn from the books by which he is best known. His works are various enough, however, that it is too limiting to consider merely one or two or even three dimensions of his career as an author—on the environment or race or politics. Here, readers can now find selections that have proven indispensable to a just appreciation of his writing career, even as they will also find examples of his prose that they might not have expected to encounter. No one has studied Roosevelt the writer with more profit than biographer Edmund Morris, who concedes that a great deal of what Roosevelt wrote would not be remembered had he not become president, so it should not be surprising that not all of Roosevelt's prose rewards today's readers as richly as it might have a century ago. To meet the challenge of representing the variety to be found in the twenty-four collected volumes of his work, this collection strives to offer a comprehensive range of Roosevelt's subject matter and of his writing style, as well as his speeches. Conceived and written for oral delivery, the latter readily disclose the author's inimitably energetic power of expression. Something of Roosevelt's charm is transacted through so much of his prose. Indeed, he was legendary in his power of personal appeal, and his charisma seemed to define modern American life. Although a line of political observers, both off and on the record, remarked on how dangerous Roosevelt's implacable ambition and his seemingly unconscious translation of his own purposes with the common good was, no one in American politics has yet rivaled the youngest U.S. president's exuberance. These qualities appear in various passages in his books about hunting, which are less about killing animals than they are about stalking them and his attentiveness to their habits. It is also apparent in the alert curiosity of his African and South American travel writing, and even in the passionate precision of Roosevelt's ornithological investigations. That vivifying power of immediate engagement also spills over again and again into the places where we do expect to find it: animating his understanding of politics, conservation, the rights of African Americans, and war. His boundless passion risks overflowing in essay after essay hammering home the importance of "preparedness," the era's buzzword for militarization. That excitability could also lead Roosevelt to exaggerate the villainy of his foes, such as his contempt for Woodrow Wilson's timidity or the cowardice of slackers, even "conscientious objectors."

In Roosevelt's later works especially, readers will detect in his style a contradictory tendency to erupt with the intensity of a conflagration and then balance it with a judicious, humane, calm tone. And sometimes Roosevelt's appeal will be too remote for us to appreciate, unless we remember that he was essentially a late-nineteenth-century mind supple and sharp enough to take the country into the first decade of a new century, but perhaps too bound to his origins to face the complexities to come. In many ways, it is perhaps fitting that he died when he did, just seven weeks after the Armistice and just as he finished a magazine piece expressing doubts about the League of Nations (included here).

Moreover, Roosevelt's audience was different from readers today, not simply because of the vast disparity in a writer's conventions for focusing attention, but also because the cultural formation of that audience has changed. Roosevelt wrote before the melting pot performed its great work of assimilating millions of southern and eastern Europeans; he could count, with assurance, even smugness, on a fairly homogenous readership, one that subscribed readily to his sense of Americans and their aspirations. So often today castigated as a racist thinker, he saw himself as enlightened about racial and ethnic differences, though he gave preference to people of his own milieu. He is criticized today for his unabashed interventionism, and many contemporaneous detractors also reproved him as an imperialist. At the same time, Roosevelt's aggressive hypermasculinity was not always regarded as a puerile limitation of his worldview. Reviewers, in praise as much as in criticism, likened his rhetorical posture to a pugilist's. Roosevelt never imagined that he was compensating for having been a weakling who had battled asthma as a child. While opponents impugned his dauntless, some would say heedless, ego, his sense of manly virtues was very much an expression of various middlebrow social philosophies of his era, and indeed he seemed to a great many Americans to exemplify the turn-of-the-century celebration of the élan vital.

Roosevelt could expect a fair response to his positions and a willing reception of his narratives, adventures, and accounts. His reviewers were confident that the general reader (as that category was then being invented) could appreciate his books with much the same grasp as an expert might. Though some of his writing was geared toward an audience seeking escapist pleasures, reviewers frequently cited how splendidly he mixed the appeal of entertainment with the reward of edification. And Roosevelt's various publishers were glad to publish his writing because his books sold reliably well.

To give Roosevelt, the writer, a twenty-first-century hearing means drawing contemporary attention to a relatively forgotten element of his indelible, manifold impact on U.S. history and society: namely, his incisive prose and its dazzling breadth. We can see that insight and range in choices not usually anthologized, such as his reflections on the character of "The American Boy"; a foray into literary criticism, "Nationalism in Literature and Art"; his deliberations over the new professionalism in sports; his tract on class division in the United States, "National Unity versus Class Cleavage"; his essay on the status of returning African American veterans, "The American Negro and the War"; his cautions about "The Control of Corporations" and their place in American political life; and the conviction evinced in the speech he delivered immediately after having been shot during the 1912 presidential campaign, "The Leader and the Cause." Moreover, we can also still enjoy Roosevelt in some of his best-known writing, including his story of hunting grizzly bears; his report of the Battle of San Juan Hill; his description of "The Strenuous Life"; his summary of "The Colonial Policy of the United States"; his vision of conservation in "Natural Resources—Their Wise Use or Their Waste"; and his testimony of political conversion, "How I Became a Progressive." From a writer so productive, these pages confirm that among Theodore Roosevelt's great gifts to his country was the legacy of a writing career unsurpassed in American history by other statesmen and whose talents should lead us to marvel at the variety, verve, and depth of his commitments.

Culture
and
Society

"The American Boy" (1900)

Theodore Roosevelt's meditation on the qualities of the American boy typifies many of his social analyses. In this essay, first published in 1900 in *St. Nicholas*, a young people's magazine, and later appearing in his collection *The Strenuous Life*, Roosevelt spells out a creed of masculine energy and discipline as the key features of what will help a boy to grow up to be the "kind of American man of whom America can be proud." Here Roosevelt's social views take the somewhat conventional perspective that a boy's vigor, developed in his commitments to both work and play, will stand him in good stead on the road to manhood. More so than in times past do American boys have opportunities to express this commitment through athletics, though Roosevelt, as we will see elsewhere, cautions boys away from preoccupations with games in the belief that all fixations are ultimately unhealthy. Roosevelt's American boy works diligently at his studies, not only for the sake of what he will learn, but also for the "effect upon his character"—of submitting to a discipline. The American men who develop out of such boys are the readily recognizable Rooseveltian figures, active and vigorous, who reject bullying and abhor any form of "cruelty or brutality."

The American Boy

Of course, what we have a right to expect of the American boy is that he shall turn out to be a good American man. Now, the chances are strong that he won't be much of a man unless he is a good deal of a boy. He must not be a coward or a weakling, a bully, a shirk, or a prig. He must work hard and play hard. He must be clean-minded and clean-lived, and able to hold his own under all circumstances and against all comers. It is only on these conditions that he will grow into the kind of American man of whom America can be really proud.

There are always in life countless tendencies for good and for evil, and each succeeding generation sees some of these tendencies strengthened and some weakened; nor is it by any means always, alas! that the tendencies for evil are weakened and those for good strengthened. But during the last few decades there certainly have been some notable changes for good in boy life. The great growth in the love of athletic sports, for instance, while fraught with danger if it becomes one-sided and unhealthy, has beyond all question had an excellent effect in in-reared manliness. Forty or fifty years ago the writer on American morals was sure to deplore the effeminacy and luxury of young Americans who were born of rich parents. The boy who was well-off then, especially in the big Eastern cities, lived too luxuriously, took to billiards as his chief innocent recreation, and felt small shame in his inability to take part in rough pastimes and field sports. Nowadays, whatever other faults the son of rich parents may tend to develop, he is at least forced by the opinion of all his associates of his own age to bear himself well in manly exercises and to develop his body—and therefore, to a certain extent, his character—in the rough sports which call for pluck, endurance, and physical address.

Of course, boys who live under such fortunate conditions that they have to do either a good deal of outdoor work or a good deal of what might be called natural outdoor play, do not need this athletic development. In the Civil War the soldiers who came from the prairie and the backwoods and the rugged farms where stumps still dotted the clearings, and who had learned to ride in their infancy, to shoot as soon as they could handle a rifle, and to camp out whenever they got the chance, were better fitted for military work than any set of mere school or college athletes could possibly be. Moreover, to mis-estimate athletics is equally bad whether their importance is magnified or minimized. The Greeks were famous athletes, and as long as their athletic training had a normal place in their lives, it was a good thing. But it was a very bad thing when they kept up their athletic games while letting the stern qualities of soldiership and statesmanship sink into disuse. Some of the boys who read this paper will certainly sometime read the famous letters of the younger Pliny, a Roman who wrote, with what seems to us a curiously modern touch, in the first century of the present era. His correspondence with the Emperor Trajan is particularly interesting; and not the least noteworthy thing in it is the tone of contempt with which he speaks of the Greek athletic sports, treating them as the diversions of an unwarlike people which it was safe to encourage in order to keep the Greeks from turning into anything formidable. So at one time the Persian kings had to forbid polo, because soldiers neglected their proper duties for the fascinations of the game. Today, some good critics have asserted that the reverses suffered by the British at the hands of the Boers in South Africa are in part due to the fact that the English officers and soldiers have carried to an unhealthy extreme the sports and pastimes which would be healthy if indulged in with moderation, and have neglected to learn as they should the business of their profession. A soldier needs to know how to shoot and take cover and shift for himself—not to box or play football. There is, of course, always the risk of thus mistaking means for ends. English fox-hunting is a first-class sport; but one of the most absurd things in real life is to note the bated breath with which certain excellent Englishmen, otherwise of quite healthy minds, speak of this admirable but not over-important pastime. They tend to make it almost as much of a fetish as, in the last century, the French and German nobles made the chase of the stag, when they carried hunting and game-preserving to a point which was ruinous to the national life. Fox-hunting is very good as a pastime, but it is about as poor a business as can be followed by any man of intelligence. Certain writers about it are fond of quoting the anecdote of a fox-hunter who, in the days of the English Civil War, was discovered pursuing his favorite sport just before a great battle between the Cavaliers and the Puritans, and right between their lines as they came together. These writers apparently consider it a merit in this man that when his country was in a death-grapple, instead of taking arms and hurrying to the defense of the cause he believed right, he should placidly have gone about his usual sports. Of course, in reality the chief serious use of fox-hunting is to encourage manliness and vigor, and keep a man so that in time of need he can show himself fit to take part in work or strife for his native land. When a man so far confuses ends and means as to think that fox-hunting, or polo, or football, or whatever else the sport may be, is to be itself taken as the end, instead of as the mere means of preparation to do work that counts when the time arises, when the occasion calls—why, that man had better abandon sport altogether.

No boy can afford to neglect his work, and with a boy, work as a rule means study. Of course, there are occasionally brilliant successes in life where the man has been worthless as a student when a boy. To take these exceptions as examples would be as unsafe as it would be to advocate blindness because some blind men have won undying honor by triumphing over their physical infirmity and accomplishing great results in the world. I am no advocate of senseless and excessive cramming in studies, but a boy should work, and should work hard, at his lessons—in the first place, for the sake of what he will learn, and in the next place, for the sake of the effect upon his own character of resolutely settling down to learn it. Shiftlessness, slackness, indifference in studying, are almost certain to mean inability to get on in other walks of life. Of course, as a boy grows older it is a good thing if he can shape his studies in the direction toward which he has a natural bent; but whether he can do this or not, he must put his whole heart into them. I do not believe in mischief-doing in school hours, or in the kind of animal spirits that results in making bad scholars; and I believe that those boys who take part in rough, hard play outside of school will not find any need for horse-play in school. While they study they should study just as hard as they play football in a match game. It is wise to obey the homely old adage, "Work while you work; play while you play."

A boy needs both physical and moral courage. Neither can take the place of the other. When boys become men they will find out that there are some soldiers very brave in the field who have proved timid and worthless as politicians, and some politicians who show an entire readiness to take chances and assume responsibilities in civil affairs, but who lack the fighting edge when opposed to physical danger. In each case, with soldiers and politicians alike, there is but half a virtue. The possession of the courage of the soldier does not excuse the lack of courage in the statesman, and even less does the possession of the courage of the statesman excuse shrinking on the field of battle. Now, this is all just as true of boys. A coward who will take a blow without returning it is a contemptible creature; but, after all, he is hardly as contemptible as the boy who dares not stand up for what he deems right against the sneers of his companions who are themselves wrong. Ridicule is one of the favorite weapons of wickedness, and it is sometimes incomprehensible how good and brave boys will be influenced for evil by the jeers of associates who have no one quality that calls for respect, but who affect to laugh at the very traits which ought to be peculiarly the cause for pride.

There is no need to be a prig. There is no need for a boy to preach about his own good conduct and virtue. If he does he will make himself offensive and ridiculous. But there is urgent need that he should practise decency; that he should be clean and straight, honest and truthful, gentle and tender, as well as brave. If he can once get to a proper understanding of things, he will have a far more hearty contempt for the boy who has begun a course of feeble dissipation, or who is untruthful, or mean, or dishonest, or cruel, than this boy and his fellows can possibly, in return, feel for him. The very fact that the boy should be manly and able to hold his own, that he should be ashamed to submit to bullying without instant retaliation, should, in return, make him abhor any form of bullying, cruelty, or brutality.

There are two delightful books, Thomas Hughes's "Tom Brown at Rugby," and Aldrich's "Story of a Bad Boy," which I hope every boy still reads; and I think American boys will always feel more in sympathy with Aldrich's story, because there is in it none of the fagging, and the bullying which goes with fagging, the account of which, and the acceptance of which, always puzzle an American admirer of Tom Brown.

There is the same contrast between two stories of Kipling's. One, called "Captains Courageous," describes in the liveliest way just what a boy should be and do. The hero is painted in the beginning as the spoiled, overindulged child of wealthy parents, of a type which we do sometimes unfortunately see, and than which there exist few things more objectionable on the face of the broad earth. This boy is afterward thrown on his own resources, amid wholesome surroundings, and is forced to work hard among boys and men who are real boys and real men doing real work. The effect is invaluable. On the other hand, if one wishes to find types of boys to be avoided with utter dislike, one will find them in another story by Kipling, called "Stalky & Co.," a story which ought never to have been written, for there is hardly a single form of meanness which it does not seem to extol, or of school mismanagement which it does not seem to applaud. Bullies do not make brave men; and boys or men of foul life cannot become good citizens, good Americans, until they change; and even after the change scars will be left on their souls.

The boy can best become a good man by being a good boy—not a goody-goody boy, but just a plain good boy. I do not mean that he must love only the negative virtues; I mean he must love the positive virtues also. "Good," in the largest sense, should include whatever is fine, straightforward, clean, brave, and manly. The best boys I know—the best men I know—are good at their studies or their business, fearless and stalwart, hated and feared by all that is wicked and depraved, incapable of submitting to wrong-doing, and equally incapable of being aught but tender to the weak and helpless. A healthy-minded boy should feel hearty contempt for the coward, and even more hearty indignation for the boy who bullies girls or small boys, or tortures animals. One prime reason for abhorring cowards is because every good boy should have it in him to thrash the objectionable boy as the need arises.

Of course, the effect that a thoroughly manly, thoroughly straight and upright boy can have upon the companions of his own age, and upon those who are younger, is incalculable. If he is not thoroughly manly, then they will not respect him, and his good qualities will count for but little; while, of course, if he is mean, cruel, or wicked, then his physical strength and force of mind merely make him so much the more objectionable a member of society. He cannot do good work if he is not strong, and does not try with his whole heart and soul to count in any contest; and his strength will be a curse to himself and to everyone else if he does not have thorough command over himself and over his own evil passions, and if he does not use his strength on the side of decency, justice, and fair dealing.

In short, in life, as in a football game, the principle to follow is:

Hit the line hard; don't foul and don't shirk, but hit the line hard!

"The Strenuous Life" (1899)

This signature essay, first published in a collection by the same title, is sure to upset the assumptions of those who regard Roosevelt as an implacable imperialist and a warmongering racist. In this address, delivered to an audience of prominent Illinois men on Appomattox Day, the thirty-fourth anniversary of the end of the Civil War, Roosevelt emphasizes all of the qualities that render him objectionable to contemporary taste. His speech begins with his characteristic gesture of enlisting his audience in a shared enterprise, in this case of valuing exertion over "ignoble ease." While Roosevelt pauses to praise nonremunerative work in science, letters, arts, and historical research—much like his own leisure activities—he primarily wishes to enjoin his audience into the common valuation of strenuousness and striving. Not only is this the path to individual success, but is it also the nation's way forward. The United States must especially strive in foreign affairs, with less concern to colonize foreign lands, such as Puerto Rico, Cuba, and the Philippines, and more to make sure that these territories are administered safely along the lines of the highest American standards of probity and fairness, an extrapolation of Roosevelt's "square deal." Familiar as this doctrine would become during his presidency, this is an earlier iteration of what Roosevelt saw as its moral underpinning. Adducing the great achievements of the Navy Department (largely the result of his unacknowledged behind-the-scenes exertions), Roosevelt advances the cause of building up the Army and its woeful lack of preparedness, a theme to which he will return again and again in the decade to come during the lead-up to the Great War. For now, however, it is enough to align the importance of the virtue of strenuousness with the new century to come, the note of destiny on which he closes.

The Strenuous Life

In speaking to you, men of the greatest city of the West, men of the State which gave to the country Lincoln and Grant, men who preeminently and distinctly embody all that is most American in the American character, I wish to preach, not the doctrine of ignoble ease, but the doctrine of the strenuous life, the life of toil and effort, of labor and strife; to preach that highest form of success which comes, not to the man who desires mere easy peace, but to the man who does not shrink from danger, from hardship, or from bitter toil, and who out of these wins the splendid ultimate triumph.

A life of slothful ease, a life of that peace which springs merely from lack either of desire or of power to strive after great things, is as little worthy of a nation as of an individual. I ask only that what every self-respecting American demands from himself and from his sons shall be demanded of the American nation as a whole. Who among you would teach your boys that ease, that peace, is to be the first consideration in their eyes—to be the ultimate goal after which they strive? You men of Chicago have made this city great, you men of Illinois have done your share, and more than your share, in making America great, because you neither preach nor practice such a doctrine. You work yourselves, and you bring up your sons to work. If you are rich and are worth your salt, you will teach your sons that though they may have leisure, it is not to be spent in idleness; for wisely used leisure merely means that those who possess it, being free from the necessity of working for their livelihood, are all the more bound to carry on some kind of non-remunerative work in science, in letters, in art, in exploration, in historical research—work of the type we most need in this country, the successful carrying out of which reflects most honor upon the nation. We do not admire the man of timid peace. We admire the man who embodies victorious effort; the man who never wrongs his neighbor, who is prompt to help a friend, but who has those virile qualities necessary to win in the stern strife of actual life. It is hard to fail, but it is worse never to have tried to succeed. In this life we get nothing save by effort. Freedom from effort in the present merely means that there has been stored up effort in the past. A man can be freed from the necessity of work only by the fact that he or his fathers before him have worked to good purpose. If the freedom thus purchased is used aright, and the man still does actual work, though of a different kind, whether as a writer or a general, whether in the field of politics or in the field of exploration and adventure, he shows he deserves his good fortune. But if he treats this period of freedom from the need of actual labor as a period, not of preparation, but of mere enjoyment, even though perhaps not of vicious enjoyment, he shows that he is simply a cumberer of the earth's surface, and he surely unfits himself to hold his own with his fellows if the need to do so should again arise. A mere life of ease is not in the end a very satisfactory life, and above all, it is a life which ultimately unfits those who follow it for serious work in the world.

In the last analysis a healthy state can exist only when the men and women who make it up lead clean, vigorous, healthy lives; when the children are so trained that they shall endeavor, not to shirk difficulties, but to overcome them; not to seek ease, but to know how to wrest triumph from toil and risk. The man must be glad to do a man's work, to dare and endure and to labor; to keep himself, and to keep those dependent upon him. The woman must be the housewife, the helpmeet of the homemaker, the wise and fearless mother of many healthy children. In one of Daudet's powerful and melancholy books he speaks of "the fear of maternity, the haunting terror of the young wife of the present day." When such words can be truthfully written of a nation, that nation is rotten to the heart's core. When men fear work or fear righteous war, when women fear motherhood, they tremble on the brink of doom; and well it is that they should vanish from the earth, where they are fit subjects for the scorn of all men and women who are themselves strong and brave and high-minded.

As it is with the individual, so it is with the nation. It is a base untruth to say that happy is the nation that has no history. Thrice happy is the nation that has a glorious history. Far better it is to dare mighty things, to win glorious triumphs, even though checkered by failure, than to take rank with those poor spirits who neither enjoy much nor suffer much, because they live in the gray twilight that knows not victory nor defeat. If in 1861 the men who loved the Union had believed that peace was the end of all things, and war and strife the worst of all things, and had acted up to their belief, we would have saved hundreds of thousands of lives, we would have saved hundreds of millions of dollars. Moreover, besides saving all the blood and treasure we then lavished, we would have prevented the heartbreak of many women, the dissolution of many homes, and we would have spared the country those months of gloom and shame when it seemed as if our armies marched only to defeat. We could have avoided all this suffering simply by shrinking from strife. And if we had thus avoided it, we would have shown that we were weaklings, and that we were unfit to stand among the great nations of the earth. Thank God for the iron in the blood of our fathers, the men who upheld the wisdom of Lincoln, and bore sword or rifle in the armies of Grant! Let us, the children of the men who proved themselves equal to the mighty days, let us, the children of the men who carried the great Civil War to a triumphant conclusion, praise the God of our fathers that the ignoble counsels of peace were rejected; that the suffering and loss, the blackness of sorrow and despair, were unflinchingly faced, and the years of strife endured; for in the end the slave was freed, the Union restored, and the mighty American republic placed once more as a helmeted queen among nations.

We of this generation do not have to face a task such as that our fathers faced, but we have our tasks, and woe to us if we fail to perform them! We cannot, if we would, play the part of China, and be content to rot by inches in ignoble ease within our borders, taking no interest in what goes on beyond them, sunk in a scrambling commercialism; heedless of the higher life, the life of aspiration, of toil and risk, busying ourselves only with the wants of our bodies for the day, until suddenly we should find, beyond a shadow of question, what China has already found, that in this world the nation that has trained itself to a career of unwarlike and isolated ease is bound, in the end, to go down before other nations which have not lost the manly and adventurous qualities. If we are to be a really great people, we must strive in good faith to play a great part in the world. We cannot avoid meeting great issues. All that we can determine for ourselves is whether we shall meet them well or ill. In 1898 we could not help being brought face to face with the problem of war with Spain.

All we could decide was whether we should shrink like cowards from the contest, or enter into it as beseemed a brave and high-spirited people; and, once in, whether failure or success should crown our banners. So it is now. We cannot avoid the responsibilities that confront us in Hawaii, Cuba, Porto Rico, and the Philippines. All we can decide is whether we shall meet them in a way that will redound to the national credit, or whether we shall make of our dealings with these new problems a dark and shameful page in our history. To refuse to deal with them at all merely amounts to dealing with them badly. We have a given problem to solve. If we undertake the solution, there is, of course, always danger that we may not solve it aright; but to refuse to undertake the solution simply renders it certain that we cannot possibly solve it aright. The timid man, the lazy man, the man who distrusts his country, the over-civilized man, who has lost the great fighting, masterful virtues, the ignorant man, and the man of dull mind, whose soul is incapable of feeling the mighty lift that thrills "stern men with empires in their brains"—all these, of course, shrink from seeing the nation undertake its new duties; shrink from seeing us build a navy and an army adequate to our needs; shrink from seeing us do our share of the world's work, by bringing order out of chaos in the great, fair tropic islands from which the valor of our soldiers and sailors has driven the Spanish flag. These are the men who fear the strenuous life, who fear the only national life which is really worth leading. They believe in that cloistered life which saps the hardy virtues in a nation, as it saps them in the individual; or else they are wedded to that base spirit of gain and greed which recognizes in commercialism the be-all and end-all of national life, instead of realizing that, though an indispensable element, it is, after all, but one of the many elements that go to make up true national greatness. No country can long endure if its foundations are not laid deep in the material prosperity which comes from thrift, from business energy and enterprise, from hard, unsparing effort in the fields of industrial activity; but neither was any nation ever yet truly great if it relied upon material prosperity alone. All honor must be paid to the architects of our material prosperity, to the great captains of industry who have built our factories and our railroads, to the strong men who toil for wealth with brain or hand; for great is the debt of the nation to these and their kind. But our debt is yet greater to the men whose highest type is to be found in a statesman like Lincoln, a soldier like Grant. They showed by their lives that they recognized the law of work, the law of strife; they toiled to win a competence for themselves and those dependent upon them; but they recognized that there were yet other and even loftier duties—duties to the nation and duties to the race.

We cannot sit huddled within our own borders and avow ourselves merely an assemblage of well-to-do hucksters who care nothing for what happens beyond. Such a policy would defeat even its own end; for as the nations grow to have ever wider and wider interests, and are brought into closer and closer contact, if we are to hold our own in the struggle for naval and commercial supremacy, we must build up our power without our own borders. We must build the isthmian canal, and we must grasp the points of vantage which will enable us to have our say in deciding the destiny of the oceans of the East and the West.

So much for the commercial side. From the standpoint of international honor the argument is even stronger. The guns that thundered off Manila and Santiago left us echoes of glory, but they also left us a legacy of duty. If we drove out a medieval tyranny only to make room for savage anarchy, we had better not have begun the task at all. It is worse than idle to say that we have no duty to perform, and can leave to their fates the islands we have conquered. Such a course would be the course of infamy. It would be followed at once by utter chaos in the wretched islands themselves. Some stronger, manlier power would have to step in and do the work, and we would have shown ourselves weaklings, unable to carry to successful completion the labors that great and high-spirited nations are eager to undertake.

The work must be done; we cannot escape our responsibility; and if we are worth our salt, we shall be glad of the chance to do the work— glad of the chance to show ourselves equal to one of the great tasks set modern civilization. But let us not deceive ourselves as to the importance of the task. Let us not be misled by vainglory into underestimating the strain it will put on our powers. Above all, let us, as we value our own self-respect, face the responsibilities with proper seriousness, courage, and high resolve. We must demand the highest order of integrity and ability in our public men who are to grapple with these new problems. We must hold to a rigid accountability those public servants who show unfaithfulness to the interests of the nation or inability to rise to the high level of the new demands upon our strength and our resources.

Of course we must remember not to judge any public servant by any one act, and especially should we beware of attacking the men who are merely the occasions and not the causes of disaster. Let me illustrate what I mean by the army and the navy. If twenty years ago we had gone to war, we should have found the navy as absolutely unprepared as the army. At that time our ships could not have encountered with success the fleets of Spain any more than nowadays we can put untrained soldiers, no matter how brave, who are armed with archaic black-powder weapons, against well-drilled regulars armed with the highest type of modern repeating rifle. But in the early eighties the attention of the nation became directed to our naval needs. Congress most wisely made a series of appropriations to build up a new navy, and under a succession of able and patriotic secretaries, of both political parties, the navy was gradually built up, until its material became equal to its splendid personnel, with the result that in the summer of 1898 it leaped to its proper place as one of the most brilliant and formidable fighting navies in the entire world. We rightly pay all honor to the men controlling the navy at the time it won these great deeds, honor to Secretary Long and Admiral Dewey, to the captains who handled the ships in action, to the daring lieutenants who braved death in the smaller craft, and to the heads of bureaus at Washington who saw that the ships were so commanded, so armed, so equipped, so well engined, as to insure the best results. But let us also keep ever in mind that all of this would not have availed if it had not been for the wisdom of the men who during the preceding fifteen years had built up the navy. Keep in mind the secretaries of the navy during those years; keep in mind the senators and congressmen who by their votes gave the money necessary to build and to armor the ships, to construct the great guns, and to train the crews; remember also those who actually did build the ships, the armor, and the guns; and remember the admirals and captains who handled battle-ship, cruiser, and torpedo-boat on the high seas, alone and in squadrons, developing the seamanship, the gunnery, and the power of acting together, which their successors utilized so gloriously at Manila and off Santiago. And, gentlemen, remember the converse, too. Remember that justice has two sides. Be just to those who built up the navy, and, for the sake of the future of the country, keep in mind those who opposed its building up. Read the "Congressional Record." Find out the senators and congressmen who opposed the grants for building the new ships; who opposed the purchase of armor, without which the ships were worthless; who opposed any adequate maintenance for the Navy Department, and strove to cut down the number of men necessary to man our fleets. The men who did these things were one and all working to bring disaster on the country. They have no share in the glory of Manila, in the honor of Santiago. They have no cause to feel proud of the valor of our sea-captains, of the renown of our flag. Their motives may or may not have been good, but their acts were heavily fraught with evil. They did ill for the national honor, and we won in spite of their sinister opposition.

Now, apply all this to our public men of today. Our army has never been built up as it should be built up. I shall not discuss with an audience like this the puerile suggestion that a nation of seventy millions of free-men is in danger of losing its liberties from the existence of an army of one hundred thousand men, three fourths of whom will be employed in certain foreign islands, in certain coast fortresses, and on Indian reserva-tions. No man of good sense and stout heart can take such a proposition seriously. If we are such weaklings as the proposition implies, then we are unworthy of freedom in any event. To no body of men in the United States is the country so much indebted as to the splendid officers and enlisted men of the regular army and navy. There is no body from which the country has less to fear, and none of which it should be prouder, none which it should be more anxious to upbuild.

Our army needs complete reorganization—not merely enlarging—and the reorganization can only come as the result of legislation. A proper general staff should be established, and the positions of ordnance, com-missary, and quartermaster officers should be filled by detail from the line. Above all, the army must be given the chance to exercise in large bodies. Never again should we see, as we saw in the Spanish war, major-generals in command of divisions who had never before commanded three com-panies together in the field. Yet, incredible to relate, Congress has shown a queer inability to learn some of the lessons of the war. There were large bodies of men in both branches who opposed the declaration of war, who opposed the ratification of peace, who opposed the upbuilding of the army, and who even opposed the purchase of armor at a reasonable price for the battle-ships and cruisers, thereby putting an absolute stop to the building of any new fighting-ships for the navy. If, during the years to come, any disaster should befall our arms, afloat or ashore, and thereby any shame come to the United States, remember that the blame will lie upon the men whose names appear upon the roll-calls of Congress on the wrong side of these great questions. On them will lie the burden of any loss of our soldiers and sailors, of any dishonor to the flag; and upon you and the people of this country will lie the blame if you do not repudiate, in no unmistakable way, what these men have done. The blame will not rest upon the untrained commander of untried troops, upon the civil officers of a department the organization of which has been left utterly inadequate, or upon the admiral with an insufficient number of ships; but upon the public men who have so lamentably failed in forethought as to refuse to remedy these evils long in advance, and upon the nation that stands behind those public men.

So, at the present hour, no small share of the responsibility for the blood shed in the Philippines, the blood of our brothers, and the blood of their wild and ignorant foes, lies at the thresholds of those who so long delayed the adoption of the treaty of peace, and of those who by their worse than foolish words deliberately invited a savage people to plunge into a war fraught with sure disaster for them—a war, too, in which our own brave men who follow the flag must pay with their blood for the silly, mock humanitarianism of the prattlers who sit at home in peace.

The army and the navy are the sword and the shield which this nation must carry if she is to do her duty among the nations of the earth—if she is not to stand merely as the China of the western hemisphere. Our proper conduct toward the tropic islands we have wrested from Spain is merely the form which our duty has taken at the moment. Of course we are bound to handle the affairs of our own household well. We must see that there is civic honesty, civic cleanliness, civic good sense in our home administration of city, State, and nation. We must strive for honesty in office, for honesty toward the creditors of the nation and of the individual; for the widest freedom of individual initiative where possible, and for the wisest control of individual initiative where it is hostile to the welfare of the many. But because we set our own household in order we are not thereby excused from playing our part in the great affairs of the world. A man's first duty is to his own home, but he is not thereby excused from doing his duty to the State; for if he fails in this second duty it is under the penalty of ceasing to be a freeman. In the same way, while a nation's first duty is within its own borders, it is not thereby absolved from facing its duties in the world as a whole; and if it refuses to do so, it merely forfeits its right to struggle for a place among the peoples that shape the destiny of mankind.

In the West Indies and the Philippines alike we are confronted by most difficult problems. It is cowardly to shrink from solving them in the proper way; for solved they must be, if not by us, then by some stronger and more manful race. If we are too weak, too selfish, or too foolish to solve them, some bolder and abler people must undertake the solution. Personally, I am far too firm a believer in the greatness of my country and the power of my countrymen to admit for one moment that we shall ever be driven to the ignoble alternative.

The problems are different for the different islands. Porto Rico is not large enough to stand alone. We must govern it wisely and well, primarily in the interest of its own people. Cuba is, in my judgment, entitled ultimately to settle for itself whether it shall be an independent state or an integral portion of the mightiest of republics. But until order and stable liberty are secured, we must remain in the island to insure them, and infinite tact, judgment, moderation, and courage must be shown by our military and civil representatives in keeping the island pacified, in relentlessly stamping out brigandage, in protecting all alike, and yet in showing proper recognition to the men who have fought for Cuban liberty. The Philippines offer a yet graver problem. Their population includes half-caste and native Christians, warlike Moslems, and wild pagans. Many of their people are utterly unfit for self-government, and show no signs of becoming fit. Others may in time become fit but at present can only take part in self-government under a wise supervision, at once firm and beneficent. We have driven Spanish tyranny from the islands. If we now let it be replaced by savage anarchy, our work has been for harm and not for good. I have scant patience with those who fear to undertake the task of governing the Philippines, and who openly avow that they do fear to undertake it, or that they shrink from it because of the expense and trouble; but I have even scanter patience with those who make a pretense of humanitarianism to hide and cover their timidity, and who cant about "liberty" and the "consent of the governed," in order to excuse themselves for their unwillingness to play the part of men. Their doctrines, if carried out, would make it incumbent upon us to leave the Apaches of Arizona to work out their own salvation, and to decline to interfere in a single Indian reservation. Their doctrines condemn your forefathers and mine for ever having settled in these United States.

England's rule in India and Egypt has been of great benefit to England, for it has trained up generations of men accustomed to look at the larger and loftier side of public life. It has been of even greater benefit to India and Egypt. And finally, and most of all, it has advanced the cause of civilization. So, if we do our duty aright in the Philippines, we will add to that national renown which is the highest and finest part of national life, will greatly benefit the people of the Philippine Islands, and, above all, we will play our part well in the great work of uplifting mankind. But to do this work, keep ever in mind that we must show in a very high degree the qualities of courage, of honesty, and of good judgment. Resistance must be stamped out. The first and all-important work to be done is to establish the supremacy of our flag. We must put down armed resistance before we can accomplish anything else, and there should be no parleying, no faltering, in dealing with our foe. As for those in our own country who encourage the foe, we can afford contemptuously to disregard them; but it must be remembered that their utterances are not saved from being treasonable merely by the fact that they are despicable.

When once we have put down armed resistance, when once our rule is acknowledged, then an even more difficult task will begin, for then we must see to it that the islands are administered with absolute honesty and with good judgment. If we let the public service of the islands be turned into the prey of the spoils politician, we shall have begun to tread the path which Spain trod to her own destruction. We must send out there only good and able men, chosen for their fitness, and not because of their partisan service, and these men must not only administer impartial justice to the natives and serve their own government with honesty and fidelity, but must show the utmost tact and firmness, remembering that, with such people as those with whom we are to deal, weakness is the greatest of crimes, and that next to weakness comes lack of consideration for their principles and prejudices.

I preach to you, then, my countrymen, that our country calls not for the life of ease but for the life of strenuous endeavor. The twentieth century looms before us big with the fate of many nations. If we stand idly by, if we seek merely swollen, slothful ease and ignoble peace, if we shrink from the hard contests where men must win at hazard of their lives and at the risk of all they hold dear, then the bolder and stronger peoples will pass us by, and will win for themselves the domination of the world. Let us therefore boldly face the life of strife, resolute to do our duty well and manfully; resolute to uphold righteousness by deed and by word; resolute to be both honest and brave, to serve high ideals, yet to use practical methods. Above all, let us shrink from no strife, moral or physical, within or without the nation, provided we are certain that the strife is justified, for it is only through strife, through hard and dangerous endeavor, that we shall ultimately win the goal of true national greatness.

"'Professionalism' in Sports" (1890)

In this article from the August 1890 issue of the *North American Review*, Roosevelt assesses the impact that athletic activities were making on American life. As much as he valued fitness, he mistrusted professionalism since it inevitably encouraged spectatorship, which he scorned. In this early piece, Roosevelt begins by naming the paramount activities of physical exertion, or individual pursuits like hunting, hiking, and camping. It might seem that he would prefer it if all Americans could find the gratification he did in such activities, but he concedes that, for many, it is more convenient to join a team or sports club, where comradeship compounds the advantages of fitness in developing character. Indeed, the primary purpose of sports, Roosevelt contends, is that the vigor and hardihood they impart make a strong people. Weak and lazy citizens cannot exercise their purchase as free men (and women) and "defend this very civilization." Although sports are enjoying a "constantly increasing prominence," they provide a happy alternative only if "they are not elevated into a fetish"—the love of spectacle he associates with the sensational tastes of bloodthirsty Roman crowds. That fundamentally passive low-mindedness is the risk of our lionizing professional athletes, and indeed Roosevelt saw the prospect in political terms. The truer American, the "more desirable citizen," he believes, is the amateur. For the greatest advantage of athletics to the nation is not to create a professional class of gifted specialists the crowd can worship but to get "as many of our people as possible to take part in manly, healthy, vigorous pastimes." Not surprisingly, fifteen years later, when the reputation of college football was suffering as a result of the many injuries and several deaths that occurred annually, causing some educational leaders to call for the sport's abolishment, then-President Roosevelt may be said to have saved it by summoning to the White House leading college authorities and coaches in order to revamp the game and make it less dangerous through such innovations as the forward pass.

"Professionalism" in Sports

It is hardly necessary at the present day to enter a plea for athletic exercise and manly out-door sports. During the last twenty-five years there has been a wonderful growth of interest in and appreciation of healthy muscular amusements; and this growth can best be promoted by stimulating, within proper bounds, the spirit of rivalry on which all our games are based. The effect upon the physique of the sedentary classes, especially in the towns and cities, has already been very marked. We are much less liable than we were to reproaches on the score of our national ill health, of the bad constitutions of our men, and of the fragility and early decay of our women.

There are still plenty of people who look down on, as of little moment, the proper development of the body; but the men of good sense sympathize as little with these as they do with the even more noxious extremists who regard physical development as an end instead of a means. As a nation we have many tremendous problems to work out, and we need to bring every ounce of vital power possible to their solution. No people has ever yet done great and lasting work if its physical type was infirm and weak. Goodness and strength must go hand in hand if the Republic is to be preserved. The good man who is ready and able to strike a blow for the right, and to put down evil with the strong arm, is the citizen who deserves our most hearty respect. There is a certain tendency in the civilization of our time to underestimate or overlook the need of the virile, masterful qualities of the heart and mind which have built up and alone can maintain and defend this very civilization, and which generally go hand in hand with good health and the capacity to get the utmost possible use out of the body. There is no better way of counteracting this tendency than by encouraging bodily exercise, and especially the sports which develop such qualities as courage, resolution, and endurance.

The best of all sports for this purpose are those which follow the Macedonian rather than the Greek model: big-game hunting, mountaineering, the chase with horse and hound, and wilderness life with all its keen, hardy pleasures. The hunter and mountaineer lead healthier lives—in time of need they would make better soldiers—than the trained athlete. Nor need these pleasures be confined to the rich. The trouble with our men of small means is quite as often that they do not know how to enjoy pleasures lying at their doors as that they cannot afford them. From New York to Minneapolis, from Boston to San Francisco, there is no large city from which it is impossible to reach a tract of perfectly wild, wooded or mountainous land within forty-eight hours; and any two young men who can get a month's holiday in August or September cannot use it to better advantage than by tramping on foot, pack on back, over such a tract. Let them go alone; a season or two will teach them much woodcraft, and will enormously increase their stock of health, hardihood, and self-reliance. If one carries a light rifle or fowling-piece, and the other a fishing rod, they will soon learn to help fill out their own bill of fare. Of course they must expect to find the life pretty hard, and filled with disappointments at first; but the cost will be very trifling, and if they have courage, their reward is sure to come.

However, most of our people, whether from lack of means, time, or inclination, do not take to feats of this kind, and must get their fun and exercise in athletics proper. The years of late boyhood and early manhood—say from twelve or fourteen to twenty-eight or thirty, and often until much later—are those in which athletic sports prove not only most attractive, but also most beneficial to the individual and the race. In college—and in most of the schools which are preparatory for college— rowing, foot-ball, base-ball, running, jumping, sparring, and the like have assumed a constantly increasing prominence. Nor is this in any way a matter for regret. Of course any good is accompanied by some evil; and a small number of college boys, who would probably turn out badly anyhow, neglect everything for their sports, and so become of little use to themselves or any one else. But as a whole college life has been greatly the gainer by the change. Only a small proportion of college boys are going to become real students and do original work in literature, science, or art;

and these are certain to study their best in any event. The others are going into business or law or some kindred occupation; and these, of course, can study but little that will be directly of use to them in afterlife. The college education of such men should be largely devoted to making them good citizens, and able to hold their own in the world; and character is far more important than intellect in making a man a good citizen or successful in his calling—meaning by character not only such qualities as honesty and truthfulness, but courage, perseverance, and self-reliance.

Now, athletic sports, if followed properly, and not elevated into a fetish, are admirable for developing character, besides bestowing on the participants an invaluable fund of health and strength. In each of the larger colleges there are from fifty to a hundred men who, on the various class and college crews and ball teams, or in the track and gymnasium games, compete for the different championships; and for every one such man who actually competes there are five or ten who take part in the practice games, train more or less, and get a great deal of benefit from the work. The careful system of measurements which have been taken at Harvard shows a marked improvement in the physique of the men even during the last ten years; and—what is more important—shows that this improvement is, if anything, more marked in the case of the average man than in that of the picked champions.

The colleges contain but a small proportion of the men interested in amateur athletics, as can be seen by the immense number of ball clubs, rowing clubs, polo clubs, hunt clubs, bicycle clubs, snow-shoe clubs, lacrosse clubs, and athletic clubs proper which are to be found scattered among our cities and towns. Almost any man of sedentary life who wishes to get exercise enough to keep him in vigorous health can readily do so at one of these clubs; and an increasing proportion of our young men are finding this out and acting accordingly. More than one of our most famous athletes originally took to athletics for his health; and, on the other hand, be it remembered always that the sports which prove most beneficial bodily to a man are those which interest and amuse him. If he belongs to a rowing club or base-ball nine, the eagerness and excitement of a contest with a rival association spur him on to keep his body in good condition; and, as with the college athletes, there are scores of outsiders, whom these championship contests attract, and whose love for athletics is increased thereby, for every individual contestant who directly participates in them.

It is needless to say that under the head of manly sports I do not include pigeon-shooting; and still less rabbit-coursing, or any other game where the man does nothing but look on.

Already this awakening of interest in manly sports, this proper care of the body, have had a good effect upon our young men; but there are, of course, accompanying dangers in any such movement. With very few exceptions the man who makes some athletic pursuit his main business, instead of turning to it as a health-giving pastime, ceases to be a particularly useful citizen. Of course I do not refer to the men who act as trainers and instructors at the different colleges and clubs; these perform a most useful and honorable function, and among them several could be named who have rendered as high service as any men in the community.

But the amateur athlete who thinks of nothing but athletics, and makes it the serious business of his life, becomes a bore, if nothing worse. A young man who has broken a running or jumping record, who has stroked a winning club crew, or played on his college nine or eleven, has a distinct claim to our respect; but if, when middle-aged, he has still done nothing more in the world, he forfeits even this claim which he originally had.

It is so in an even more marked degree with the "professional" athlete. In America the difference between amateurs and professionals is in one way almost the reverse of what it is in England, and accords better with the ways of life of our democratic community. In England the average professional is a man who works for his living, and the average amateur is one who does not; whereas with us the amateur usually is, and always ought to be, a man who, like other American citizens, works hard at some regular calling—it matters not what, so long as it is respectable—while the professional is very apt to be a gentleman of more or less elegant leisure, aside from his special pursuit.

The mere statement of the difference is enough to show that the amateur, and not the professional, is the desirable citizen, the man who should be encouraged. Our object is to get as many of our people as possible to take part in manly, healthy, vigorous pastimes, which will benefit the whole nation; it is not to produce a limited class of athletes who shall make it the business of their lives to do battle with one another for the popular amusement. Most masterful nations have shown a strong taste for manly sports. In the old days, when we ourselves were still a people of backwoodsmen, at every merrymaking there were sure to be trials of skill and strength, at running, wrestling, and rifle-shooting, among the young men. We should encourage by every method the spirit which makes such trials popular; it is a very excellent revival of old-time American ways. But the existence of a caste of gladiators in the midst of a population which does not itself participate in any manly sports is usually, as it was at Rome, a symptom of national decadence.

The Romans who, when the stern and simple strength of Rome was departing, flocked to the gladiatorial shows, were influenced only by a ferocious craving for bloody excitement; not by any sympathy with men of stout heart and tough sinew. So it is, to a lesser extent, today. In base-ball alone, the professional teams, from a number of causes, have preserved a fairly close connection with non-professional players, and have done good work in popularizing a most admirable and characteristic American game; but even here the outlook is now less favorable, and, aside from this one pastime, professionalism is the curse of many an athletic sport, and the chief obstacle to its healthy development. Professional rowing is under a dark cloud of suspicion because of the crooked practices which have disgraced it. Horse-racing is certainly not in an ideal condition. A prize-fight is simply brutal and degrading. The people who attend it, and make a hero of the prize-fighter, are—excepting boys who go for fun and don't know any better—to a very great extent, men who hover on the border-line of criminality; and those who are not are speedily brutalized, and are never rendered more manly. They form as ignoble a body as do the kindred frequenters of rat-pit and cock-pit. The prize-fighter and his fellow professional athletes of the same ilk are, together with their patrons in every rank of life, the very worst foes with whom the cause of general athletic development has to contend.

"At the Dedication Ceremonies
of the Louisiana Purchase Exposition,
St. Louis" (1903)

Less than a week after Roosevelt spoke at Yellowstone, he visited the
St. Louis World's Fair to honor the centennial of President Jefferson's
famous act of land acquisition. Roosevelt used this occasion to celebrate
the American commitment to growth that he equates with the character
of national life. Indeed, the Purchase marked the signal act in the effort
to define the United States as a "great expanding nation," and the work
of exploring and settling "Louisiana" was the most significant feature of
American life until the Civil War and of the shaping of our political state.
For Roosevelt, no other great country had sought to expand the way the
United States had, by absorbing new lands into its political identity. Only
the United States had had the wisdom to assimilate the inhabitants of new
territories with the same standing as current citizens, a model that today
other countries ignore to their peril. Roosevelt is thus contradistinguish-
ing the U.S. example from imperialist regimes taking dominion throughout the world through colonization. Of course, the ominous absence in
Roosevelt's speech is his omission of the nation's policy of Indian-killing,
land-grabbing, and legal sleight of hand. Such an acknowledgment would
have had to temper Roosevelt's homage to the "aggressive and masterful
character of the hardy pioneer folk." In addition, Roosevelt wants also to
honor the great civilizing spirit of those pioneers whose "restless energy"
had led to a "marvelous material prosperity." That success laid the ground-
work for an even "higher life," the challenge of which it is up to the future
to create. Roosevelt closes by dramatically insisting that Americans draw

not only on their heritage of the "strong virile virtues," so regularly associated with his vision, but also on the virtues of "self-restraint, self-mastery, regard for the rights of others . . . our abhorrence of cruelty, brutality, and corruption, in public and in private life alike," if the nation will truly flourish in the future.

At the Dedication Ceremonies of the Louisiana Purchase Exposition, St. Louis, April 30, 1903

Mr. President, ladies, and gentlemen:

At the outset of my address let me recall to the minds of my hearers that the soil upon which we stand, before it was ours, was successively the possession of two mighty empires, Spain and France, whose sons made a deathless record of heroism in the early annals of the New World. No history of the Western country can be written without paying heed to the wonderful part played therein in the early days by the soldiers, missionaries, explorers, and traders, who did their work for the honor of the proud banners of France and Castile. While the settlers of English-speaking stock, and those of Dutch, German, and Scandinavian origin who were associated with them, were still clinging close to the Eastern seaboard, the pioneers of Spain and of France had penetrated deep into the hitherto unknown wilderness of the West, had wandered far and wide within the boundaries of what is now our mighty country. The very cities themselves—St. Louis, New Orleans, Santa Fe—bear witness by their titles to the nationalities of their founders. It was not until the Revolution had begun that the English-speaking settlers pushed west across the Alleghenies, and not until a century ago that they entered in to possess the land upon which we now stand.

We have met here today to commemorate the hundredth anniversary of the event which more than any other, after the foundation of the Government and always excepting its preservation, determined the character of our national life—determined that we should be a great expanding Nation instead of relatively a small and stationary one.

Of course it was not with the Louisiana Purchase that our career of expansion began. In the middle of the Revolutionary War the Illinois region, including the present States of Illinois and Indiana, was added to our domain by force of arms, as a sequel to the adventurous expedition of George Rogers Clark and his frontier riflemen. Later the treaties of Jay and Pinckney materially extended our real boundaries to the West. But none of these events was of so striking a character as to fix the popular imagination. The old thirteen colonies had always claimed that their rights stretched westward to the Mississippi, and vague and unreal though these claims were until made good by conquest, settlement, and diplomacy, they still served to give the impression that the earliest westward movements of our people were little more than the filling in of already existing national boundaries.

But there could be no illusion about the acquisition of the vast territory beyond the Mississippi, stretching westward to the Pacific, which in that day was known as Louisiana. This immense region was admittedly the territory of a foreign power, of a European kingdom. None of our people had ever laid claim to a foot of it. Its acquisition could in no sense be treated as rounding out any existing claims. When we acquired it we made evident once and for all that consciously and of set purpose we had embarked on a career of expansion, that we had taken our place among those daring and hardy nations who risk much with the hope and desire of winning high position among the great powers of the earth. As is so often the case in nature, the law of development of a living organism showed itself in its actual workings to be wiser than the wisdom of the wisest.

This work of expansion was by far the greatest work of our people during the years that intervened between the adoption of the Constitution and the outbreak of the Civil War. There were other questions of real moment and importance, and there were many which at the time seemed such to those engaged in answering them; but the greatest feat of our forefathers of those generations was the deed of the men who, with pack train or wagon train, on horseback, on foot, or by boat, pushed the frontier ever westward across the continent.

Never before had the world seen the kind of national expansion which gave our people all that part of the American continent lying west of the thirteen original States; the greatest landmark in which was the Louisiana Purchase. Our triumph in this process of expansion was indissolubly bound up with the success of our peculiar kind of federal government; and this success has been so complete that because of its very completeness we now sometimes fail to appreciate not only the all-importance but the tre-mendous difficulty of the problem with which our Nation was originally faced.

When our forefathers joined to call into being this Nation, they under-took a task for which there was but little encouraging precedent. The development of civilization from the earliest period seemed to show the truth of two propositions: In the first place, it had always proved exceed-ingly difficult to secure both freedom and strength in any government; and in the second place, it had always proved well-nigh impossible for a nation to expand without either breaking up or becoming a centralized tyranny. With the success of our effort to combine a strong and efficient national union, able to put down disorder at home and to maintain our honor and interest abroad, I have not now to deal. This success was signal and all-important, but it was by no means unprecedented in the same sense that our type of expansion was unprecedented. The history of Rome and of Greece illustrates very well the two types of expansion which had taken place in ancient time and which had been universally accepted as the only possible types up to the period when as a Nation we ourselves began to take possession of this continent. The Grecian States performed remarkable feats of colonization, but each colony as soon as created became entirely independent of the mother State, and in after years was almost as apt to prove its enemy as its friend. Local self-government, local independence, was secured, but only by the absolute sacrifice of anything resembling national unity. In consequence, the Greek world, for all its wonderful brilliancy and the extraordinary artistic, literary, and philo-sophical development which has made all mankind its debtors for the ages, was yet wholly unable to withstand a formidable foreign foe, save spasmodically. As soon as powerful, permanent empires arose on its out-skirts, the Greek states in the neighborhood of such empires fell under their sway. National power and greatness were completely sacrificed to local liberty.

With Rome the exact opposite occurred. The imperial city rose to absolute dominion over all the peoples of Italy and then expanded her rule over the entire civilized world by a process which kept the nation strong and united, but gave no room whatever for local liberty and self-government. All other cities and countries were subject to Rome. In con-sequence this great and masterful race of warriors, rulers, road-builders, and administrators stamped their indelible impress upon all the afterlife of our race, and yet let an over-centralization eat out the vitals of their empire until it became an empty shell; so that when the barbarians came they destroyed only what had already become worthless to the world.

The underlying viciousness of each type of expansion was plain enough and the remedy now seems simple enough. But when the fathers of the Republic first formulated the Constitution under which we live this remedy was untried and no one could foretell how it would work. They themselves began the experiment almost immediately by adding new States to the original thirteen. Excellent people in the East viewed this initial expansion of the country with great alarm. Exactly as during the colonial period many good people in the mother-country thought it highly important that settlers should be kept out of the Ohio Valley in the interest of the fur companies, so after we had become a Nation many good people on the Atlantic Coast felt grave apprehension lest they might somehow be hurt by the westward growth of the Nation. These good people shook their heads over the formation of States in the fertile Ohio Valley which now forms part of the heart of our Nation; and they declared that the destruction of the Republic had been accomplished when through the Louisiana Purchase we acquired nearly half of what is now that same Republic's present territory. Nor was their feeling unnatural. Only the adventurous and the far-seeing can be expected heartily to welcome the process of expansion, for the nation that expands is a nation which is entering upon a great career, and with greatness there must of necessity come perils which daunt all save the most stout-hearted.

We expanded by carving the wilderness into Territories and out of these Territories building new States when once they had received as permanent settlers a sufficient number of our own people. Being a practical Nation we have never tried to force on any section of our new territory an unsuitable form of government merely because it was suitable for another section under different conditions. Of the territory covered by the Louisiana Purchase a portion was given Statehood within a few years. Another portion has not been admitted to Statehood, although a century has elapsed—although doubtless it soon will be. In each case we showed the practical governmental genius of our race by devising methods suitable to meet the actual existing needs; not by insisting upon the application of some abstract shibboleth to all our new possessions alike, no matter how incongruous this application might sometimes be.

Over by far the major part of the territory, however, our people spread in such numbers during the course of the nineteenth century that we were able to build up State after State, each with exactly the same complete local independence in all matters affecting purely its own domestic interests as in any of the original thirteen States—each owing the same absolute fealty to the Union of all the States which each of the original thirteen States also owes—and finally each having the same proportional right to its share in shaping and directing the common policy of the Union which is possessed by any other State, whether of the original thirteen or not.

This process now seems to us part of the natural order of things, but it was wholly unknown until our own people devised it. It seems to us a mere matter of course, a matter of elementary right and justice, that in the deliberations of the national representative bodies the representatives of a State which came into the Union but yesterday stand on a footing of exact and entire equality with those of the Commonwealths whose sons once signed the Declaration of Independence. But this way of looking at the matter is purely modern, and in its origin purely American. When Washington during his Presidency saw new States come into the Union on a footing of complete equality with the old, every European nation which had colonies still administered them as dependencies, and every other mother-country treated the colonist not as a self-governing equal but as a subject.

The process which we began has since been followed by all the great peoples who were capable both of expansion and of self-government, and now the world accepts it as the natural process, as the rule; but a century and a quarter ago it was not merely exceptional; it was unknown.

This, then, is the great historic significance of the movement of continental expansion in which the Louisiana Purchase was the most striking single achievement. It stands out in marked relief even among the feats of a nation of pioneers, a nation whose people have from the beginning been picked out by a process of natural selection from among the most enterprising individuals of the nations of western Europe. The acquisition of the territory is a credit to the broad and far-sighted statesmanship of the great statesmen to whom it was immediately due, and above all to the aggressive and masterful character of the hardy pioneer folk to whose rest-less energy these statesmen gave expression and direction, whom they fol-lowed rather than led. The history of the land comprised within the limits of the Purchase is an epitome of the entire history of our people. Within these limits we have gradually built up State after State until now they many times surpass in wealth, in population, and in many-sided devel-opment the original thirteen States as they were when their delegates met in the Continental Congress. The people of these States have shown themselves mighty in war with their fellow-man, and mighty in strength to tame the rugged wilderness. They could not thus have conquered the forest and the prairie, the mountain and the desert, had they not possessed the great fighting virtues, the qualities which enable a people to overcome the forces of hostile men and hostile nature. On the other hand, they could not have used aright their conquest had they not in addition pos-sessed the qualities of self-mastery and self-restraint, the power of acting in combination with their fellows, the power of yielding obedience to the law and of building up an orderly civilization. Courage and hardihood are indispensable virtues in a people; but the people which possesses no others can never rise high in the scale either of power or of culture. Great peoples must have in addition the governmental capacity which comes only when individuals fully recognize their duties to one another and to the whole body politic, and are able to join together in feats of construc-tive statesmanship and of honest and effective administration.

The old pioneer days are gone, with their roughness and their hard-ship, their incredible toil and their wild half-savage romance. But the need for the pioneer virtues remains the same as ever. The peculiar fron-tier conditions have vanished; but the manliness and stalwart hardihood of the frontiersmen can be given even freer scope under the conditions surrounding the complex industrialism of the present day. In this great region acquired for our people under the Presidency of Jefferson, this region stretching from the Gulf to the Canadian border, from the Missis-sippi to the Rockies, the material and social progress has been so vast that alike for weal and for woe its people now share the opportunities and bear the burdens common to the entire civilized world. The problems before us are fundamentally the same east and west of the Mississippi, in the new States and in the old, and exactly the same qualities are required for their successful solution.

We meet here today to commemorate a great event, an event which marks an era in statesmanship no less than in pioneering. It is fitting that we should pay our homage in words; but we must in honor make our words good by deeds. We have every right to take a just pride in the great deeds of our forefathers; but we show ourselves unworthy to be their descendants if we make what they did an excuse for our lying supine instead of an incentive to the effort to show ourselves by our acts worthy of them. In the administration of city, State, and Nation, in the management of our home life and the conduct of our business and social relations, we are bound to show certain high and fine qualities of character under penalty of seeing the whole heart of our civilization eaten out while the body still lives.

We justly pride ourselves on our marvelous material prosperity, and such prosperity must exist in order to establish a foundation upon which a higher life can be built; but unless we do in very fact build this higher life thereon, the material prosperity itself will go for but very little. Now, in 1903, in the altered conditions, we must meet the changed and changing problems with the spirit shown by the men who in 1803 and in the subsequent years gained, explored, conquered, and settled this vast territory, then a desert, now filled with thriving and populous States.

The old days were great because the men who lived in them had mighty qualities; and we must make the new days great by showing these same qualities. We must insist upon courage and resolution, upon hardihood, tenacity, and fertility in resource; we must insist upon the strong, virile virtues; and we must insist no less upon the virtues of self-restraint, self-mastery, regard for the rights of others; we must show our abhorrence of cruelty, brutality, and corruption, in public and in private life alike. If we come short in any of these qualities we shall measurably fail; and if, as I believe we surely shall, we develop these qualities in the future to an even greater degree than in the past, then in the century now beginning we shall make of this Republic the freest and most orderly, the most just and most mighty nation which has ever come forth from the womb of time.

"National Unity versus Class Cleavage" (1903)

In the address to the New York State Fair on September 7, 1903, later published under this title, President Roosevelt describes a vision of a healthy and hardy populace, one where wage earners and farmers alike understand their shared place in the American order of things. Roosevelt used this occasion to elaborate how U.S. economic and social policies can succeed by reminding workers up and down the ranks that "we all of us tend to go up or go down together" and that we might strive in our own pursuits for the good of all. In this way, the speech responds to specters of disunity and class antagonism that emerged during periods when economic growth and social opportunities were available only to some. Our country's ideals flourish, says Roosevelt, when each group enjoys the public bounty and no group is excluded. Otherwise, our self-interest becomes suspicious and contemptuous; our view of the Republic's potential too narrow; our regard for our fellows too prejudiced. Moreover, we must look to leaders who appreciate this fair-mindedness or risk demagoguery. Such leaders will vanquish the "envy" of the striving classes and the "arrogance" of the propertied ones by promoting a just and free society where mutual respect, hard work, and common sense prevail. For Roosevelt, "We must see that each man is given a square deal," which is the only way to ensure the continuation of our "orderly liberty."

National Unity versus Class Cleavage

Governor Higgins, my fellow citizens:

In speaking on Labor Day at the annual fair of the New York State Agricultural Association, it is natural to keep especially in mind the two bodies who compose the majority of our people and upon whose welfare depends the welfare of the entire State. If circumstances are such that thrift, energy, industry, and forethought enable the farmer, the tiller of the soil, on the one hand, and the wage worker, on the other, to keep themselves, their wives, and their children in reasonable comfort, then the State is well off, and we can be assured that the other classes in the community will likewise prosper. On the other hand, if there is in the long run a lack of prosperity among the two classes named, then all other prosperity is sure to be more seeming than real. It has been our profound good fortune as a nation that hitherto, disregarding exceptional periods of depression and the normal and inevitable fluctuations, there has been, on the whole, from the beginning of our Government to the present day a progressive betterment alike in the condition of the tiller of the soil and in the condition of the man who, by his manual skill and labor, supports himself and his family, and endeavors to bring up his children so that they may be at least as well off as, and if possible better off than, he himself has been. There are, of course, exceptions, but as a whole the standard of living among the farmers of our country has risen from generation to generation, and the wealth represented on the farms has steadily increased, while the wages of labor have likewise risen, both as regards the actual money paid and as regards the purchasing power which that money represents.

Side by side with this increase in the prosperity of the wage-worker and the tiller of the soil has gone on a great increase in prosperity among the business men and among certain classes of professional men; and the prosperity of these men has been partly the cause and partly the consequence of the prosperity of farmer and wage-worker. It can not be too often repeated that in this country, in the long run, we all of us tend to go up or go down together. If the average of well-being is high, it means that the average wage-worker, the average farmer, and the average business man are all alike well off. If the average shrinks, there is not one of these classes which will not feel the shrinkage. Of course there are always some men who are not affected by good times, just as there are some men who are not affected by bad times. But speaking broadly, it is true that if prosperity comes all of us tend to share more or less therein, and that if adversity comes each of us, to a greater or less extent, feels the tension. Unfortunately, in this world the innocent frequently find themselves obliged to pay some of the penalty for the misdeeds of the guilty; and so if hard times come, whether they be due to our own fault or to our misfortune, whether they be due to some burst of speculative frenzy that has caused a portion of the business world to lose its head—a loss which no legislation can possibly supply—or whether they be due to any lack of wisdom in a portion of the world of labor—in each case the trouble once started is felt more or less in every walk of life.

It is all-essential to the continuance of our healthy national life that we should recognize this community of interest among our people. The welfare of each of us is dependent fundamentally upon the welfare of all of us, and therefore in public life that man is the best representative of each of us who seeks to do good to each by doing good to all; in other words, whose endeavor it is, not to represent any special class and promote merely that class's selfish interests, but to represent all true and honest men of all sections and all classes and to work for their interests by working for our common country.

We can keep our government on a sane and healthy basis, we can make and keep our social system what it should be, only on condition of judging each man, not as a member of a class, but on his worth as a man. It is an infamous thing in our American life, and fundamentally treacherous to our institutions, to apply to any man any test save that of his personal worth, or to draw between two sets of men any distinction save the distinction of conduct, the distinction that marks off those who do well and wisely from those who do ill and foolishly. There are good citizens and bad citizens in every class as in every locality, and the attitude of decent people toward great public and social questions should be determined, not by the accidental questions of employment or locality, but by those deep-set principles which represent the innermost souls of men.

The failure in public and in private life thus to treat each man on his own merits, the recognition of this government as being either for the poor as such or for the rich as such, would prove fatal to our Republic, as such failure and such recognition have always proved fatal in the past to other republics. A healthy republican government must rest upon individuals, not upon classes or sections. As soon as it becomes government by a class or by a section it departs from the old American ideal.

It is, of course, the merest truism to say that free institutions are of avail only to people who possess the high and peculiar characteristics needed to take advantage of such institutions. The century that has just closed has witnessed many and lamentable instances in which people have seized a government free in form, or have had it bestowed upon them, and yet have permitted it under the forms of liberty to become some species of despotism or anarchy, because they did not have in them the power to make this seeming liberty one of deed instead of one merely of word. Under such circumstances the seeming liberty may be supplanted by a tyranny or despotism in the first place, or it may reach the road of despotism by the path of license and anarchy. It matters but little which road is taken. In either case the same goal is reached. People show themselves just as unfit for liberty whether they submit to anarchy or to tyranny; and class government, whether it be the government of a plutocracy or the government of a mob, is equally incompatible with the principles established in the days of Washington and perpetuated in the days of Lincoln.

Many qualities are needed by a people which would preserve the power of self-government in fact as well as in name. Among these qualities are forethought, shrewdness, self-restraint, the courage which refuses to abandon one's own rights, and the disinterested and kindly good sense which enables one to do justice to the rights of others. Lack of strength and lack of courage unfit men for self-government on the one hand; and on the other, brutal arrogance, envy, in short, any manifestation of the spirit of selfish disregard, whether of one's own duties or of the rights of others, are equally fatal.

In the history of mankind many republics have risen, have flourished for a less or greater time, and then have fallen because their citizens lost the power of governing themselves and thereby of governing their state; and in no way has this loss of power been so often and so clearly shown as in the tendency to turn the government into a government primarily for the benefit of one class instead of a government for the benefit of the people as a whole.

Again and again in the republics of ancient Greece, in those of mediæval Italy and mediæval Flanders, this tendency was shown, and wherever the tendency became a habit it invariably and inevitably proved fatal to the state. In the final result it mattered not one whit whether the movement was in favor of one class or of another. The outcome was equally fatal, whether the country fell into the hands of a wealthy oligarchy which exploited the poor or whether it fell under the domination of a turbulent mob which plundered the rich. In both cases there resulted violent alternations between tyranny and disorder, and a final complete loss of liberty to all citizens—destruction in the end overtaking the class which had for the moment been victorious as well as that which had momentarily been defeated. The death knell of the Republic had rung as soon as the active power became lodged in the hands of those who sought, not to do justice to all citizens, rich and poor alike, but to stand for one special class and for its interests as opposed to the interests of others.

The reason why our future is assured lies in the fact that our people are genuinely skilled in and fitted for self-government and therefore will spurn the leadership of those who seek to excite this ferocious and foolish class antagonism. The average American knows not only what he himself intends to do about what is right, but that his average fellow-countryman has the same intention and the same power to make his intention effective. He knows, whether he be business man, professional man, farmer, mechanic, employer, or wage-worker, that the welfare of each of these men is bound up with the welfare of all the others; that each is neighbor to the other, is actuated by the same hopes and fears, has fundamentally the same ideals, and that all alike have much the same virtues and the same faults. Our average fellow-citizen is a sane and healthy man, who believes in decency and has a wholesome mind. He therefore feels an equal scorn alike for the man of wealth guilty of the mean and base spirit of arrogance toward those who are less well off, and for the man of small means who in his turn either feels, or seeks to excite in others the feeling of mean and base envy for those who are better off. The two feelings envy and arrogance are but opposite sides of the same shield, but different developments of the same spirit. Fundamentally, the unscrupulous rich man who seeks to exploit and oppress those who are less well off is in spirit not opposed to, but identical with, the unscrupulous poor man who desires to plunder and oppress those who are better off. The courtier and the demagogue are but developments of the same type under different conditions, each manifesting the same servile spirit, the same desire to rise by pandering to base passions; though one panders to power in the shape of a single man and the other to power in the shape of a multitude. So likewise the man who wishes to rise by wronging others must by right be contrasted, not with the man who likewise wishes to do wrong, although to a different set of people, but with the man who wishes to do justice to all people and to wrong none.

The line of cleavage between good and bad citizenship lies, not between the man of wealth who acts squarely by his fellows and the man who seeks each day's wage by that day's work, wronging no one and doing his duty by his neighbor; nor yet does this line of cleavage divide the unscrupulous wealthy man who exploits others in his own interest, from the demagogue, or from the sullen and envious being who wishes to attack all men of property, whether they do well or ill. On the contrary, the line of cleavage between good citizenship and bad citizenship separates the rich man who does well from the rich man who does ill, the poor man of good conduct from the poor man of bad conduct. This line of cleavage lies at right angles to any such arbitrary line of division as that separating one class from another, one locality from another, or men with a certain degree of property from those of a less degree of property.

The good citizen is the man who, whatever his wealth or his poverty, strives manfully to do his duty to himself, to his family, to his neighbor, to the State; who is incapable of the baseness which manifests itself either in arrogance or in envy, but who while demanding justice for himself is no less scrupulous to do justice to others. It is because the average American citizen, rich or poor, is of just this type that we have cause for our profound faith in the future of the Republic.

Ours is a government of liberty, by, through, and under the law. Lawlessness and connivance at law-breaking—whether the law-breaking take the form of a crime of greed and cunning or of a crime of violence—are destructive not only of order, but of the true liberties which can only come through order. If alive to their true interests rich and poor alike will set their faces like flint against the spirit which seeks personal advantage by overriding the laws, without regard to whether this spirit shows itself in the form of bodily violence by one set of men or in the form of vulpine cunning by another set of men.

Let the watchwords of all our people be the old familiar watchwords of honesty, decency, fair-dealing, and common sense. The qualities denoted by these words are essential to all of us, as we deal with the complex industrial problems of today, the problems affecting not merely the accumulation but even more the wise distribution of wealth. We ask no man's permission when we require him to obey the law; neither the permission of the poor man nor yet of the rich man. Least of all can the man of great wealth afford to break the law, even for his own financial advantage; for the law is his prop and support, and it is both foolish and profoundly unpatriotic for him to fail in giving hearty support to those who show that there is in very fact one law, and one law only, alike for the rich and the poor, for the great and the small.

Men sincerely interested in the due protection of property, and men sincerely interested in seeing that the just rights of labor are guaranteed, should alike remember not only that in the long run neither the capitalist nor the wage-worker can be helped in healthy fashion save by helping the other; but also that to require either side to obey the law and do its full duty toward the community is emphatically to that side's real interest.

There is no worse enemy of the wage-worker than the man who condones mob violence in any shape or who preaches class hatred; and surely the slightest acquaintance with our industrial history should teach even the most short-sighted that the times of most suffering for our people as a whole, the times when business is stagnant, and capital suffers from shrinkage and gets no return from its investments, are exactly the times of hardship, and want, and grim disaster among the poor. If all the existing instrumentalities of wealth could be abolished, the first and severest suffering would come among those of us who are least well off at present. The wage-worker is well off only when the rest of the country is well off; and he can best contribute to this general well-being by showing sanity and a firm purpose to do justice to others.

In his turn the capitalist who is really a conservative, the man who has forethought as well as patriotism, should heartily welcome every effort, legislative or otherwise, which has for its object to secure fair dealing by capital, corporate or individual, toward the public and toward the employee. Such laws as the franchise-tax law in this State, which the Court of Appeals recently unanimously decided constitutional—such a law as that passed in Congress last year for the purpose of establishing a Department of Commerce and Labor, under which there should be a bureau to oversee and secure publicity from the great corporations which do an interstate business—such a law as that passed at the same time for the regulation of the great highways of commerce so as to keep these roads clear on fair terms to all producers in getting their goods to market—these laws are in the interest not merely of the people as a whole, but of the propertied classes. For in no way is the stability of property better assured than by making it patent to our people that property bears its proper share of the burdens of the State; that property is handled not only in the interest of the owner, but in the interest of the whole community.

In other words, legislation to be permanently good for any class must also be good for the Nation as a whole, and legislation which does injustice to any class is certain to work harm to the Nation. Take our currency system for example. This Nation is on a gold basis. The treasury of the public is in excellent condition. Never before has the per capita of circulation been as large as it is this day; and this circulation, moreover, is of money every dollar of which is at par with gold. Now, our having this sound currency system is of benefit to banks, of course, but it is of infinitely more benefit to the people as a whole, because of the healthy effect on business conditions.

In the same way, whatever is advisable in the way of remedial or corrective currency legislation—and nothing revolutionary is advisable under present conditions—must be undertaken only from the standpoint of the business community as a whole, that is, of the American body politic as a whole. Whatever is done, we can not afford to take any step backward or to cast any doubt upon the certain redemption in standard coin of every circulating note.

Among ourselves we differ in many qualities of body, head, and heart; we are unequally developed, mentally as well as physically. But each of us has the right to ask that he shall be protected from wrongdoing as he does his work and carries his burden through life. No man needs sympathy because he has to work, because he has a burden to carry. Far and away the best prize that life offers is the chance to work hard at work worth doing; and this is a prize open to every man, for there can be no work better worth doing than that done to keep in health and comfort and with reasonable advantages those immediately dependent upon the husband, the father, or the son.

There is no room in our healthy American life for the mere idler, for the man or the woman whose object it is throughout life to shirk the duties which life ought to bring. Life can mean nothing worth meaning, unless its prime aim is the doing of duty, the achievement of results worth achieving. A recent writer has finely said: "After all, the saddest thing that can happen to a man is to carry no burdens. To be bent under too great a load is bad; to be crushed by it is lamentable; but even in that there are possibilities that are glorious. But to carry no load at all—there is nothing in that. No one seems to arrive at any goal really worth reaching in this world who does not come to it heavy laden."

Surely from our own experience each one of us knows that this is true. From the greatest to the smallest, happiness and usefulness are largely found in the same soul, and the joy of life is won in its deepest and truest sense only by those who have not shirked life's burdens. The men whom we most delight to honor in all this land are those who, in the iron years from '61 to '65, bore on their shoulders the burden of saving the Union. They did not choose the easy task. They did not shirk the difficult duty. Deliberately and of their own free will they strove for an ideal, upward and onward across the stony slopes of greatness. They did the hardest work that was then to be done; they bore the heaviest burden that any generation of Americans ever had to bear; and because they did this they have won such proud joy as it has fallen to the lot of no other men to win, and have written their names for evermore on the golden honor roll of the Nation. As it is with the soldier, so it is with the civilian. To win success in the business world, to become a first-class mechanic, a successful farmer, an able lawyer or doctor, means that the man has devoted his best energy and power through long years to the achievement of his ends. So it is in the life of the family, upon which in the last analysis the whole welfare of the Nation rests. The man or woman who as bread-winner and home-maker, or as wife and mother, has done all that he or she can do, patiently and uncomplainingly, is to be honored; and is to be envied by all those who have never had the good fortune to feel the need and duty of doing such work. The woman who has borne, and who has reared as they should be reared, a family of children, has in the most emphatic manner deserved well of the Republic. Her burden has been heavy, and she has been able to bear it worthily only by the possession of resolution, of good sense, of conscience, and of unselfishness. But if she has borne it well, then to her shall come the supreme blessing, for in the words of the oldest and greatest of books, "Her children shall rise up and call her blessed"; and among the benefactors of the land her place must be with those who have done the best and the hardest work, whether as law-givers or as soldiers, whether in public or private life.

This is not a soft and easy creed to preach. It is a creed willingly learned only by men and women who, together with the softer virtues, possess also the stronger; who can do, and dare, and die at need, but who while life lasts will never flinch from their allotted task. You farmers, and wage-workers, and business men of this great State, of this mighty and wonderful Nation, are gathered together today, proud of your State and still prouder of your Nation, because your forefathers and predecessors have lived up to just this creed. You have received from their hands a great inheritance, and you will leave an even greater inheritance to your children, and your children's children, provided only that you practice alike in your private and your public lives the strong virtues that have given us as a people greatness in the past. It is not enough to be well-meaning and kindly, but weak; neither is it enough to be strong, unless morality and decency go hand in hand with strength. We must possess the qualities which make us do our duty in our homes and among our neighbors, and in addition we must possess the qualities which are indispensable to the make-up of every great and masterful nation—the qualities of courage and hardihood, of individual initiative and yet of power to combine for a common end, and above all, the resolute determination to permit no man and no set of men to sunder us one from the other by lines of caste or creed or section. We must act upon the motto of "all for each and each for all." There must be ever present in our minds the fundamental truth that in a republic such as ours the only safety is to stand neither for nor against any man because he is rich or because he is poor, because he is engaged in one occupation or another, because he works with his brains or because he works with his hands. We must treat each man on his worth and merits as a man. We must see that each is given a square deal, because he is entitled to no more and should receive no less. Finally we must keep ever in mind that a republic such as ours can exist only by virtue of the orderly liberty which comes through the equal domination of the law over all men alike, and through its administration in such resolute and fearless fashion as shall teach all that no man is above it and no man below it.

"The Parasite Woman;
the Only Indispensable Citizen" (1917)

Readers expecting to discover in Theodore Roosevelt the makings of a feminist will be disappointed in his various writings on the place of women in American life, and his position will strike readers today as all too limited. Indeed, he wrote little about the national conversation leading up to the Nineteenth Amendment, but his attitude toward women's issues was hardly conventional, since he thought there was as much chance of women neglecting their duties in order to exercise the right to vote as there was for men. As Roosevelt saw it, the question of the relation between the sexes was inevitably a question of fairness: women did have the right to education, and extraordinary women should have the right to pursue their extraordinariness if that lay outside the home, just as ambitious men might forswear mere moneymaking if their talents took them into the arts, just as honest men might do the same if their interest was politics. But Roosevelt stops short of the radical implications of his vision. He avers that most men are fitted for "home-making" in the sense of meeting the challenge of supporting a household, and that the largest majority of women are suited to the right conduct of practical homemaking, even as they are morally entitled to share in the disposal of the husband's earnings. Indeed, Roosevelt holds particular scorn for the extremes: it is acceptable for a man of Roosevelt's upbringing to lose patience with radical feminists, but wrong for husbands to deny wives their rights as anything less than their full equal. The key role for women is, as always, upholding the strength of the Republic and national ideals, and so the following excerpt from the essay, which is collected in *The Foes of Our Own Household* (1917), ends with a burst of patriotic fervor and the importance of women in shouldering this civic responsibility.

The Parasite Woman;
the Only Indispensable Citizen

Of all species of silliness the silliest is the assertion sometimes made that the woman whose primary life-work is taking care of her home and children is somehow a "parasite woman." It is such a ridiculous inversion of the truth that it ought not to be necessary even to allude to it. Nevertheless, it is acted upon by a large number of selfish, brutal, or thoughtless men, and it is screamed about by a number of foolish women. Therefore a word of common sense on the matter may not be out of place.

There are men so selfish, so short-sighted, or so brutal, that they speak and act as if the fact of the man's earning money for his wife and children, while the woman bears the children, rears them and takes care of the house for them and for the man, somehow entitles the man to be known as the head of the family, instead of a partner on equal terms with his wife, and entitles him to the exclusive right to dispose of the money and, as a matter of fact, to dispose of it primarily in his own interest.

There are professional feminists and so-called woman's-rights women who, curiously enough, seem to accept so much of this male attitude as implies that the partner who earns the money is the superior partner and that therefore the woman, who is physically weaker than the man, should accept as her primary duty the rivaling of him in the money-making business in which he will normally do better than she will; and they stigmatize as parasites the women who do the one great and all-essential work, without which no other activity by either sex amounts to anything.

Apply common sense and common decency to both attitudes. It is entirely right that any woman should be allowed to make any career for herself of which she is capable, whether or not it is a career followed by a man. She has the same right to be a lawyer, a doctor, a farmer, or a storekeeper that the man has to be a poet, an explorer, a politician, or a painter. There are women whose peculiar circumstances or whose peculiar attributes render it advisable that they should follow one of the professions named, just as there are men who can do most good to their fellows by following one of the careers above indicated for men. More than this. It is indispensable that such careers shall be open to women and that certain women shall follow them, if the women of a country, and therefore if the country itself, expect any development. In just the same way, it is indispensable that some men shall be explorers, artists, sculptors, literary men, politicians, if the country is to have its full life. Some of the best farmers are women just as some of the best exploring work and scientific work has been done by women. There is a real need for a certain number of women doctors and women lawyers. Whether a writer or a painter or a singer is a man or a woman makes not the slightest difference, provided that the work he or she does is good.

All this I not merely admit; I insist upon it. But surely it is a mere statement of fact to add that the primary work of the average man and the average woman—and of all exceptional men and women whose lives are to be really full and happy—must be the great primal work of home-making and home-keeping, for themselves and their children.

The primary work of the man is to earn his own livelihood and the livelihood of those dependent upon him, to do his own business, whether his business is on a farm or in a shop, in the counting-room of a bank or the engine-cab of a train, in a mine or on a fishing-boat, or at the head of a telegraph or telephone line; whether he be an engineer or an inventor, a surgeon or a railway president, or a carpenter or a brakeman. In other words, the man must do his business and do it well in order to support himself and his wife and children and in order that the nation may continue to exist. I appreciate to the full the work of the politician, the poet, the sculptor, and the explorer; and yet it is mere common sense to say that they cannot do any work at all unless their average fellow countryman does his business, whether with hand or brain, pen or pick, in such fashion that the country is on a decent industrial basis. If it is not, nobody will have any house or anything to eat or any means of getting around; and therefore there won't be any poets or politicians. This is not exalting one class at the expense of another. On the contrary, it recognizes the absolute need from the standpoint of national greatness and permanent achievement, that there shall be some men in a state the worth of whose activities cannot be and is not measured or expressed by money. But there is also the absolute need that this shall not be true of the average man— and, as a matter of fact, it is a great deal better even if it is not true of the exceptional man—if, in addition to his non-remunerative work, he is able by his activities to pay his way as he goes.

Now, this also applies to women. Exceptional women—like Julia Ward Howe or Harriet Beecher Stowe or Mrs. Homer—are admirable wives and mothers, admirable keepers of the home, and yet workers of genius outside the home. Such types, of course, are rare whether among men or women. There are also exceptional—and less happy, and normally less useful—women whose great service to the state and community is rendered outside the home, and who have no family life; just as is true of exceptional—and normally less happy and less useful—men. But exactly as it is true that no nation will prosper unless the average man is a home-maker; that is, unless at some business or trade or profession he earns enough to make a home for himself and his wife and children, and is a good husband and father; so no nation can exist at all unless the average woman is the home-keeper, the good wife, and unless she is the mother of a sufficient number of healthy children to insure the race going forward and not backward. The indispensable work for the community is the work of the wife and the mother. It is the most honorable work. It is literally and exactly the vital work, the work which of course must be done by the average woman or the whole nation goes down with a crash.

Foolish men treat this fact as warranting them in all kinds of out-cries against what they call "unwomanly" activities, including the outcry against the "higher education." This is nonsense. The woman is entitled to just as much education as the man; and it will not hurt her one par-ticle more than it hurts the man. It may hurt a fool in either case; but no one else. However, justification is given these people who cry against the "higher education" by such utterances as those made the other day by a president of a women's college who fatuously announced, in advocacy of a small birthrate, that it was better to have one child brought up in the best way than several not thus brought up. In the first place, there is no such antithesis as is thus implied, for, as a matter of fact, children in a fam-ily of children are usually better brought up than the only child, or than the child of a two-child family. In the next place, the statement, which must of course be taken to apply to the average individual, is on its face false, and the woman making it is not only unfit to be at the head of a female college, but is not fit to teach the lowest class in a kindergarten, for such teaching is not merely folly, but a peculiarly repulsive type of mean and selfish wickedness. The one-child family as an average ideal of course spells death; and death means the end of all hope. It is only while there is life that there is hope. A caste or a race or a nation, where the average family consists of one child, faces immediate extinction, and therefore it matters not one particle how this child is brought up. But if there are plenty of children then there is always hope. Even if they have not been very well brought up, they *have been brought up*; and so there is something to work on.

Just as the prime work for the average man must be earning his livelihood and the livelihood of those dependent upon him, so the prime work for the average woman must be keeping the home and bearing and rearing her children. This woman is not a parasite on society. She *is* society. She is the one indispensable component part of society. Socially, the same standard of moral obligation applies both to her and to the man; and in addition she is entitled to all the chivalry of love and tenderness and reverence, if in gallant and fearless fashion she faces the risk and wearing labor entailed by her fulfilment of duty; but if she shirks her duty she is entitled to no more consideration than the man who shirks his. Unless she does her duty, the whole social system collapses. If she does her duty, she is entitled to all honor.

This last statement is the crucial statement. The one way to honor this indispensable woman, the wife and mother, is to insist that she be treated as the full equal of her husband. The birth pangs make all men the debtors of all women; and the man is a wretched creature who does not live up to this obligation. Marriage should be a real partnership; a partnership of the soul, the spirit, and the mind, no less than of the body. An immediately practical feature of this partnership should be the full acknowledgment that the woman who keeps the home has exactly the same right to a say in the disposal of the money as the man who earns the money. Earning the money is not one whit more indispensable than keeping the home. Indeed, I am inclined to put it in the second place. The husband who does not give his wife, as a matter of right, her share in the disposal of the common funds is false to his duty. It is not a question of favor at all. Aside from the money to be spent on common account, for the household and the children, the wife has just the same right as the husband to her pin money, her spending money. It is not his money that he gives to her as a gift. It is hers as a matter of right. He may earn it; but he earns it because she keeps the house; and she has just as much right to it as he has. This is not a hostile right; it is a right which it is every woman's duty to ask and which it should be every man's pride and pleasure to give without asking. He is a poor creature if he grudges it; and she in her turn is a poor creature if she does not insist upon her rights, just exactly as she is worse than a poor creature if she does not do her duty.

It is the men who insist upon women doing their full duty, who insist that the primary duty of the woman is in the home, who also have a right to insist that she is just as much entitled to the suffrage as is the man. We believe in equality of right, not in identity of functions. The woman must bear and rear the children, as her first duty to the state; and the man's first duty is to take care of her and the children. In neither case is it the exclusive duty. In neither case does it exclude the performance of other duties. The right to vote no more implies that a woman will neglect her home than that a man will neglect his business. Indeed, as regards one of the greatest and most useful of all professions, that of surgery and medicine, it is probably true that the average doctor's wife has more time for the performance of political duties than the average doctor himself.

There was a capital article recently in *The Britannia*, the official organ of the Women's Social and Political Union in England, by Mrs. Emmeline Pankhurst. She was urging the full performance of duty in the war both by men and by women. In it she denounced the laboring men who did not whole-heartedly do everything in their power to aid the cause of England in the war. She spoke of the fact that workingmen and women in France could not understand how there could be strikes among workers in England during the war. She insisted that the prime duty during the war was for the men and women alike to put aside all other grievances and make common cause on behalf of the nation, and then to try to make the country a better one for their children to live in. It was a capital article, and it should be read by men and women here just as much as by men and women in England. It is because I believe that the American woman will in time of need and when the facts are brought home to her take such a position as Mrs. Pankhurst has thus taken, that I emphatically believe that she should have the right just as much as the man to vote, and, what is even more important, that she shall be given her full rights in connection with the performance by her as wife and mother of those indispensable duties which make her the one absolutely indispensable citizen of this Republic.

I end as I began by speaking of the good woman who is the best of all good citizens. I speak of goodness in the largest sense, as implying also wisdom and courage—for the woman who is either a fool or a coward is not a really useful member of the commonwealth. I ask that we search our hearts, that we cast aside selfish sloth and craven love of ease, and dare to live nobly and bravely. I make my appeal to all the good and wise and brave men and women of our Republic. I make it in the name of the larger Americanism, which means fealty to the highest national ideal. I speak for those who greatly prize peace, but who prize duty and justice and honor even more than peace. I believe in that ardent patriotism which will make a nation true to itself by making it secure justice for all within its own borders, and then so far as may be, aid in every way in securing just and fair treatment for all the nations of mankind. I believe that the people of the United States have in them the power to rise to the level of their needs, their opportunities, and their obligations. But they can only do so if they face the facts, however unpleasant. For some years we have as a people shown an appalling unfitness for world leadership on behalf of the democratic ideal; for, especially during the last three years, we have played a mean and sordid part among the nations, and have been faithless to our obligations and to all the old-time ideals of American patriotism. Women, as much as men, must put righteousness and justice before peace. We must prepare at once in amplest fashion to defend ourselves against outside aggression from any source, and the women must do their part just as much as the men. Then, in addition to striving for material well-being and reasonable equality of opportunity for our own people, in addition to making ready to defend our own rights with our own strength, surely the heirs of Washington and Lincoln, the women just as much as the men, must, as regards the rest of the world, stand at any cost for justice and righteousness for and among the peoples and the nations of mankind. . . .

"The American Negro and the War" (1918)

Although Roosevelt's record on race was not particularly sturdy, he understood that racism and injustices against African Americans violated his vision of a "square deal." At various points in his presidency and afterward, he sought, largely through famous symbolic gestures such as diverting a portion of his Nobel Prize money to African American relief organizations or by inviting Booker T. Washington to dine with him at the White House, to signal his fundamental sympathy for "colored" Americans. Heartfelt as such acts were, Roosevelt was also cognizant of the importance of sustaining African American support of the Republican Party, especially in the Deep South, where he saw the potential for overcoming Democratic control of those states. The speech below—his last public address—made less than two weeks before the Armistice in aid of a war-relief charity he supported, congratulates the honorable participation of African American soldiers, testifies to his faith in their valiance, and pays tribute to women's support at home. Most important, however, is Roosevelt's sense that, as horrible as this war has been, it will be especially worth the combatants' sacrifices if it leads to further reflection on our "national soul," including the country's treatment of the Negro. Trying throughout to avoid patronizing his African American audience (though perhaps not always succeeding), Roosevelt urges African Americans to take pride in their service and to be cognizant of their rights, even as he urges them to continue to set such high standards that the white man will ultimately be forced to recognize their rights instead of insisting on the stereotype of the dangers of the African American criminal to perpetuate inequality.

The American Negro and the War

Remarks made at a meeting held under the auspices of the Circle for Negro War Relief, at Carnegie Hall, New York, on November 2, 1918.

At this time I would not willingly speak for any cause not connected with our direct and immediate duty of winning the war and caring for those who are to win the war. (*Applause.*) I take peculiar pleasure in coming to speak for the Circle for Negro War Relief. And now if any of you haven't given, turn in a pledge card, and if any one is likely to forget the admirable adjuration at the end of one line of the song before the last, be sure that you pay what you pledge!

I wish to mention that when it became my duty to divide the Nobel Peace Prize among our war activities I gave an equal share to the work being done by Negro women for war relief (*Applause*) with the shares I had given to such organizations as the Y.M.C.A., the Knights of Columbus, and the Salvation Army, and in doing it I tried to follow out the counsel so wisely given by one of our speakers this evening, to remember that the Negro has a right to sit at the council board where questions vitally affecting him are considered—and at the same time that as a matter of expediency it is well to have white men at the board too. (*Laughter and applause.*) And I say that though I know there are many colored men—Mr. Scott is one and the chairman is another—whom I would be delighted to have sit at the council board where only the affairs of white men are concerned. As things are now, the wisest course to follow is that followed in the organization of this Circle. And so when I gave the $4,100 from the Nobel Peace Prize I mentioned two women, one white and one colored, as the ones whose advice I wished to have followed in the actual disposition of the fund. Now, I only mention this to show that I tried by works to show the faith that is in me. And I want you to do the same with the pledge cards!

I wish to congratulate you on the dignity and self-restraint with which the appeal of the Circle is issued. You have put what I would like to say better than I could have put it, when you say that you would like the men at the front and in the camps to know that there is a distinctively colored organization working for them. The people at home ought to know that this organization, though started and maintained with friendly coöperation from white friends, is intended to prove to the world that the colored people themselves can manage war relief in an efficient, honest, and dignified way, and so bring honor to their race. (*Applause.*) Every organization like the Circle for Negro War Relief is doing its part in bringing about the right solution for the great problem which the chairman has spoken of this evening. I do not for one moment wish to be understood as excusing the white man from his full responsibility for what he has done to keep the black man down; but I do wish to say with all the emphasis and all the earnestness at my command that the greatest work the colored man can do to help his race upward is by his own person, and through coöperation with his fellows, showing the dignity of service by the colored man and colored woman for all our people. (*Applause.*)

Let me illustrate by an example suggested to me by one name I see both on your list of vice-presidents and on your list of directors, to show just what I mean when I say the advisability of white coöperation and the occasional advisability of doing without white coöperation. Had I been permitted to raise troops to go to the other side in what will soon be the "late war," I should have asked permission to raise two colored regiments. It is perfectly possible of course that there is more than one colored man in the country fit for the extraordinarily difficult task of commanding one such regiment which would contain nothing but colored officers. But it happened that I only knew of one, and that was Colonel Charles Young. (*Applause.*) I had intended, and Colonel Young had been so notified, to offer him the colonelship of one regiment, telling him that I expected him to choose only colored officers and that, while I was sure he would understand the extreme difficulty and extreme responsibility of his task, I intended to try to impress it upon him still more; to tell him that under those conditions I put a heavier responsibility upon him than upon any other colored man in the country; that he was to be given an absolutely free hand in choosing his officers; and that on the other hand he would have to treat them absolutely mercilessly if they didn't come right up to the highest level. On the other hand, with the other colored regiment I should have had a colonel and a lieutenant-colonel and three majors who would have been white men. One of them, Hamilton Fish, is over there now. He was offered promotion in another regiment; but he said no, he would stay with his sun-burned Yankees. (*Laughter and applause.*) He stayed accordingly.

Mr. Cobb has spoken to you as an eyewitness of what has been done by the colored troops across the seas. I am well prepared to believe it. In the very small war in which I served, which was a kind of pink tea affair compared to this, I was in a division, a small dismounted cavalry division, where in addition to my own regiment we had three white regular regiments and two colored regiments; and when we had gotten through the campaign my own men, who were probably two-thirds southerners and southwesterners, used to say "The Ninth and Tenth Cavalry are good enough to drink out of our canteens." (*Laughter and applause.*)

Terrible though this war has been, I think it has been also fraught with the greatest good for our national soul. We went to war, as Mr. Cobb has said, to maintain our own national self-respect. And, friends, it would have been dreadful if we hadn't gone in. Materially, because the fight was so even that I don't think it is boasting, I think it is a plain statement of fact, Mr. Cobb, that our going in turned the scale. Isn't that so? (*Applause.*) I think the Germans and their vassal allies would have been victorious if we hadn't gone in. And if they had been victorious and we had stayed out—soft, flabby, wealthy—they would have eaten us without saying grace. (*Laughter and applause.*) Well, thank Heaven! we went in, and our men on the other side, our sons and brothers on the other side, white men and black, white soldiers and colored soldiers, have done such admirable work that every American can now walk with his head up and look the citizen of any other country in the world straight in the eyes. (*Applause.*) We have the satisfaction of knowing that we have played the decisive part. I am not saying this in any spirit of self-flattery. If any of you have heard me speak during the preceding four years, you know that I have not addressed the American people in a vein of undiluted eulogy. But without self-flattery we can say that it was our going in that turned the scale for freedom and against the most dangerous tyranny that the world has ever seen. We acted as genuine friends of liberty in so doing.

Now, after the war, friends, I think all of us in this country, white and black alike, have also got to set an example to the rest of the world in steering a straight course equally distant from kaiserism and bolshevism. (*Applause*.)

And, friends, I wish as an American to thank you, and as your fellow-American to congratulate you, upon the honor won and the services rendered by the colored troops on the other side; by the men, such as the soldier we have with us tonight who won the cross of war, the French war cross for gallantry in action; by the many others like him who acted with equal gallantry and who for one reason or another never attracted the attention of their superiors, and, well though they did, did not receive the outward and visible token to prove what they had done. I congratulate you on what all those men have done. I congratulate you on what the colored nurses at home have done and have been ready to do (*Applause*), and I express my very sincere regret that some way was not found to put them on the other side at the front. I congratulate you upon it in the name of our country, and above all in the name of the colored people of our country. For in the end services of this kind have a cumulative effect in winning the confidence and the respect of your fellows of another color. And I hope—and I wish to use a stronger expression than "hope"; I expect—and I am going to do whatever small amount I can to bring about the realization of the expectation—I expect that as a result of this great war, intended to secure a greater justice internationally among the peoples of mankind, we shall apply at home the lessons that we have been learning and helping teach abroad (*Applause*); that we shall work sanely, not foolishly, but resolutely, toward securing a juster and fairer treatment in this country of colored people, basing that treatment upon the only safe rule to be followed in American life, of treating each individual accordingly as his conduct or her conduct requires you to treat them. (*Applause*.)

I don't ask for any man that he shall, because of his race, be given any privilege. All I ask is that in his ordinary civil and political rights, in his right to work, to enjoy life and liberty and the pursuit of happiness, that as regards these rights he be given the same treatment that we would give him if he was an equally good man of another color. (*Applause*.)

Now, friends, both the white and the black man in moments of exultation are apt to think that the millennium is pretty near; that the "sweet chariot" has swung so low that everybody can get upon it at once. I don't think that my colored fellow-citizens are a bit worse than my white fellow-citizens as regards that particular aspiration! But mine is the ungrateful task of warning both that they must not expect too much. They must have their eyes on the stars but their feet on the ground. I have to warn my white fellow-citizens on this point when they say "Well now, at the end of this war we are going to have universal peace, and everybody will always hereafter love everybody else!" I wish you to remember that the strongest professional exponents of international love in public life today are Lenin and Trotsky; and when these professed internationalists got control of Russia they ruined Russia and betrayed the liberty-loving nations of mankind. I wish to help forward the cause of internationalism; and for that very reason I decline to indulge in dreams that might turn to nightmares. Now, in the same way, I will do everything I can to aid, to help bring about, to bring nearer, the day when justice, the square-deal, will be given as between black man and white. (*Applause.*) And yet I want to warn you that that is only going to come gradually; that there will be very much injustice; injustice that must not overmuch disappoint you; that must not cow you; and, above all, must not make you feel sullen and hopeless. And one thing I wish to say, not to you here, but to the colored men who live where the bulk of colored men do, in the south: always remember the lesson which I learned from Booker Washington: that in the long run the white man who can give most help to the colored man is the white man who lives next to him. And in consequence I have always felt it my duty, in or out of office, and I have always tried—not always successfully, but I always tried—to work so that I could command the assistance and respect of the bulk of the white men who are decent and square, in what I attempted to do for the colored man who is decent and square. I say I did not always succeed. Sometimes I had most intricate rows with one side, and sometimes with the other—there were moments when I thought I had committed both in an offensive alliance against myself.

But at any rate such is the ideal I have had before me. It is the ideal all of us must have before us: to try never to be content unless we have gone forward; never to be content unless we are trying to make things better, but always to be taking into account just how far it is possible to press things forward so as not to invite a reaction that would make things worse than they were before. It is not an easy task; but it is a task that every one of us must set himself to perform. The prime thing for the white man to remember is that it is his business to treat the colored man, and even more the colored woman, squarely; to give him or her not only the proper treatment in material things, but also the respect to which every decent man or woman is entitled as a matter of right. (*Applause.*) And the prime thing for the colored man is to conduct himself so that the unjust suspicions of the white may not be given any foundation of justice so far as his colored neighbor is concerned. To each side I preach the doctrine of thinking more of its duties than of its rights. I don't mean that you shan't think of your rights. I want you to do so. But it is awfully easy, if you begin to dwell all the time on your rights, to find that you suffer from an ingrowing sense of your own perfections and wrongs and that you forget what you owe to any one else. To the white man I never speak of the Negro's failings at all. When I speak to the white man I speak to him about his duty to give the colored man a square deal in industry, in self-respect, in matters like housing, in everything of the kind, and just so far as possible to aid him to preserve, as is said here, "his dignity so that he shall live and work in an efficient, honest, and dignified way." In other words, so that he or she shall keep and maintain his or her self-respect, the most valuable quality that any citizen can have. That's the advice that I give to the white man.

To the colored man I say, "Stand up for your rights of course, but be perfectly certain that the right-thinking white man understands what your point of view is and that he is given a full opportunity to know your rights so that he can join you in standing up for them. And set your faces like flint against the Negro criminal." And I ask that because of the very fact that too often the white man is guilty of the dreadful injustice of putting on the whole Negro race the responsibility for the Negro criminal, as he never dreams of doing in the case of the white race and the white criminal. But as colored men I wish to impress upon you to the limit of my power that the colored criminal is peculiarly an enemy of the colored race; because of the very fact that the white man and white woman who hear of him inevitably symbolize him as the race. They ought not to do it; but they do! And therefore the worst offender against the colored race is the colored criminal. He is the man who does more to keep the Negro down than any white man can possibly do. And I ask you colored men to of all things hunt down, hunt out, the colored criminal of every type. Thereby you will render the greatest service to the colored race that can possibly be rendered.

Well, friends, you see I have suffered from my usual temptation to drop into a sermon. I didn't intend to preach it. I have come here simply to wish you well and to congratulate all colored men and women, and all their white fellow-Americans upon the gallantry and efficiency with which the colored men have behaved at the front, and the efficiency and wish to render service which has been shown by both the colored men and the colored women behind them in this country.

NATIONAL
POLITICS

"The Control of Corporations" (1902)

Perhaps the single most vexing feature of American economic life that President Roosevelt encountered was the rise of corporations and their emerging power and influence. Roosevelt understood how this change in business had come about and the prosperity that corporations might help to stimulate, but he was also mindful of the "evil" corporations could do. He begins this speech—given August 23, 1902, in Providence, Rhode Island, and now known by the above title—urging their regulation with an agricultural metaphor to underscore how with the advantages of great wealth comes the risk of adversity: "When the weather is good for the crops it is good for the weeds." The new economic conditions that bring so much wealth are also bringing starker divisions, "class cleavage" he calls it elsewhere, that the new urban landscape makes especially graphic. Corporations may shower money on more Americans, but how few get rich and how many remain poor are questions that Roosevelt believed right-thinking legislation must consider. States themselves will not exert constraints adequate to regulate these new engines of wealth that drive corporate growth. Any control must be exerted on the national level. If the federal government currently lacks the means to do so, it should remedy that at once. So mindful was Roosevelt of how corporations had the capacity to generate deep and long-term changes in American social life that he also warned against their presence in politics. He sought—after his reelection to the presidency—to prohibit corporations from making campaign contributions. It is especially ironic that a hundred years after Roosevelt sought to forbid the practice, corporations gained the right to contribute as much as they choose.

The Control of Corporations

Mr. Governor, and you, my fellow citizens:

We are passing through a period of great commercial prosperity, and such a period is as sure as adversity itself to bring mutterings of discontent. At a time when most men prosper somewhat some men always prosper greatly; and it is as true now as when the tower of Siloam fell upon all alike, that good fortune does not come solely to the just, nor bad fortune solely to the unjust. When the weather is good for crops it is good for weeds. Moreover, not only do the wicked flourish when the times are such that most men flourish, but, what is worse, the spirit of envy and jealousy springs up in the breasts of those who, though they may be doing fairly well themselves, see others no more deserving, who do better.

Wise laws and fearless and upright administration of the laws can give the opportunity for such prosperity as we see about us. But that is all that they can do. When the conditions have been created which make prosperity possible, then each individual man must achieve it for himself by his own energy and thrift and business intelligence. If when people wax fat they kick, as they have kicked since the days of Jeshurun, they will speedily destroy their own prosperity. If they go into wild speculation and lose their heads they have lost that which no laws can supply. If in a spirit of sullen envy they insist upon pulling down those who have profited most in the years of fatness, they will bury themselves in the crash of the common disaster. It is difficult to make our material condition better by the best laws, but it is easy enough to ruin it by bad laws.

The upshot of all this is that it is peculiarly incumbent upon us in a time of such material well-being, both collectively as a nation and individually as citizens, to show, each on his own account, that we possess the qualities of prudence, self-knowledge, and self-restraint. In our government we need above all things stability, fixity of economic policy; while remembering that this fixity must not be fossilization, that there must not be inability to shift our laws so as to meet our shifting national needs. There are real and great evils in our social and economic life, and these evils stand out in all their ugly baldness in time of prosperity; for the wicked who prosper are never a pleasant sight. There is every need of striving in all possible ways, individually and collectively, by combinations among ourselves and through the recognized governmental agencies, to cut out those evils. All I ask is to be sure that we do not use the knife with an ignorant zeal which would make it more dangerous to the patient than to the disease.

One of the features of the tremendous industrial development of the last generation has been the very great increase in private, and especially in corporate fortunes. We may like this or not, just as we choose, but it is a fact nevertheless; and as far as we can see it is an inevitable result of the working of the various causes, prominent among them steam and electricity. Urban population has grown in this country, as in all civilized countries, much faster than the population as a whole during the last century. If it were not for that Rhode Island could not today be the State she is. Rhode Island has flourished as she has flourished because of the conditions which have brought about the great increase in urban life. There is evil in these conditions, but you can't destroy it unless you destroy the civilization they have brought about. Where men are gathered together in great masses it inevitably results that they must work far more largely through combinations than where they live scattered and remote from one another. Many of us prefer the old conditions of life, under which the average man lived more to himself and by himself, where the average community was more self-dependent, and where even though the standard of comfort was lower on the average, yet there was less of the glaring inequality in worldly conditions which we now see about us in our great cities. It is not true that the poor have grown poorer; but some of the rich have grown so very much richer that, where multitudes of men are herded together in a limited space, the contrast strikes the onlooker as more violent than formerly. On the whole, our people earn more and live better than ever before, and the progress of which we are so proud could not have taken place had it not been for the upbuilding of industrial centres, such as this in which I am speaking.

But together with the good there has come a measure of evil. Life is not so simple as it was; and surely, both for the individual and the community, the simple life is normally the healthy life. There is not in the great cities the feeling of brotherhood which there is still in country localities; and the lines of social cleavage are far more deeply marked.

For some of the evils which have attended upon the good of the changed conditions we can at present see no complete remedy. For others the remedy must come by the action of men themselves in their private capacity, whether merely as individuals or by combination. For yet others some remedy can be found in legislative and executive action—national, State, or municipal. Much of the complaint against combinations is entirely unwarranted. Under present-day conditions it is as necessary to have corporations in the business world as it is to have organizations, unions, among wage-workers. We have a right to ask in each case only this: that good, and not harm, shall follow. Exactly as labor organizations, when managed intelligently and in a spirit of justice and fair play, are of very great service not only to the wage-workers, but to the whole community, as has been shown again and again in the history of many such organizations; so wealth, not merely individual, but corporate, when used aright is not merely beneficial to the community as a whole, but is absolutely essential to the upbuilding of such a series of communities as those whose citizens I am now addressing. This is so obvious that it ought to be too trite to mention, and yet it is necessary to mention it when we see some of the attacks made upon wealth, as such.

Of course a great fortune if used wrongly is a menace to the community. A man of great wealth who does not use that wealth decently is, in a peculiar sense, a menace to the community, and so is the man who does not use his intellect aright. Each talent—the talent for making money, the talent for showing intellect at the bar, or in any other way—if unaccompanied by character, makes the possessor a menace to the community. But such a fact no more warrants us in attacking wealth than it does in attacking intellect. Every man of power, by the very fact of that power, is capable of doing damage to his neighbors; but we can not afford to discourage the development of such men merely because it is possible they may use their power for wrong ends. If we did so we should leave our history a blank, for we should have no great statesmen, soldiers, merchants, no great men of arts, of letters, of science. Doubtless on the average the most useful citizen to the community as a whole is the man to whom has been granted what the Psalmist asked for—neither poverty nor riches. But the great captain of industry, the man of wealth, who, alone or in combination with his fellows, drives through our great business enterprises, is a factor without whom the civilization that we see round about us here could not have been built up. Good, not harm, normally comes from the upbuilding of such wealth. Probably the greatest harm done by vast wealth is the harm that we of moderate means do ourselves when we let the vices of envy and hatred enter deep into our own natures.

But there is other harm; and it is evident that we should try to do away with that. The great corporations which we have grown to speak of rather loosely as trusts are the creatures of the State, and the State not only has the right to control them, but it is in duty bound to control them wherever the need of such control is shown. There is clearly need of supervision—need to possess the power of regulation of these great corporations through the representatives of the public—wherever, as in our own country at the present time, business corporations become so very powerful alike for beneficent work and for work that is not always benefi-cent. It is idle to say that there is no need for such supervision. There is, and a sufficient warrant for it is to be found in any one of the admitted evils appertaining to them. We meet a peculiar difficulty under our system of government, because of the division of governmental power between the Nation and the States. When the industrial conditions were simple, very little control was needed, and the difficulties of exercising such con-trol under our Constitution were not evident. Now the conditions are complicated and we find it hard to frame national legislation which shall be adequate; while as a matter of practical experience it has been shown that the States either can not or will not exercise a sufficient control to meet the needs of the case. Some of our States have excellent laws—laws which it would be well indeed to have enacted by the National Legisla-ture. But the widespread differences in these laws, even between adjacent States, and the uncertainty of the power of enforcement, result practically in altogether insufficient control. I believe that the nation must assume this power of control by legislation; if necessary by constitutional amend-ment. The immediate necessity in dealing with trusts is to place them under the real, not the nominal, control of some sovereign to which, as its creatures, the trusts shall owe allegiance, and in whose courts the sovereign's orders may be enforced.

This is not the case with the ordinary so-called trust today; for the trust nowadays is a large State corporation, which generally does business in other States, often with a tendency toward monopoly. Such a trust is an artificial creature not wholly responsible to or controllable by any legislation, either by State or nation, and not subject to the jurisdiction of any one court. Some governmental sovereign must be given full power over these artificial, and very powerful, corporate beings. In my judgment this sovereign must be the National Government. When it has been given full power, then this full power can be used to control any evil influence, exactly as the government is now using the power conferred upon it by the Sherman anti-trust law.

Even when the power has been granted it would be most unwise to exercise it too much, to begin by too stringent legislation. The mechanism of modern business is as delicate and complicated as it is vast, and nothing would be more productive of evil to all of us, and especially to those least well off in this world's goods, than ignorant meddling with this mechanism—above all, meddling in a spirit of class legislation or hatred or rancor. It is eminently necessary that the power should be had, but it is just as necessary that it should be exercised with wisdom and self-restraint. The first exercise of that power should be the securing of publicity among all great corporations doing an interstate business. The publicity, though non-inquisitorial, should be real and thorough as to all important facts with which the public has concern. Daylight is a powerful discourager of evil. Such publicity would by itself tend to cure the evils of which there is just complaint; it would show us if evils existed, and where the evils are imaginary, and it would show us what next ought to be done.

Above all, let us remember that our success in accomplishing anything depends very much upon our not trying to accomplish everything. Distrust whoever pretends to offer you a patent cure-all for every ill of the body politic, just as you would a man who offers a medicine which would cure every evil of your individual body. A medicine that is recommended to cure both asthma and a broken leg is not good for either. Mankind has moved slowly upward through the ages, sometimes a little faster, sometimes a little slower, but rarely indeed by leaps and bounds. At times a great crisis comes in which a great people, perchance led by a great man, can at white heat strike some mighty blow for the right—make a long stride in advance along the path of justice and of orderly liberty. But normally we must be content if each of us can do something—not all that we wish, but something—for the advancement of those principles of righteousness which underlie all real national greatness, all true civilization and freedom. I see no promise of any immediate and complete solution of all the problems we group together when we speak of the trust question. But we can make a beginning in solving these problems, and a good beginning, if only we approach the subject with a sufficiency of resolution, of honesty, and of that hard common-sense which is one of the most valuable, and not always one of the most common, assets in any nation's greatness. The existing laws will be fully enforced as they stand on the statute books without regard to persons, and I think good has already come from their enforcement. I think, furthermore, that additional legislation should be had and can be had, which will enable us to accomplish much more along the same lines. No man can promise a perfect solution, at least in the immediate future. But something has already been done, and much more can be done if our people temperately and determinedly will that it shall be done.

In conclusion let me add one word. While we are not to be excused if we fail to do whatever is possible through the agency of government, we must keep ever in mind that no action of the government, no action by combination among ourselves, can take the place of the individual qualities to which in the long run every man must owe the success he can make of life. There never has been devised, and there never will be devised, any law which will enable a man to succeed save by the exercise of those qualities which have always been the prerequisites of success—the qualities of hard work, of keen intelligence, of unflinching will. Such action can supplement those qualities but it can not take their place. No action by the State can do more than supplement the initiative of the individual; and ordinarily the action of the State can do no more than to secure to each individual the chance to show under as favorable conditions as possible the stuff that there is in him.

"The Colonial Policy of the United States" from *African and European Addresses* (1910)

Only after he was out of office for two years did Roosevelt travel to Sweden to claim his Nobel Prize, which had been awarded in 1906, for his role in settling the Russo-Japanese War of 1905. At nearby Christiania, Norway, he offered the following remarks that he hoped would forestall the charges of imperialism so often levied against him. The talk, which later appeared in a volume edited by Lawrence Fraser Abbott, who accompanied Roosevelt on this foreign journey, bristles with his characteristic confidence in justifying the United States taking a more prominent role on the world stage and his willingness to undertake actions where there is need and when no one else will. To that end, he brings forward the leading examples of his international interventionism, in Cuba, the Philippines, and in San Domingo (now called the Dominican Republic). In each case, Roosevelt means to parry any accusation that the actions he called for were in any way conceived as forwarding the nation's own commercial or political interests over those of other nations. In the case of Cuba, he articulates a justification with which contemporary Americans themselves have grown familiar: the need to enter into military action in order to "help" a country to its "feet," to leave it "in better shape to maintain its permanent independent existence." Roosevelt closes his speech with an appeal to history, but now with the hindsight of a century, critics can see how sadly wrong was his confidence in several foreign policy decisions, as successful as each may have seemed in its day, such as the aggressive actions he sanctioned in creating the Panama Canal.

The Colonial Policy of the United States

An address delivered at Christiania,
Norway, on the Evening of May 5, 1910

When I first heard that I was to speak again this evening, my heart failed me. But directly after hearing Mr. Bratlie I feel that it is a pleasure to say one or two things; and before saying them, let me express my profound acknowledgment for your words. You have been not only more than just but more than generous. Because I have been so kindly treated, I am going to trespass on your kindness still further, and say a word or two about my own actions while I was President. I do not speak of them, my friends, save to illustrate the thesis that I especially uphold, that the man who has the power to act is to be judged not by his words but by his acts—by his words in so far as they agree with his acts. All that I say about peace I wish to have judged and measured by what I actually did as President.

I was particularly pleased by what you said about our course, the course of the American people, in connection with the Philippines and Cuba. I believe that we have the Cuban Minister here with us tonight? (A voice: "Yes.") Well, then, we have a friend who can check off what I am going to say. At the close of the war of '98 we found our army in possession of Cuba, and man after man among the European diplomats of the old school said to me: "Oh, you will never go out of Cuba. You said you would, of course, but that is quite understood; nations don't expect promises like that to be kept." As soon as I became President, I said, "Now you will see that the promise will be kept." We appointed a day when we would leave Cuba. On that day Cuba began its existence as an independent republic. Later there came a disaster, there came a revolution, and we were obliged to land troops again, while I was President, and then the same gentlemen with whom I had conversed before said: "Now you are relieved from your promise; your promise has been kept, and now you will stay in Cuba." I answered: "No, we shall not. We will keep the promise not only in the letter but in the spirit. We will stay in Cuba to help it on its feet, and then we will leave the island in better shape to maintain its permanent independent existence." And before I left the Presidency Cuba resumed its career as a separate republic, holding its head erect as a sovereign state among the other nations of the earth. All that our people want is just exactly what the Cuban people themselves want—that is, a continuance of order within the island, and peace and prosperity, so that there shall be no shadow of an excuse for any outside intervention.

We acted along the same general lines in the case of San Domingo. We intervened only so far as to prevent the need of taking possession of the island. None of you will know of this, so I will just tell you briefly what it was that we did. The Republic of San Domingo, in the West Indies, had suffered from a good many revolutions. In one particular period when I had to deal with the island, while I was President, it was a little difficult to know what to do, because there were two separate governments in the island, and a revolution going on against each. A number of dictators, under the title of President, had seized power at different times, had borrowed money at exorbitant rates of interest from Europeans and Americans, and had pledged the custom-houses of the different towns to different countries; and the chief object of each revolutionary was to get hold of the custom-houses. Things got to such a pass that it became evident that certain European Powers would land and take possession of parts of the island. We then began negotiations with the Government of the island. We sent down ships to keep within limits various preposterous little manifestations of the revolutionary habit, and, after some negotiations, we concluded an agreement. It was agreed that we should put a man in as head of the custom-houses, that the collection of customs should be entirely under the management of that man, and that no one should be allowed to interfere with the custom-houses. Revolutions could go on outside them without interference from us; but the custom-houses were not to be touched. We agreed to turn over to the San Domingo Government forty-five per cent of the revenue, keeping fifty-five per cent as a fund to be applied to a settlement with the creditors. The creditors also acquiesced in what we had done, and we started the new arrangement. I found considerable difficulty in getting the United States Senate to ratify the treaty, but I went ahead anyhow and executed it until it was ratified. Finally it was ratified, for the opposition was a purely factious opposition, representing the smallest kind of politics with a leaven of even baser motive. Under the treaty we have turned over to the San Domingo Government forty-five per cent of the revenues collected, and yet we have turned over nearly double as much as they ever got when they collected it *all* themselves. In addition, we have collected sufficient to make it certain that the creditors will receive every cent to which they are entitled. It is self-evident, therefore, that in this affair we gave a proof of our good faith. We might have taken possession of San Domingo. Instead of thus taking possession, we put into the custom-houses one head man and half a dozen assistants, to see that the revenues were honestly collected, and at the same time served notice that they should not be forcibly taken away; and the result has been an extraordinary growth of the tranquillity and prosperity of the islands, while at the same time the creditors are equally satisfied, and all danger of outside interference has ceased.

That incident illustrates two things: First, if a nation acts in good faith, it can often bring about peace without abridging the liberties of another nation. Second, our experience emphasizes the fact (which every Peace Association should remember) that the hysterical sentimentalist for peace is a mighty poor person to follow. I was actually assailed, right and left, by the more extreme members of the peace propaganda in the United States for what I did in San Domingo; most of the other professional peace advocates took no interest in the matter, or were tepidly hostile; however, I went straight ahead and did the job. The ultra-peace people attacked me on the ground that I had "declared war" against San Domingo, the "war" taking the shape of the one man put in charge of the custom-houses! This will seem to you incredible, but I am giving you an absolutely accurate account of what occurred. I disregarded those foolish people, as I shall always disregard sentimentalists of that type when they are guilty of folly. At the present we have comparative peace and prosperity in the island, in consequence of my action, and of my disregard of these self-styled advocates of peace.

The same reasoning applies in connection with what we did at the Isthmus of Panama, and what we are doing in the Philippines. Our colonial problems in the Philippines are not the same as the colonial problems of other Powers. We have in the Philippines a people mainly Asiatic in blood, but with a streak of European blood and with the traditions of European culture, so that their ideals are largely the ideals of Europe. At the moment when we entered the islands the people were hopelessly unable to stand alone. If we had abandoned the islands, we should have left them a prey to anarchy for some months, and then they would have been seized by some other Power ready to perform the task that we had not been able to perform. Now I hold that it is not worthwhile being a big nation if you cannot do a big task; I care not whether that task is digging the Panama Canal or handling the Philippines. In the Philippines I feel that the day will ultimately come when the Philippine people must settle for themselves whether they wish to be entirely independent, or in some shape to keep up a connection with us. The day has not yet come; it may not come for a generation or two. One of the greatest friends that liberty has ever had, the great British statesman Burke, said on one occasion that there must always be government, and that if there is not government from within, then it must be supplied from without. A child has to be governed from without, because it has not yet grown to a point when it can govern itself from within; and a people that shows itself totally unable to govern itself from within must expect to submit to more or less of government from without, because it cannot continue to exist on other terms—indeed, it cannot be permitted permanently to exist as a source of danger to other nations. Our aim in the Philippines is to train the people so that they may govern themselves from within. Until they have reached this point they cannot have self-government. I will never advocate self-government for a people so long as their self-government means crime, violence, and extortion, corruption within, lawlessness among themselves and towards others. If that is what self-government means to any people then they ought to be governed by others until they can do better.

What I have related represents a measure of practical achievement in the way of helping forward the cause of peace and justice, and of giving to different peoples freedom of action according to the capacities of each. It is not possible, as the world is now constituted, to treat every nation as one private individual can treat all other private individuals, because as yet there is no way of enforcing obedience to law among nations as there is among private individuals. If in the streets of this city a man walks about with the intent to kill somebody, if he manages his house so that it becomes a source of infection to the neighborhood, the community, with its law officers, deals with him forthwith. That is just what happened at Panama, and, as nobody else was able to deal with the matter, I dealt with it myself, on behalf of the United States Government, and now the Canal is being dug, and the people of Panama have their independence and a prosperity hitherto unknown in that country.

In the end, I firmly believe that some method will be devised by which the people of the world, as a whole, will be able to insure peace, as it cannot now be insured. How soon that end will come I do not know; it may be far distant; and until it does come I think that, while we should give all the support that we can to any possible feasible scheme for quickly bringing about such a state of affairs, yet we should meanwhile do the more practicable, though less sensational, things. Let us advance step by step; let us, for example, endeavor to increase the number of arbitration treaties and enlarge the methods for obtaining peaceful settlements. Above all, let us strive to awaken the public international conscience, so that it shall be expected, and expected efficiently, of the public men responsible for the management of any nation's affairs that those affairs shall be conducted with all proper regard for the interests and well-being of other Powers, great or small.

"The New Nationalism" (1910)

The appeal of this speech, first published in a collection of the same name, is how forcefully and effectively it communicates Roosevelt's fundamental political vision. In this address to the Union veterans of the Civil War, Roosevelt pauses several times to praise their sacrifice and valor of fifty years ago while adducing their example as a model for citizenship in the present. Yet the main object of Roosevelt's attack is, again, the exercise of economic or social privilege that only the powerful few, by virtue of their cunning, can exercise. The bulk of the speech is Roosevelt's case for the "square deal," his vision of fairness of opportunity and government's responsibility to intervene when unjust circumstances prevail. The square deal means giving a chance to those who would not ordinarily get a chance to make the most of their talents. Plank by plank, Roosevelt explains his platform, and with each explanation one feels his bristling scorn for privilege. It isn't so much that he detests inheritance or achievement; Roosevelt's contempt is reserved for the descendant who does not extend himself in the spirit of his antecedent and for the businessman who rigs the system, buying influence or bending laws, acting in combination to gain unfair advantages. Nor does Roosevelt merely champion workers or their unions; they too must abide by laws; they too must not seek their own undue influence or grow lawless. Roosevelt's "new nationalism" issues a call for centralizing powers to act when it is inefficient for state governments in their "utter confusion" to do so, to treat national problems by seeking national solutions. Roosevelt thus hopes that this modern nationalism will be "broad and far-reaching," dealing with "new problems" and putting "national needs" above "sectional or personal advantage." In the twenty-first century President Obama, in another speech at Osawatomie, Kansas, at the beginning of his reelection campaign, effectively sought to channel Roosevelt's demand that we turn to a "square deal" government over an unregulated free market to solve economic and social injustice and raise Americans' hopes.

The New Nationalism

Speech at Osawatomie, 31 August, 1910

We come here today to commemorate one of the epoch-making events of the long struggle for the rights of man—the long struggle for the uplift of humanity. Our country—this great republic—means nothing unless it means the triumph of a real democracy, the triumph of popular government, and, in the long run, of an economic system under which each man shall be guaranteed the opportunity to show the best that there is in him. That is why the history of America is now the central feature of the history of the world; for the world has set its face hopefully toward our democracy; and, O my fellow citizens, each one of you carries on your shoulders not only the burden of doing well for the sake of your own country, but the burden of doing well and of seeing that this nation does well for the sake of mankind.

There have been two great crises in our country's history: first, when it was formed, and then, again, when it was perpetuated; and, in the second of these great crises—in the time of stress and strain which culminated in the Civil War, on the outcome of which depended the justification of what had been done earlier, you men of the Grand Army, you men who fought through the Civil War, not only did you justify your generation, not only did you render life worth living for our generation, but you justified the wisdom of Washington and Washington's colleagues. If this republic had been founded by them only to be split asunder into fragments when the strain came, then the judgment of the world would have been that Washington's work was not worth doing. It was you who crowned Washington's work, as you carried to achievement the high purpose of Abraham Lincoln.

Now, with this second period of our history the name of John Brown will be forever associated; and Kansas was the theater upon which the first act of the second of our great national life dramas was played. It was the result of the struggle in Kansas which determined that our country should be in deed as well as in name devoted to both union and freedom; that the great experiment of democratic government on a national scale should succeed and not fail. In name we had the Declaration of Independence in 1776; but we gave the lie by our acts to the words of the Declaration of Independence until 1865; and words count for nothing except in so far as they represent acts. This is true everywhere; but, O my friends, it should be truest of all in political life. A broken promise is bad enough in private life. It is worse in the field of politics. No man is worth his salt in public life who makes on the stump a pledge which he does not keep after election; and, if he makes such a pledge and does not keep it, hunt him out of public life. I care for the great deeds of the past chiefly as spurs to drive us onward in the present. I speak of the men of the past partly that they may be honored by our praise of them, but more that they may serve as examples for the future.

It was a heroic struggle; and, as is inevitable with all such struggles, it had also a dark and terrible side. Very much was done of good, and much also of evil; and, as was inevitable in such a period of revolution, often the same man did both good and evil. For our great good fortune as a nation, we, the people of the United States as a whole, can now afford to forget the evil, or, at least, to remember it without bitterness, and to fix our eyes with pride only on the good that was accomplished. Even in ordinary times there are very few of us who do not see the problems of life as through a glass, darkly; and when the glass is clouded by the murk of furious popular passion, the vision of the best and the bravest is dimmed. Looking back, we are all of us now able to do justice to the valor and the disinterestedness and the love of the right, as to each it was given to see the right, shown both by the men of the North and the men of the South in that contest which was finally decided by the attitude of the West. We can admire the heroic valor, the sincerity, the self-devotion shown alike by the men who wore the Blue and the men who wore the Gray; and our sadness that such men should have had to fight one another is tempered by the glad knowledge that ever hereafter their descendants shall be found fighting side by side, struggling in peace as well as in war for the uplift of their common country, all alike resolute to raise to the highest pitch of honor and usefulness the nation to which they all belong. As for the veterans of the Grand Army of the Republic, they deserve honor and recognition such as is paid to no other citizens of the republic; for to them the republic owes its all; for to them it owes its very existence. It is because of what you and your comrades did in the dark years that we of today walk, each of us, head erect, and proud that we belong, not to one of a dozen little squabbling contemptible commonwealths, but to the mightiest nation upon which the sun shines.

I do not speak of this struggle of the past merely from the historic standpoint. Our interest is primarily in the application today of the lessons taught by the contest of half a century ago. It is of little use for us to pay lip loyalty to the mighty men of the past unless we sincerely endeavor to apply to the problems of the present precisely the qualities which in other crises enabled the men of that day to meet those crises. It is half melancholy and half amusing to see the way in which well-meaning people gather to do honor to the men who, in company with John Brown, and under the lead of Abraham Lincoln, faced and solved the great problems of the nineteenth century, while, at the same time, these same good people nervously shrink from, or frantically denounce, those who are trying to meet the problems of the twentieth century in the spirit which was accountable for the successful solution of the problems of Lincoln's time.

Of that generation of men to whom we owe so much, the man to whom we owe most is, of course, Lincoln. Part of our debt to him is because he forecast our present struggle and saw the way out. He said:—

I hold that while man exists it is his duty to improve not only his own condition, but to assist in ameliorating mankind.

And again:—

Labor is prior to, and independent of, capital. Capital is only the fruit of labor, and could never have existed if labor had not first existed. Labor is the superior of capital, and deserves much the higher consideration.

If that remark was original with me, I should be even more strongly denounced as a communist agitator than I shall be anyhow. It is Lincoln's.

I am only quoting it; and that is one side; that is the side the capitalist should hear. Now, let the workingman hear his side.

> *Capital has its rights, which are as worthy of protection as any other rights. . . . Nor should this lead to a war upon the owners of property. Property is the fruit of labor; . . . property is desirable; is a positive good in the world.*

And then comes a thoroughly Lincolnlike sentence:—

> *Let not him who is houseless pull down the house of another, but let him work diligently and build one for himself, thus by example assuring that his own shall be safe from violence when built.*

It seems to me that, in these words, Lincoln took substantially the attitude that we ought to take; he showed the proper sense of proportion in his relative estimates of capital and labor, of human rights and property rights. Above all, in this speech, as in many others, he taught a lesson in wise kindliness and charity; an indispensable lesson to us of today. But this wise kindliness and charity never weakened his arm or numbed his heart. We cannot afford weakly to blind ourselves to the actual conflict which faces us today. The issue is joined, and we must fight or fail.

In every wise struggle for human betterment one of the main objects, and often the only object, has been to achieve in large measure equality of opportunity. In the struggle for this great end, nations rise from barbarism to civilization, and through it people press forward from one stage of enlightenment to the next. One of the chief factors in progress is the destruction of special privilege. The essence of any struggle for healthy liberty has always been, and must always be, to take from some one man or class of men the right to enjoy power, or wealth, or position, or immunity, which has not been earned by service to his or their fellows. That is what you fought for in the Civil War, and that is what we strive for now.

At many stages in the advance of humanity, this conflict between the men who possess more than they have earned and the men who have earned more than they possess is the central condition of progress. In our day it appears as the struggle of free men to gain and hold the right of self-government as against the special interests, who twist the methods of free government into machinery for defeating the popular will. At every stage, and under all circumstances, the essence of the struggle is to equalize opportunity, destroy privilege, and give to the life and citizenship of every individual the highest possible value both to himself and to the commonwealth. That is nothing new. All I ask in civil life is what you fought for in the Civil War. I ask that civil life be carried on according to the spirit in which the army was carried on. You never get perfect justice, but the effort in handling the army was to bring to the front the men who could do the job. Nobody grudged promotion to Grant, or Sherman, or Thomas, or Sheridan, because they earned it. The only complaint was when a man got promotion which he did not earn.

Practical equality of opportunity for all citizens, when we achieve it, will have two great results. First, every man will have a fair chance to make of himself all that in him lies; to reach the highest point to which his capacities, unassisted by special privilege of his own and unhampered by the special privilege of others, can carry him, and to get for himself and his family substantially what he has earned. Second, equality of opportunity means that the commonwealth will get from every citizen the highest service of which he is capable. No man who carries the burden of the special privileges of another can give to the commonwealth that service to which it is fairly entitled.

I stand for the square deal. But when I say that I am for the square deal, I mean not merely that I stand for fair play under the present rules of the game, but that I stand for having those rules changed so as to work for a more substantial equality of opportunity and of reward for equally good service. One word of warning, which, I think, is hardly necessary in Kansas. When I say I want a square deal for the poor man, I do not mean that I want a square deal for the man who remains poor because he has not got the energy to work for himself. If a man who has had a chance will not make good, then he has got to quit. And you men of the Grand Army, you want justice for the brave man who fought, and punishment for the coward who shirked his work. Is not that so?

Now, this means that our government, national and state, must be freed from the sinister influence or control of special interests. Exactly as the special interests of cotton and slavery threatened our political integrity before the Civil War, so now the great special business interests too often control and corrupt the men and methods of government for their own profit. We must drive the special interests out of politics. That is one of our tasks today. Every special interest is entitled to justice—full, fair, and complete—and, now, mind you, if there were any attempt by mob violence to plunder and work harm to the special interest, whatever it may be, that I most dislike, and the wealthy man, whomsoever he may be, for whom I have the greatest contempt, I would fight for him, and you would if you were worth your salt. He should have justice. For every special interest is entitled to justice, but not one is entitled to a vote in Congress, to a voice on the bench, or to representation in any public office. The Constitution guarantees protection to property, and we must make that promise good. But it does not give the right of suffrage to any corporation.

The true friend of property, the true conservative, is he who insists that property shall be the servant and not the master of the commonwealth; who insists that the creature of man's making shall be the servant and not the master of the man who made it. The citizens of the United States must effectively control the mighty commercial forces which they have themselves called into being.

There can be no effective control of corporations while their political activity remains. To put an end to it will be neither a short nor an easy task, but it can be done.

We must have complete and effective publicity of corporate affairs, so that the people may know beyond peradventure whether the corporations obey the law and whether their management entitles them to the confidence of the public. It is necessary that laws should be passed to prohibit the use of corporate funds directly or indirectly for political purposes; it is still more necessary that such laws should be thoroughly enforced. Corporate expenditures for political purposes, and especially such expenditures by public service corporations, have supplied one of the principal sources of corruption in our political affairs.

It has become entirely clear that we must have government supervision of the capitalization, not only of public service corporations, including, particularly, railways, but of all corporations doing an interstate business. I do not wish to see the nation forced into the ownership of the railways if it can possibly be avoided, and the only alternative is thoroughgoing and effective regulation, which shall be based on a full knowledge of all the facts, including a physical valuation of property. This physical valuation is not needed, or, at least, is very rarely needed, for fixing rates; but it is needed as the basis of honest capitalization.

We have come to recognize that franchises should never be granted except for a limited time, and never without proper provision for compensation to the public. It is my personal belief that the same kind and degree of control and supervision which should be exercised over public service corporations should be extended also to combinations which control necessaries of life, such as meat, oil, and coal, or which deal in them on an important scale. I have no doubt that the ordinary man who has control of them is much like ourselves. I have no doubt he would like to do well, but I want to have enough supervision to help him realize that desire to do well.

I believe that the officers, and, especially, the directors, of corporations should be held personally responsible when any corporation breaks the law.

Combinations in industry are the result of an imperative economic law which cannot be repealed by political legislation. The effort at prohibiting all combination has substantially failed. The way out lies, not in attempting to prevent such combinations, but in completely controlling them in the interest of the public welfare. For that purpose the Federal Bureau of Corporations is an agency of first importance. Its powers, and, therefore, its efficiency, as well as that of the Interstate Commerce Commission, should be largely increased. We have a right to expect from the Bureau of Corporations and from the Interstate Commerce Commission a very high grade of public service. We should be as sure of the proper conduct of the interstate railways and the proper management of interstate business as we are now sure of the conduct and management of the national banks, and we should have as effective supervision in one case as in the other. The Hepburn Act, and the amendment to the Act in the shape in which it finally passed Congress at the last session, represent a long step in advance, and we must go yet further.

There is a widespread belief among our people that, under the methods of making tariffs which have hitherto obtained, the special interests are too influential. Probably this is true of both the big special interests and the little special interests. These methods have put a premium on selfishness, and, naturally, the selfish big interests have gotten more than their smaller, though equally selfish, brothers. The duty of Congress is to provide a method by which the interest of the whole people shall be all that receives consideration. To this end there must be an expert tariff commission, wholly removed from the possibility of political pressure or of improper business influence. Such a commission can find the real difference between cost of production, which is mainly the difference of labor cost here and abroad. As fast as its recommendations are made, I believe in revising one schedule at a time. A general revision of the tariff almost inevitably leads to log-rolling and the subordination of the general public interest to local and special interests.

The absence of effective state, and, especially, national, restraint upon unfair money getting has tended to create a small class of enormously wealthy and economically powerful men, whose chief object is to hold and increase their power. The prime need is to change the conditions which enable these men to accumulate power which it is not for the general welfare that they should hold or exercise. We grudge no man a fortune which represents his own power and sagacity, when exercised with entire regard to the welfare of his fellows. Again, comrades over there, take the lesson from your own experience. Not only did you not grudge, but you gloried in the promotion of the great generals who gained their promotion by leading the army to victory. So it is with us. We grudge no man a fortune in civil life if it is honorably obtained and well used. It is not even enough that it should have been gained without doing damage to the community. We should permit it to be gained only so long as the gaining represents benefit to the community. This, I know, implies a policy of a far more active governmental interference with social and economic conditions in this country than we have yet had, but I think we have got to face the fact that such an increase in governmental control is now necessary.

No man should receive a dollar unless that dollar has been fairly earned. Every dollar received should represent a dollar's worth of service rendered—not gambling in stocks, but service rendered. The really big fortune, the swollen fortune, by the mere fact of its size acquires qualities which differentiate it in kind as well as in degree from what is possessed by men of relatively small means. Therefore, I believe in a graduated income tax on big fortunes, and in another tax which is far more easily collected and far more effective—a graduated inheritance tax on big fortunes, properly safeguarded against evasion and increasing rapidly in amount with the size of the estate. . . .

The people of the United States suffer from periodical financial panics to a degree substantially unknown among the other nations which approach us in financial strength. There is no reason why we should suffer what they escape. It is of profound importance that our financial system should be promptly investigated, and so thoroughly and effectively revised as to make it certain that hereafter our currency will no longer fail at critical times to meet our needs.

It is hardly necessary for me to repeat that I believe in an efficient army and a navy large enough to secure for us abroad that respect which is the surest guarantee of peace. A word of special warning to my fellow citizens who are as progressive as I hope I am. I want them to keep up their interest in our internal affairs; and I want them also continually to remember Uncle Sam's interests abroad. Justice and fair dealing among nations rest upon principles identical with those which control justice and fair dealing among the individuals of which nations are composed, with the vital exception that each nation must do its own part in international police work. If you get into trouble here, you can call for the police; but if Uncle Sam gets into trouble, he has got to be his own policeman, and I want to see him strong enough to encourage the peaceful aspirations of other peoples in connection with us. I believe in national friendships and heartiest good will to all nations; but national friendships, like those between men, must be founded on respect as well as on liking, on forbearance as well as upon trust. I should be heartily ashamed of any American who did not try to make the American government act as justly toward the other nations in international relations as he himself would act toward any individual in private relations. I should be heartily ashamed to see us wrong a weaker power, and I should hang my head forever if we tamely suffered wrong from a stronger power.

Of conservation I shall speak more at length elsewhere. Conservation means development as much as it does protection. I recognize the right and duty of this generation to develop and use the natural resources of our land; but I do not recognize the right to waste them, or to rob, by wasteful use, the generations that come after us. I ask nothing of the nation except that it so behave as each farmer here behaves with reference to his own children. That farmer is a poor creature who skins the land and leaves it worthless to his children. The farmer is a good farmer who, having enabled the land to support himself and to provide for the education of his children, leaves it to them a little better than he found it himself. I believe the same thing of a nation.

Moreover, I believe that the natural resources must be used for the benefit of all our people, and not monopolized for the benefit of the few, and here again is another case in which I am accused of taking a revolutionary attitude. People forget now that one hundred years ago there were public men of good character who advocated the nation selling its public lands in great quantities, so that the nation could get the most money out of it, and giving it to the men who could cultivate it for their own uses. We took the proper democratic ground that the land should be granted in small sections to the men who were actually to till it and live on it. Now, with the water power, with the forests, with the mines, we are brought face to face with the fact that there are many people who will go with us in conserving the resources only if they are to be allowed to exploit them for their benefit. That is one of the fundamental reasons why the special interests should be driven out of politics. Of all the questions which can come before this nation, short of the actual preservation of its existence in a great war, there is none which compares in importance with the great central task of leaving this land even a better land for our descendants than it is for us, and training them into a better race to inhabit the land and pass it on. Conservation is a great moral issue, for it involves the patriotic duty of insuring the safety and continuance of the nation. Let me add that the health and vitality of our people are at least as well worth conserving as their forests, waters, lands, and minerals, and in this great work the national government must bear a most important part.

I have spoken elsewhere also of the great task which lies before the farmers of the country to get for themselves and their wives and children not only the benefits of better farming, but also those of better business methods and better conditions of life on the farm. The burden of this great task will fall, as it should, mainly upon the great organizations of the farmers themselves. I am glad it will, for I believe they are all well able to handle it. In particular, there are strong reasons why the Departments of Agriculture of the various states, the United States Department of Agriculture, and the agricultural colleges and experiment stations should extend their work to cover all phases of farm life, instead of limiting themselves, as they have far too often limited themselves in the past, solely to the question of the production of crops. And now a special word to the farmer. I want to see him make the farm as fine a farm as it can be made; and let him remember to see that the improvement goes on indoors as well as out; let him remember that the farmer's wife should have her share of thought and attention just as much as the farmer himself.

Nothing is more true than that excess of every kind is followed by reaction; a fact which should be pondered by reformer and reactionary alike. We are face to face with new conceptions of the relations of property to human welfare, chiefly because certain advocates of the rights of property as against the rights of men have been pushing their claims too far. The man who wrongly holds that every human right is secondary to his profit must now give way to the advocate of human welfare, who rightly maintains that every man holds his property subject to the general right of the community to regulate its use to whatever degree the public welfare may require it.

But I think we may go still further. The right to regulate the use of wealth in the public interest is universally admitted. Let us admit also the right to regulate the terms and conditions of labor, which is the chief element of wealth, directly in the interest of the common good. The fundamental thing to do for every man is to give him a chance to reach a place in which he will make the greatest possible contribution to the public welfare. Understand what I say there. Give him a chance, not push him up if he will not be pushed. Help any man who stumbles; if he lies down, it is a poor job to try to carry him; but if he is a worthy man, try your best to see that he gets a chance to show the worth that is in him. No man can be a good citizen unless he has a wage more than sufficient to cover the bare cost of living, and hours of labor short enough so that after his day's work is done he will have time and energy to bear his share in the management of the community, to help in carrying the general load. We keep countless men from being good citizens by the conditions of life with which we surround them. We need comprehensive workmen's compensation acts, both state and national laws to regulate child labor and work for women, and, especially, we need in our common schools not merely education in book learning, but also practical training for daily life and work. We need to enforce better sanitary conditions for our workers and to extend the use of safety appliances for our workers in industry and commerce, both within and between the states. Also, friends, in the interest of the workingman himself we need to set our faces like flint against mob violence just as against corporate greed; against violence and injustice and lawlessness by wage workers just as much as against lawless cunning and greed and selfish arrogance of employers. If I could ask but one thing of my fellow countrymen, my request would be that, whenever they go in for reform, they remember the two sides, and that they always exact justice from one side as much as from the other. I have small use for the public servant who can always see and denounce the corruption of the capitalist, but who cannot persuade himself, especially before election, to say a word about lawless mob violence. And I have equally small use for the man, be he a judge on the bench, or editor of a great paper, or wealthy and influential private citizen, who can see clearly enough and denounce the lawlessness of mob violence, but whose eyes are closed so that he is blind when the question is one of corruption in business on a gigantic scale. Also remember what I said about excess in reformer and reactionary alike. If the reactionary man, who thinks of nothing but the rights of property, could have his way, he would bring about a revolution; and one of my chief fears in connection with progress comes because I do not want to see our people, for lack of proper leadership, compelled to follow men whose intentions are excellent, but whose eyes are a little too wild to make it really safe to trust them. Here in Kansas there is one paper which habitually denounces me as the tool of Wall Street, and at the same time frantically repudiates the statement that I am a Socialist on the ground that that is an unwarranted slander of the Socialists.

National efficiency has many factors. It is a necessary result of the principle of conservation widely applied. In the end it will determine our failure or success as a nation. National efficiency has to do, not only with natural resources and with men, but it is equally concerned with institutions. The state must be made efficient for the work which concerns only the people of the state; and the nation for that which concerns all the people. There must remain no neutral ground to serve as a refuge for law-breakers, and especially for lawbreakers of great wealth, who can hire the vulpine legal cunning which will teach them how to avoid both jurisdictions. It is a misfortune when the national legislature fails to do its duty in providing a national remedy, so that the only national activity is the purely negative activity of the judiciary in forbidding the state to exercise power in the premises.

I do not ask for overcentralization; but I do ask that we work in a spirit of broad and far-reaching nationalism when we work for what concerns our people as a whole. We are all Americans. Our common interests are as broad as the continent. I speak to you here in Kansas exactly as I would speak in New York or Georgia, for the most vital problems are those which affect us all alike. The national government belongs to the whole American people, and where the whole American people are interested, that interest can be guarded effectively only by the national government. The betterment which we seek must be accomplished, I believe, mainly through the national government.

The American people are right in demanding that New Nationalism, without which we cannot hope to deal with new problems. The New Nationalism puts the national need before sectional or personal advantage. It is impatient of the utter confusion that results from local legislatures attempting to treat national issues as local issues. It is still more impatient of the impotence which springs from overdivision of governmental powers, the impotence which makes it possible for local selfishness or for legal cunning, hired by wealthy special interests, to bring national activities to a deadlock. This New Nationalism regards the executive power as the steward of the public welfare. It demands of the judiciary that it shall be interested primarily in human welfare rather than in property, just as it demands that the representative body shall represent all the people rather than any one class or section of the people.

I believe in shaping the ends of government to protect property as well as human welfare. Normally, and in the long run, the ends are the same; but whenever the alternative must be faced, I am for men and not for property, as you were in the Civil War. I am far from underestimating the importance of dividends; but I rank dividends below human character. Again, I do not have any sympathy with the reformer who says he does not care for dividends. Of course, economic welfare is necessary, for a man must pull his own weight and be able to support his family. I know well that the reformers must not bring upon the people economic ruin, or the reforms themselves will go down in the ruin. But we must be ready to face temporary disaster, whether or not brought on by those who will war against us to the knife. Those who oppose all reform will do well to remember that ruin in its worst form is inevitable if our national life brings us nothing better than swollen fortunes for the few and the triumph in both politics and business of a sordid and selfish materialism.

If our political institutions were perfect, they would absolutely prevent the political domination of money in any part of our affairs. We need to make our political representatives more quickly and sensitively responsive to the people whose servants they are. More direct action by the people in their own affairs under proper safeguards is vitally necessary. The direct primary is a step in this direction, if it is associated with a corrupt practices act effective to prevent the advantage of the man willing recklessly and unscrupulously to spend money over his more honest competitor. It is particularly important that all moneys received or expended for campaign purposes should be publicly accounted for, not only after election, but before election as well. Political action must be made simpler, easier, and freer from confusion for every citizen. I believe that the prompt removal of unfaithful or incompetent public servants should be made easy and sure in whatever way experience shall show to be most expedient in any given class of cases.

One of the fundamental necessities in a representative government such as ours is to make certain that the men to whom the people delegate their power shall serve the people by whom they are elected, and not the special interests. I believe that every national officer, elected or appointed, should be forbidden to perform any service or receive any compensation, directly or indirectly, from interstate corporations; and a similar provision could not fail to be useful within the states.

The object of government is the welfare of the people. The material progress and prosperity of a nation are desirable chiefly so far as they lead to the moral and material welfare of all good citizens. Just in proportion as the average man and woman are honest, capable of sound judgment and high ideals, active in public affairs—but, first of all, sound in their home life, and the father and mother of healthy children whom they bring up well—just so far, and no farther, we may count our civilization a success. We must have—I believe we have already—a genuine and permanent moral awakening, without which no wisdom of legislation or administration really means anything; and, on the other hand, we must try to secure the social and economic legislation without which any improvement due to purely moral agitation is necessarily evanescent. Let me again illustrate by a reference to the Grand Army. You could not have won simply as a disorderly and disorganized mob. You needed generals; you needed careful administration of the most advanced type; and a good commissary—the cracker line. You well remember that success was necessary in many different lines in order to bring about general success. You had to have the administration at Washington good, just as you had to have the administration in the field; and you had to have the work of the generals good. You could not have triumphed without that administration and leadership; but it would all have been worthless if the average soldier had not had the right stuff in him. He had to have the right stuff in him, or you could not get it out of him. In the last analysis, therefore, vitally necessary though it was to have the right kind of organization and the right kind of generalship, it was even more vitally necessary that the average soldier should have the fighting edge, the right character. So it is in our civil life. No matter how honest and decent we are in our private lives, if we do not have the right kind of law and the right kind of administration of the law, we cannot go forward as a nation. That is imperative; but it must be an addition to, and not a substitution for, the qualities that make us good citizens. In the last analysis, the most important elements in any man's career must be the sum of those qualities which, in the aggregate, we speak of as character. If he has not got it, then no law that the wit of man can devise, no administration of the law by the boldest and strongest executive, will avail to help him. We must have the right kind of character—character that makes a man, first of all, a good man in the home, a good father, a good husband—that makes a man a good neighbor. You must have that, and, then, in addition, you must have the kind of law and the kind of administration of the law which will give to those qualities in the private citizen the best possible chance for development. The prime problem of our nation is to get the right type of good citizenship, and, to get it, we must have progress, and our public men must be genuinely progressive.

"National Preparedness— Military—Industrial—Social" (1916)

For much of Roosevelt's time in national politics, he turned frequently to the theme of military preparedness, a mission he had pursued as Assistant Secretary of the Navy. That particular time of his career is a fascinating chapter of how he used, and some say abused, his office to put into practice a great many improvements to modernize the Navy. There is good reason to suppose that those innovations proved decisive during the Spanish-American War of 1898. From the outset of World War I in 1914, Roosevelt championed "preparedness" in his increasingly furious critiques of President Wilson's passivity, which Roosevelt thought put the nation at risk. Modern nations need only look to the atrocities in Belgium, about which he also wrote, to see how warfare had changed so markedly for the worse. Throughout the first years of the war, Roosevelt heartily campaigned for a military buildup, a faith in having a fully operating standing army, not limited to a mere 100,000 but large enough to protect a nation of 100 million. The triumph of Roosevelt's vision is that the U.S. military converted into a much stronger, more centralized institution, whose vision of continuous readiness instructed Americans in the virtue of sacrifice over the course of the century. The case for preparedness, however, is even more complex insofar as it also meant being able to execute the international duties of a great power. Rooseveltian preparedness was crucial for the country's moral and social well-being as well as its safety. It included universal service as well as a model of what shared national duties and a strong central government should resemble. At the beginning and close of this speech, Roosevelt addresses the men of both the Blue and the Gray, the veterans of fifty-five years before, to remind all: "Let us not from laziness or lack of foresight create a situation where brave men shall die to make good our shortsightedness."

National Preparedness—
Military—Industrial—Social

Speech at Kansas City, May 30, 1916

I come to Kansas City, here in the Great West, to speak on Memorial Day to the farmers and merchants and wage workers and manufacturers who dwell west of the Mississippi. What I have to say to you is exactly what I should say to your fellows who dwell on the Atlantic Coast, or the Pacific Slope, or beside the Great Lakes, or on the shores of the Gulf of Mexico. My message is a message to all Americans. My appeal is to the spirit of thorough-going Americanism in all our people in whatever portion of the land they dwell. In thanking all the organizations—business, political, and social—whose invitation I have accepted, including my comrades of the Spanish War, I know that none of you will object to my putting first the Grand Army of the Republic and the Confederate Veterans. I come here to speak on behalf of the spirit which, in the early sixties, burned in the hearts of the men who wore the Blue and of the men who wore the Gray. In what I have to say I shall appeal with equal emphasis to the soul qualities of the men who followed Grant and of the men who followed Lee; of all who, in the great crisis, proved their truth by their endeavor and showed themselves willing to sacrifice everything for the right, as God gave them to see the right. But I make no appeal to the spirit of the peace-at-any-price men of '61 to '65. I ask that we in this generation prove ourselves the spiritual heirs both of the men who wore the Blue and of the men who wore the Gray. But I make no appeal to the memory of the copperhead pacifists who put peace above duty, who put love of ease and love of money-getting before devotion to country, and whose convictions were too weak to stir to action their tepid souls.

This Is a Great Year of Decision.

This is one of the great years of decision in our national history. The way in which we now decide will largely determine whether we are to go forward in righteousness and power or backward in degradation and weakness. We are face to face with elemental facts of right and wrong, of force or feebleness. According to the spirit in which we face these facts and govern our actions, we shall determine whether in the future we shall enjoy a growing national life or suffer a lingering national decay.

First and foremost, friends, I ask you to beware of the false prophets, both the prophets of sordid materialism, and the prophets of that silly sentimentalism which refuses to look truths in the face if the truths are unpleasant. We cannot meet the future either by mere gross materialism or by mere silly sentimentalism; above all we cannot meet it if we attempt to balance gross materialism in action by silly sentimentalism in words. In actual practice the professional pacifists do not serve good. They serve evil. They do not serve high ideals. It is not righteous to fail to fight on behalf of assailed righteousness. Such a course probably means sheer cowardice, and certainly means moral surrender. The men who are the torch carriers of world civilization are those, and only those, who acknowledge the supreme duty of protecting sacred spiritual things when attacked. In actual practice the professional pacifist is merely the tool of the sensual materialist who has no ideals, whose shriveled soul is wholly absorbed in automobiles, and the movies, and money making, and in the policies of the cash register and the stock ticker, and the life of fatted ease.

Two years ago any number of persons were assuring us that the day of great wars had passed; that it was impossible that there ever should be great wars again; that preparedness brought on war; that we did not need to take any steps in our own defense; that the capitalists of the world, because high finance had become internationalized, would never permit a great war; that the opinion of the civilized world was enough to stop all international outrages. This was only two years ago. During these two years we have seen the most destructive war in all history waged on a wider scale than ever in history before. Never before has there been such slaughter as has been compressed into the last twenty-two months; and, alas that it should be written, the brutality, the ruthlessness, the disregard for International Law, and the callous and calculated atrocities committed on non-combatants, including women and children, have been such as the civilized world has not even approached during the past century.

Two years ago the false prophets who said that there never would be another war were applauded by all our people who were wholly absorbed in money-getting; by all who cared only for lives of soft ease and vapid pleasure; by all who liked to satisfy their emotions cheaply and safely by applauding high-sounding phrases; and by the great mass of well-meaning men who had not thought out the matter with conscientious thoroughness.

Let Us Not Be Misled.

Let us not be misled again. Undoubtedly as soon as this war ends all the well-meaning, short-sighted persons, who two years ago said there never would be a war again, and who have been obliged to be silent on this particular point during the past two years, will once more begin their shrill pipings that the last war has occurred. Once more they will demand or announce the invention of some patent device by which strong and ruthless and cunning men will be held in place by timid men without any preparedness, without any display of courage or acceptance of endurance, risk, labor, and hardship.

When this war is over it is possible that some one of the combatants, being fully armed, will assail us because we offer ourselves as a rich and helpless prize. On the other hand it is also possible that there will be temporary exhaustion among the combatants, and a willingness, even on the part of the most brutal and ruthless, to go through the form of saying that they are peaceful and harmless. In such event there will be real danger lest our people be influenced by the foolish apostles of unpreparedness to accept this condition as permanent, and once more to shirk our duty of getting ready.

I wish to say, with all the emphasis in my power, that if peace in Europe should come tomorrow, it ought not, in the smallest degree, to affect our policy of preparedness. As a matter of fact, we probably cannot now prepare in any way that will have a material effect upon the present war. Our folly has been such that it is now too late for us to do this. All we can now do is to prepare so that the war shall leave no aftermath of horror and disaster for our nation. If we fail so to prepare then assuredly some day we or our children will have bitter cause to rue our folly, and to remember too late the words of old Sir Thomas Browne: "For since we cannot be wise by teachings . . . there is an unhappy necessity that we must smart in our own skins."

I wish especially to call the attention of all people who may be momentarily misled by the statements of the peace-at-any-price men, the professional pacifists of today, to the actual results of our policy of unpreparedness. Twenty-two months have gone by since this war began. Nearly five years have gone by since the revolution in Mexico loosed on Americans in Mexico, and on Americans on our own side of the border, the forces of murder and misrule. Yet, during these five years we have taken no efficient steps to control the situation in Mexico, and during these twenty-two months, since the world has been in such a cataclysm of fear and blood as never before in its history, we of this Republic, with literally astounding folly, with a folly criminal from the national standpoint, have refused in any way to prepare. The professional pacifists said, and even now say, that such preparedness would have invited trouble with Mexico and trouble with Germany and perhaps with other old world powers. Look at the facts! We kept ourselves helpless to do justice to or for Mexico; we refused to make ready in any way to protect our citizens in Mexico, or even on our own side of the Mexican border. We submitted tamely to the murder of our men and the rape of our women. We bore with spiritless submission outrages upon outrages, until the number of our citizens killed mounted into the hundreds. Yet, so far from securing the good-will of the Mexicans, this policy of unpreparedness and of tame submission to insult and injury, merely aroused both their anger and contempt to such a degree that we are now engaged in a harassing little war along the border.

We have not the forces to make that war effective. We have actually drained the Coast Artillery from the seaboard defense, to serve as infantry down on the Mexican border. This nation of one hundred million people with a territory as large as all Europe, and more wealth than any other nation in the world possesses, has to strip its seacoast forts of their defenders and put these defenders at work which they are not trained to do. Even thus we are wholly unable to make good our complete lack of preparedness.

The Price of Irresolution.

If at the outset, if three years ago, we had resolutely and with foresight prepared to act, and then, if necessary, acted, in Mexico, that country would
today be as peaceful and prosperous as Cuba—where we actually did take
the very action I advocate for Mexico. If, the instant that the great war
broke out in July, 1914, our fleet had been mobilized, a competent man
put at the head of the Navy Department, our army put into proper trim,
and steps taken by our representatives at Washington, both Executive and
Legislative, to show that we were making ready to meet any exigency that
arose, there would have been no trouble of any kind with any belligerent.
Of course, when we submitted to wrongdoing from one side, we invited
a repetition of that wrongdoing by that side, and the infliction of similar
wrongs by the other side. The thousands of non-combatants, men, women
and children, including many hundreds of American men, women, and
children, who have been killed on the high seas, owe the loss of their lives
primarily to the supine inaction of this nation; to our failure to prepare,
and our failure in instant insistence on our own rights and on those rights
of others which we had guaranteed to protect.

The professional pacifists insisted that such lack of preparedness on
our part, and the observance by us of that kind of neutrality which consists in tame acceptance of injury from all sides, would make us popular
with all the combatants and insure our well-being. On the contrary, the
only effect has been to earn for us the contemptuous dislike of all the
warring nations and to bring us to the verge of trouble with them. If we
had prepared we would have saved thousands of lives and we would have
guaranteed our own peace. The failure to prepare, the failure to stand
up for the rights of ourselves and of others, the yielding to wrongdoing,
resulted both in deferring the day when it was possible for this nation to
act as peacemaker, and in bringing us measurably nearer to the danger
of ourselves being involved in the conflict. Weakness invites contempt.
Weakness combined with bluster invites both contempt and aggression.
Self-respecting strength that respects the rights of others is the only quality that secures respect from others. If, in our foreign policy, we are weak,
if we use lofty words at the same time that we commit mean or unworthy
actions, and above all, if we fail to protect our own rights, we shall not
secure the good-will of any one, and we shall incur the contempt of other

nations; and contempt of that kind is easily turned into active international violence. If we cannot protect ourselves we may be sure that no one else will protect us. If we are not prepared in advance, we cannot be true to ourselves; and if we are not true to ourselves we shall certainly be false to every one else.

International Duty.

I believe in International Duty. I hold that we cannot assert that we are entirely guiltless of responsibility for the outrages committed on well-behaved nations, particularly on Belgium, and on non-combatants, particularly on women and children, in the present war. Prior to the war we had become parties to the various conventions and treaties designed to mitigate the horrors of war, and to limit the offenses that can, with impunity, be committed by belligerents either on neutrals or non-combatants. When we declined to take any action under these conventions and treaties we ourselves treated them as "scraps of paper." Such being the case, while our guilt is not as great as that of the strong and ruthless nations who committed the misdeeds, we nevertheless occupy, in some respects, an even meaner position. For we possess strength, and yet we refuse to make ready this strength and we refuse to use it for righteousness. We possess strength, and yet we decline to put it behind our plighted word when the interests and honor of others are involved.

Performance of international duty to others means that in international affairs, in the commonwealth of nations, we shall not only refrain from wronging the weak, but shall, according to our capacity, and as opportunity offers, stand up for the weak when the weak are wronged by the strong. Most emphatically it does not mean that we shall submit to wrong-doing by other nations. To do so is a proof not of virtue, but of weakness, and of a mean and abject national spirit. To submit to wrongdoing is to encourage wrongdoing; and it is, therefore, itself, a form of iniquity—and a peculiarly objectionable form of iniquity, for it is based on cowardice. The first step in securing international justice is that every peaceful, well-behaved nation shall develop its own strength and its intelligent will power, so as to prevent ill-behaved nations from wrong-doing. The second step is that the strong among these well-behaved nations shall, in some way or shape extend aid and comfort to their weak well-behaved brothers, when the latter are wronged. The duty of a nation like ours cannot be considered as if we stood alone in the world. We are one of a community of nations and the effective condemnation of wrong-doing by that community is the great force of civilization. If we shirk our part of that duty to condemn, and if necessary more than condemn, the wrong, we are aiding to break down the force of the public opinion of mankind in the support of justice and righteousness, and with that we are helping to destroy the forces of peace and justice which serve to prevent others from doing wrong towards us and thus serve to preserve our peace and safety. It is, however, worse than idle, it is mischievous, to indulge in visionary plans about world-action in the future, until, in the present, we act as we should in two vital matters; in the first place by abandoning the pernicious habit of making reckless promises which cannot, or ought not, or will not be kept, and in the second place, and most important of all, by preparing our own strength so that we can protect our own rights.

Preparedness Secures Justice.

Preparedness, instead of being provocative of war and injustice, tells in favor of peace and justice. Only through preparedness can we do justice to others. Only through preparedness can we secure justice for ourselves. Well-meaning persons who have not thought seriously or deeply on the subject sometimes assert that we are too far away from the old world ever to fear assault or invasion. The answer is two-fold. In the first place we have under our flag the Canal Zone and Alaska, and various islands. These it is absolutely impossible to protect from any formidable foe except by a first-class navy and army. In the next place, the events of the present war show that the ocean is now a highway for any power whose ships control it. We have just witnessed the transfer by sea of a Russian army from Eastern Siberia to France—a sea voyage three times as long as that across the Atlantic. We have seen a huge army gathered at the Dardanelles from England, France, and Australia; and the distance from Australia to the Dardanelles is far greater than the distance from Asia to our shores. There gathered for the attack on Constantinople a host of fighting men drawn from the great island-continent of the South Pacific, and they were joined by the fighting men of the British Isles, who dwelt on the opposite side of the world. From the northern and the southern hemispheres, the transport steamers have carried with speed and safety, over the two greatest oceans, masses of troops ten times as numerous as our whole mobile army. If any army half the size of that which attacked the Dardanelles was landed near New York or San Francisco in a time no longer than that occupied by the British and Australians in reaching the Dardanelles, we should in the present condition of our forces be utterly at its mercy. The immediate loss would fall on the Atlantic or Pacific coast; but we are all Americans, and the disgrace would be shared by all of us wherever we live, and the blow to our self-respect and our material well-being would shake our whole country to its foundations.

Those who confidently assert that there is no danger of our ever being attacked are either ignorant or forgetful of the multitude of examples which show how international conflicts arise. The pressure of population and a desire for wealth and power now as in former ages are urging nations in the old world to get possession of all the unoccupied or weakly held parts of the earth from which profit can be derived. This is what has often brought rival European nations face to face and to the verge of war in Asia and Africa. It has played a great part in bringing on the present war. It is possible that some nation will attack us out of hand, making of some action on the part of our people a plausible cause of quarrel. It is much more likely that if we are not strong enough to maintain our rights, including the assertion of the Monroe Doctrine, we shall be subjected to a series of aggressions upon our rights growing more and more grievous until we reach a point where we ourselves shall be obliged to resent the aggression or else to abandon policies essential to our national greatness and well-being.

The Prime Needs in Preparedness.

The prime needs in preparedness, the needs which can be immediately met, are to give us, first, the navy we require, and second the regular army we require. I have elsewhere given the reasons why we require the second navy in the world and a small, highly efficient regular army of 250,000 men, with a proper reserve. Here let it suffice to say that such a navy and such an army would be our best insurance against war and for peace.

But the navy and the regular army are not enough. Exactly as back of the navy should stand the regular army, so back of the regular army should stand the nation. I speak to, and on behalf of, a nation of freemen. Freemen fit to be freemen do not have to hire other men to do their fighting. I speak here on the invitation of the men who wore the Blue and the men who wore the Gray of fifty years ago; of the men who fought in the two great citizen armies when, North and South, the bravest and best in the land went forth to battle for their deep convictions. I ask that we of this generation be loyal to the memories of our fathers, and be ready at need to pay with our own bodies for our own principles. When I ask you to prepare by seeing that your representatives provide a first-class navy and a first-class regular army, I am merely asking you to prepare to have the other fellow do your fighting for you. This does not satisfy me. It ought not to satisfy you. You and I, friends, cannot be loyal to the memory of Washington, and of Grant, and of Lee, unless we are fit and ready to do our own fighting in time of need. I do not wish us, the people, to sink into a condition where we are so soft, so ease loving, so fond of pleasures, or so wrapped up in money-getting that we cannot do the hard work that brave men must do when the need calls. I speak for universal service based on universal training.

Universal Training and Universal Service.

Universal training and universal service represent the only service and training a democracy should accept. It is the plain people, it is the farmers, the working men, the small business men, the professional men, who above all others should back up this plan. I have just received a letter from a friend, a farmer in North Carolina, who is arranging to have six farmers' boys from his neighborhood sent to one of the training camps for boys this summer. He writes that he has been besieged by farmers and their wives to send their sons to that camp. They wish them to get the training, to have the value of the trip, and of the association with boys from other parts of the country. They realize how much good it would do them in every way. They realize that the kind of training for preparedness that their boys would receive would help them industrially in time of peace just as much as in war. These farmers and their wives do not wish war. They do not wish their sons to go to war if the war can legitimately be avoided. But they feel that if the nation does get into a fight they wish their sons to take part in that fight, and in such event they wish them to be able to take care of themselves and not merely be helpless victims of fever or of bullets.

The farmers and wage workers, the business men and professional men who are not men of large means, and whose wives have to exercise proper economy in order to keep their homes happy and comfortable—these are the people who, beyond all others, should realize that such training should not be reserved for the boys whose fathers or friends are rich enough to pay for it, but should be given to all American boys at the expense of the nation. It is the present lack of system, the present method of allowing only those boys to train whose fathers have money, which is unfair and undemocratic. It breeds class distinction, among other unhealthy things. I do not believe as a permanent thing in a system that merely puts the Harvard boy alongside the Yale boy or the Princeton boy, the big merchant's son or railroad president's son beside the big lawyer's son or, perhaps, beside the employee of the rich man who is patriotic enough to pay his expenses. All this is the best that we can get at present; and until the people as a whole wake up. But it is not enough. I believe in the system that will put all the boys I have mentioned alongside the boy whose father is a brakeman here in Missouri, or a hardworking farmer in Kansas, or a factory operative in Massachusetts or New Jersey, or a bookkeeper or stenographer in New York or Chicago; that will put all of them beside the boy from the mountains of North Carolina who has never seen a railway train and has always gone barefoot. Let all these boys be given the same kind of training, and let the best boy out of the bunch become an officer. Let no one be allowed to shirk the duty of preparing himself, for if he does, he is putting on the shoulders of a better man the burden which he himself should carry.

The Volunteer Training Camps.

We have heard a good deal of talk about the officer class, that we are getting from the volunteer training camps of the present day. As long as we do not have universal military service these camps offer the only chance for young men to prepare so as to serve the country. The man who goes to them renders a high and patriotic service and incidentally profits immensely by the training and experience. My sons have gone and are going to these camps. I believe in these camps with all my heart and soul. They are supplying by private initiative what our governmental representatives have not the foresight to provide for everybody. As long as our citizens do not insist upon everybody being trained, upon everyone going to such camps, why, the boys that do go to them will inevitably get the commissions if war comes.

In other words, as long as our people do not make the training universal, and do not make it paid for by the commonwealth, only the men of means will be trained as officers at these camps. At present this is the only way to provide that, in the event of war, we shall have officers worth having. But such a system is fundamentally undemocratic. It is our own fault, the fault of our people, that we do not establish the really democratic system, for the only way to establish the democratic system is through universal service. Napoleon drew his marshals from the humblest ranks, simply because they were the best men for the job; and in a democratic army promotion should go by merit. Here, at present, the son of the farmer and the son of the wage worker know that they have little chance to become officers in the event of war because they cannot afford the time and the money to get themselves trained in advance. I ask the plain people of the United States, I ask the farmers, the wage workers, the ordinary men, to give their sons the same chance that the sons of wealthier men have. Make the opportunity open to all; to your sons, to my sons; to all on an even basis. A system of universal training for universal service would be one of the biggest things ever done in this country to preserve our democratic institutions in spirit and in fact.

The Spirit the Country Needs.

The other day when I spoke on universal service in Detroit a woman in the gallery called out: "I have two sons and they shall both go if the country needs them." I answered her, "Madam, I take off my hat to you. That is the spirit this country needs, and if all the mothers of the country will do as you do and raise their boys so that they shall be able and ready at need to fight for the country, there will never be any need for any of them to fight for the country. No nation will ever attack a unified and prepared America."

And to you men of the Grand Army, and you, Confederate Veterans, I need not say that this was in effect what was done in our Civil War. Of course, the men who had been trained at West Point had an initial advantage; but every one went into the ranks on even terms and men from the ranks rose to the highest positions on their merits. Let me illustrate this by an incident out of my own experience. I was colonel of a volunteer regiment at Santiago in the Spanish War. I served under the then Brigadier-General Sam Young, and I served beside the then Brigadier-General Adna Chaffee. Later, as President, it was my good fortune to give, first to Sam Young, and afterwards to Adna Chaffee, the appointment of Lieutenant-General of the United States, the highest office in the United States Army. On the day that Sam Young retired, and that Adna Chaffee was to take his place and be presented as Lieutenant-General at the White House, it happened that Chaffee's epaulettes had not come and Sam Young sent him around his own epaulettes with a little note reading, "These are presented by Private Young, '61, to Private Chaffee, '61." The two fine old boys had entered the army in the same year at the beginning of the Civil War as privates in the ranks, and they had worked their way up by sheer force of courage and character, and perseverance and ability, until they stood in succession in the highest position at the head of the army in which they had once served as enlisted men. That symbolized what the American army should be, and what we could make the American army under a system of universal service based on universal training. It is a system which will give every man an equal chance, which will make it the duty of each man to learn how to serve his country, and which will secure to each man the right to serve that country in the capacity to which his ability entitles him. Such an army would be a people's army; and it would never be used except in a people's war.

Remember always that what I ask is asked in the name of peace and in the name of democracy, no less than in the name of national honor and interest. It is the men who do not believe in peace at any price who are most apt to secure the peace which self-respecting men and women can accept. I ask that this nation prepare, in the first place, because if war should be thrust upon us, we must be able to emerge victorious from the trial, and we cannot do so unless we are prepared; and in the second place I ask that we prepare because it is the surest way to secure peace, the surest way to keep war from our borders. Little Switzerland is at peace at this moment because she prepared and only because she prepared. In the Napoleonic wars Switzerland was overrun by French, German, and Russian armies; great battles were fought within her limits and she became an appanage of the French Empire—and all this purely and solely because at that time she had not prepared, she was not able to hold her own against invaders. A century later a war even greater bursts over Europe. Switzerland's natural boundaries and defenses are precisely what they were; the temptation to use her territory is precisely as great for the belligerents, but Switzerland had prepared, and therefore Switzerland today is at peace.

All-Round Preparedness the Need.

Military preparedness is only one side of all-round preparedness. It would be worthless unless based on industrial preparedness, and both would be worthless unless based on preparedness of the soul and the spirit. You men who wore the Blue and the Gray, when once the war was over, turned to the farm and the shop and the counting house, and again took up your life work of earning your living and supporting your families, and making provision for the generation that was to come after you. You did this work thoroughly, as you had thoroughly done the work of war.

Our people of today must apply your spirit to the changed circumstances of today. It is never possible to treat the past as giving the exact precedent for given action in the present. But the spirit shown by the men who in the great crises in the past rose level to those crises, must be shown by the men of the present in the crisis of the present. In this country we have the double duty of training ourselves so as to be willing to die for the country and of developing our internal policy so as to make the country worth living in. In the long run the country *must* be worth living in if it is worth dying for.

In order to make this country worth living in we must develop a real national purpose controlled not only by moral motives but by cool intelligence. If our people put a premium upon the demagogue by supporting the man who makes impossible promises, and who either does not attempt to reduce these promises to action, or else fails in attempting to do so, then we shall go down. The people must choose as their executive and legislative leaders at Washington men absolutely national in spirit; men whose theory of government is as far as the poles from the pork-barrel theory—and this, whether the pork-barrel be considered from a personal, political, or sectional standpoint—men who look forward and not back; men who face the facts as they actually are. After this war we shall see a new Europe; a Europe energetically developing new social and economic means of meeting new problems. If, under these circumstances, we take refuge in formulae dug out as fossils from the workings of principles in the past, instead of developing these principles so as to meet the future, we shall be as foolish as if we were to arm our soldiers with flintlocks and send them against an army possessing machine guns, high-power rifles, and modern artillery. The time for flintlock theories of statesmanship in this country is past.

This applies as much to industry as to national defense. To let the interstate transportation systems of the country, for example, be regulated by forty-eight small conflicting sovereignties, is just as foolish as to trust to forty-eight conflicting sovereignties in military matters. The nation must regulate the arteries of traffic for the whole country in the interests of the whole country. It must control the armed forces of the whole country in the interests of the whole country. In such matters there cannot be divided sovereignty without national weakness. Moreover, what applies to railways directly or indirectly concerned in interstate business, also applies to all great corporations engaged in interstate or international business.

Two Dominating Truths.

I stand with all my heart for military preparedness; but no one knows better than I that military preparedness alone can neither make nor maintain a great nation. It is merely the essential safeguard for a nation industrially efficient and prosperous, and with a prosperity justly distributed; a safeguard for a national life organized in all points for national ends and national ideals. This national life must be dominated by the two great truths; first, that in a successful democracy, every man must, in reasonable measure, be his "brother's keeper," and second, that every citizen in such a democracy must accept with his whole heart the principle that his first duty in war or in peace is to serve the nation.

Occasionally it is said by some one blind to industrial tendencies that the nation has no right to regulate the activities of the great successful business men. Occasionally it is said by some unworthy would-be labor leader that the workingman owes nothing to the country, because there is not enough of such regulation in his interest. Each statement must be emphatically repudiated by every patriot. If any man, whether workingman or capitalist, believes that he owes nothing to this country, then the sooner he gets out of the country the better, for he is unfit to do good to himself or to anyone else. Such a man is not entitled to claim companionship with you veterans of the Civil War who are here today. He is unfit to live in the land which is proud of the memory of your deeds. On the other hand the great business men must recognize more and more, that there must be full and frank co-operation between them and the government to secure the public welfare. On the part of the government this co-operation must be given with the sincere desire to increase the efficiency of our industrial organization, not to hamper it, and with full recognition of the fact that much of modern industry must be carried on by great industrial units. The aim of government should be not to destroy these units but, while encouraging them, to regulate them in the interests of the people as a whole. At the same time the big business man must with equal frankness recognize the fact that his business activities, while beneficial to himself and his associates, must also justify themselves by being beneficial to the men who work for him, and to the public which he serves.

Other National Needs.

A nation to survive must stand for the principles of social and industrial justice.

If any class is here oppressed, or so neglected that the neglect becomes in effect oppression, the ideals of patriotism in that class will assuredly be dwarfed and stunted. We must not let any man think that he can shirk his own duties, or blame his own failure and shortcomings on others; and yet we must shape our collective action, so that as far as possible each man shall have a fair chance to show the stuff that is in him, unhelped and unhampered by special privilege. Legislation to help the business man is eminently proper, but only on condition that we show equal zeal for the working and living rights, the social and economic rights, of farmer and wage earner; in short, the rights of all productive citizens must be safeguarded with equal care. A protective tariff with the duties adjusted outside of factional politics is essential in the industrial world of today. But the protective tariff by itself means nothing but the rudimentary beginning of the needed policy, or rather policies, for the broadest national development of our economic life, along lines designed to secure real, substantial justice. Our national resources must be conserved, but the conservation must be in the public interest, and on this as on all other points the prosperity and growth of industry must, so far as possible, be made to go hand in hand with a reasonably equitable distribution of its returns.

In addition to treating our brother man and sister woman as we would wish them to treat us, we must also endeavor, so far as we are able, to secure them just treatment by others. This is why we must try to abolish child labor. This is why we must see that women in industry are protected from inhuman treatment of any kind. This is why we must try to secure, not merely for women and children, but for men also, conditions of life and labor, such that the head of the family will not be ground under foot by excessive toil, nor kept to a wage that will not permit him to bring up his family in the way it should be brought up, that will not permit him to save his wife from prostrating drudgery. It does not mean that we shall try to give to the shiftless the same reward as to the energetic and hard working. It does not mean that we shall permit the vicious to commit wrong with impunity. It does not mean that we shall excuse any wage worker, or any other man for failure to honor the United States flag and wholeheartedly to serve the nation—for the privileges of citizenship should be conditioned on the possession and exercise of patriotism. But it does mean that for the sake of our children and children's children who are to come after us, we shall strive to bring about conditions in this country such as to free every hard working and right thinking man from the sense of injustice and oppression, from the feeling that the laws do not secure him justice, but do give an advantage over against him to unscrupulous cunning and unscrupulous force. In the long run our children's children will find that this is not a good country for any one to live in unless we and they make it a reasonably good country for every one to live in.

Performance Not Promise Needed.

What I thus say does not represent anything new in principle. On the contrary, the principles thus set forth have received the lip loyalty of many men before election, who, after election, forgot their pre-election promises. What we need in our public men is performance, not promise; to treat a platform merely as a means of getting office, not as a covenant to be kept in office, is demoralizing both to the public and to the servants of the public.

Now, friends, the men here today whom I have particularly addressed, the men who wore the Blue, and the men who wore the Gray in the Civil War, proved that they had convictions worth dying for. They thereby made this a land worth living in. They showed that they were willing to sacrifice everything, including life itself, for certain great ideals. They thereby ranged themselves among the great peoples of mankind. No nation is really great, no race is entitled to a permanent position of leadership or of equality on this earth, unless its sons are willing to die at need for great ideals. But it is equally important that they shall show a like power of fealty to ideals in the way they live their ordinary lives. If after the close of the Civil War the soldiers who fought in it on both sides had shown themselves so demoralized by the four years of fighting that they could not settle down to civil life, but insisted on continuing in arms and plunging the country into anarchy, the net result of their former heroism would have been destruction for this nation.

Such a result would have proved that, although we could produce soldiers, we could not produce citizens—and the soldier who is a bad citizen, and the citizen who cannot, at need, serve as a soldier are equally unfit to live in a free, self-governing commonwealth.

The Lesson of Heroism.

This is Memorial Day. You have today decorated the graves of gallant men who paid by their death for the lack of wisdom and foresight shown by their forefathers. This is a day of homage to heroism. But it is also a day of mourning. For forty years prior to the Civil War our people refused to face facts and soberly bend their energies to make war impossible. Heroes shed their blood, and women walked all their lives in the shadow, because there had been such lack of foresight, such slothful, lazy optimism. Let the lesson thus taught sink into the minds of us of this generation. Let us not from laziness and lack of foresight create a situation where brave men shall die to make good our shortsightedness. I ask that we prepare, not because I wish war, but because with all my heart I desire to keep war afar from us; and only by forethought and by preparation of soul and body can we thus keep it afar off.

The end we have in view is a high and fine national life based on an industrial efficiency which shall be accompanied by social and economic justice. Military preparedness against war is merely a means to this end. But it is an indispensable means. We are not fit to be free men unless we show the forethought and will power necessary to insure that we ourselves shall have the right to decide our own destinies, and not be forced helplessly to submit to have them decided by alien conquerors.

If we are true to the men of the mighty past we shall guide ourselves by what Lowell wrote to the pacifists of his time, who—to use his own words—wished to "knuckle down" to their foes. He said:

> "Peace won't keep house with Fear!
> If you want peace the thing you've got to do
> Is just to show you're up to fighting too;
> Better that all our ships with all their crews
> Should sink to rot in ocean's dreamless ooze,
> Each torn flag waving challenge as it went
> And each dumb gun a brave man's monument,
> Than seek such peace as only cowards crave;
> Give me the peace of dead men or of brave."

———

> "Come Peace! Not like a mourner bowed
>   For honor lost and dear ones wasted,
> But proud to meet a people proud,
>   With eyes that tell of triumph tasted!

> "Come, while our country feels the lift
>   Of a great instinct shouting 'Forwards!'
> And knows that freedom's not a gift
>   That tarries long in hands of cowards!"

"The League of Nations" (1919)

Noteworthy as Roosevelt's last published work, this editorial for the *Kansas City Star* reveals the former president's anxiety that the current president, Woodrow Wilson, had an insufficient grasp of how to ensure peace in the future. Roosevelt had been steadily attacking Wilson for years on what he thought of as the Democrat's passivity, even fecklessness, in the face of German aggression, and, here, the vagueness of his vision of international cooperation. Any such plan, from Roosevelt's point of view, needed to be backed up with a resolve never to be caught unprepared again. So he uses this occasion once again to urge a new militarization to take place after the war, including the implementing of a universal military service—the Swiss model to which he refers. Interestingly, Roosevelt's sense of how a new organization should grow only faintly resembles what the League of Nations might have been had that organization begun with a Security Council as its center, much like its successor, the United Nations. We see here how Roosevelt could not foresee the inclusiveness that, a quarter of a century later, would help make a new scheme for an international "league" more viable.

The League of Nations

January 13, 1919

It is, of course, a serious misfortune that our people are not getting a clear idea of what is happening on the other side.[*] For the moment the point as to which we are foggy is the League of Nations. We all of us earnestly desire such a league, only we wish to be sure that it will help and not hinder the cause of world peace and justice. There is not a young man in this country who has fought, or an old man who has seen those dear to him fight, who does not wish to minimize the chance of future war. But there is not a man of sense who does not know that in any such movement if too much is attempted the result is either failure or worse than failure.

The trouble with Mr. Wilson's utterances, so far as they are reported, and the utterances of acquiescence in them by European statesmen, is that

---

[*] This article on "The League of Nations" is the last contribution that Colonel Roosevelt prepared for *The Star*. It was dictated at his home in Oyster Bay, January 3, the Friday before his death. His secretary expected to take the typed copy to him for correction Monday. Instead she was called on the telephone early Monday morning and told of his death. A delay of several days naturally ensued, before the editorial reached the office of *The Star*.

In view of the immense moment of the issues before the Peace Conference, *The Star* had asked Colonel Roosevelt to give his countrymen the benefit of his discussion of the possibilities of a League of Nations as a preventive of war. He consented, although, as he wrote, he expected to follow this editorial with one "on what I regard as infinitely more important, namely, our business to prepare for our own self-defense." That article, however, was never written.

This article, then, his final contribution to *The Star*, represents his matured judgment based on protracted discussion and correspondence. It is of peculiar importance as the last message of a man who, above every other American of his generation, combined high patriotism, practical sense, and a positive genius for international relations.

they are still absolutely in the stage of rhetoric precisely like the "fourteen points." Some of the fourteen points will probably have to be construed as having a mischievous significance, a smaller number might be construed as being harmless, and one or two even as beneficial, but nobody knows what Mr. Wilson really means by them, and so all talk of adopting them as basis for a peace or a league is nonsense and, if the talker is intelligent, it is insincere nonsense to boot. So Mr. Wilson's recent utterances give us absolutely no clue as to whether he really intends that at this moment we shall admit Germany, Russia—with which, incidentally, we are still waging war—Turkey, China, and Mexico into the League on full equality with ourselves. Mr. Taft has recently defined the purposes of the League and the limitations under which it would act, in a way that enables most of us to say we very heartily agree in principle with his theory and can, without doubt, come to an agreement on specific details.

Would it not be well to begin with the League which we actually have in existence, the League of the Allies who have fought through this great war? Let us at the peace table see that real justice is done as among these Allies, and that while the sternest reparation is demanded from our foes for such horrors as those committed in Belgium, Northern France, Armenia, and the sinking of the *Lusitania*, nothing should be done in the spirit of mere vengeance. Then let us agree to extend the privileges of the League, as rapidly as their conduct warrants it, to other nations, doubtless discriminating between those who would have a guiding part in the League and the weak nations who would be entitled to the privileges of membership, but who would not be entitled to a guiding voice in the councils. Let each nation reserve to itself and for its own decision, and let it clearly set forth questions which are nonjusticiable. Let nothing be done that will interfere with our preparing for our own defense by introducing a system of universal obligatory military training modeled on the Swiss plan.

Finally make it perfectly clear that we do not intend to take a position of international Meddlesome Matty. The American people do not wish to go into an overseas war unless for a very great cause and where the issue is absolutely plain. Therefore, we do not wish to undertake the responsibility of sending our gallant young men to die in obscure fights in the Balkans or in Central Europe, or in a war we do not approve of. Moreover, the American people do not intend to give up the Monroe Doctrine.

Let civilized Europe and Asia introduce some kind of police system in the weak and disorderly countries at their thresholds. But let the United States treat Mexico as our Balkan Peninsula and refuse to allow European or Asiatic powers to interfere on this continent in any way that implies permanent or semi-permanent possession. Every one of our allies will with delight grant this request if President Wilson chooses to make it, and it will be a great misfortune if it is not made.

I believe that such an effort made moderately and sanely, but sincerely and with utter scorn for words that are not made good by deeds, will be productive of real and lasting international good.

The End

Campaigns
and
Controversies

———————◆◆◆———————

"The Enforcement of Law" (1895)

One of the highlights of Roosevelt's political career in New York was his term as a member of the New York City Police Commission, which for many politicians might have been seen as sinecure, a place to do no harm by winking at the various subterfuges through which the police managed their affairs. His tenure there was short but eventful: he succeeded in securing numerous reforms, especially concerning police hiring practices and the making of a truly professional police force, and in general made himself a substantial inconvenience to the machine politicians ruling the city. Perhaps the most notorious episode of Rooseveltian honesty and probity versus Tammany corruption and greed concerned enforcement of the laws against selling liquor on Sundays, which he describes in the following article for *The Forum*. Fines for violations were exacted from those saloonkeepers who would not bribe authorities to overlook the misdemeanor; violators under Tammany protection were free to scoff. Roosevelt found this state of affairs untenable as a practice that came within his purview and sought to make enforcement fairer. So complete was his victory that he eventually lost the backing of his party. Indeed, the position was his last in city politics. Next, he would go to Washington to serve as Assistant Secretary of the Navy, an office he filled with perhaps an even greater zeal than the relish clearly present in this account of his Police Commission activities.

The Enforcement of Law

September, 1895

The question at issue in New York City just at present is much more important than the question of a more or less liberal Sunday excise law. The question is as to whether public officials are to be true to their oaths of office, and see that the law is administered in good faith. The Police Board stands squarely in favor of the honest enforcement of the law. Our opponents of every grade and of every shade of political belief take the position that government officials, who have sworn to enforce the law, shall violate their oaths whenever they think it will please a sufficient number of the public to make the violation worthwhile. It seems almost incredible that in such a controversy it should be necessary to do more than state in precise terms both propositions. Yet it evidently is necessary. Not only have the wealthy brewers and liquor-sellers, whose illegal business was interfered with, venomously attacked the Commissioners for enforcing the law; but they have been joined by the major portion of the New York press and by the very large mass of voters who put the gratification of appetite above all law. These men have not dared to meet the issue squarely and fairly. They have tried to befog it and to raise false issues. They have especially sought to change the fight from the simple principle of the enforcement of law into a contest as to the extent of the restrictions which should properly be placed on the sale of liquors. They do not deny that we have enforced the law with fairness and impartiality, but they insist that we ought to connive at law-breaking.

Very many friends of the reform movement, and very many politicians of the party to which I belong, have become frightened at the issue thus raised; and the great bulk of the machine leaders of the Democracy profess to be exultant at it, and to see in it a chance for securing their own return to power. Senator Hill and Tammany in particular have loudly welcomed the contest. On the other hand certain Republican politicians, and certain Republican newspapers, have contended that our action in honestly doing our duty as public officers of the municipality of New York will jeopardize the success of the Republican party, with which I, the President of the Board, am identified. The implication is that for the sake of the Republican party, a party of which I am a very earnest member, I should violate my oath of office and connive at law-breaking. To this I can only answer that I am far too good a Republican to be willing to believe that the honest enforcement of law by a Republican can redound to the discredit of the party to which he belongs. This applies as much to the weak-kneed municipal reformers who fear that we have hurt the cause of municipal reform, as it does to the Republicans. I am not an impractical theorist; I am a practical politician. But I do not believe that practical politics and foul politics are necessarily synonymous terms. I never expect to get absolute perfection; and I have small sympathy with those people who are always destroying good men and good causes because they are not the best of all possible men and all possible causes; but on a naked issue of right and wrong, such as the performance or non-performance of one's official duty, it is not possible to compromise. Indeed, according to the way we present Commissioners feel, we have nothing to do with Republicanism or Democracy in the administration of the police force of the city of New York. Personally, I think I can best serve the Republican party by taking the police force absolutely out of politics. Our duty is to preserve order, to protect life and property, to arrest criminals, and to secure honest elections. In striving to attain these ends we recognize no party; we pay no heed to any man's political predilections, whether he is within or without the police force. In the past, "Politics," in the base sense of the term, has been the curse of the police force of New York; and the present Board has done away with such politics.

The position of Senator Hill and the Tammany leaders, when reduced to its simplest terms, is merely the expression of the conviction that it does not pay to be honest. They believe that advocacy of law-breaking is a good card before the people. As one of their newspapers frankly put it, the machine Democratic leaders intend to bid for the support of the voters on the ground that their party "will not enforce laws" which are distasteful to any considerable section of the public. Senator Hill declaims against the Board because it honestly enforces the law which was put on the statute-book but three years ago by his legislature and his governor (for he owned them both). This is of course a mere frank avowal that Senator Hill and the Democratic leaders who think with him believe that a majority in the State can be built up out of the combined votes of the dishonest men, the stupid men, the timid weaklings, and the men who put appetite above principle—who declare, in the language of Scripture, that their god is their belly, and who rank every consideration of honor, justice, and public morality below the gratification of their desire to drink beer at times when it is prohibited by law.

When such are the fears of our friends and the hopes of our foes, it is worthwhile briefly to state exactly what the condition of affairs was when the present Board of Police Commissioners in New York took office, and what that course of conduct was which has caused such violent excite-ment. The task is simple. On entering office we found—what indeed had long been a matter of common notoriety—that various laws, and notably the excise law, were enforced rigidly against people who had no political pull, but were not enforced at all against the men who had a political pull, or who possessed sufficient means to buy off the high officials who controlled, or had influence in, the Police Department. All that we did was to enforce these laws, not against some wrong-doers, but honestly and impartially against all wrong-doers. We did not resurrect dead laws; we did not start a crusade to enforce blue laws. All that we did was to take a law which was very much alive, but which had been used only for purposes of blackmail, and to do away entirely with the blackmail feature by enforcing it equitably as regards all persons. Looked at soberly, this scarcely seems a revolutionary proceeding; and still less does it seem like one which needs an elaborate justification.

In an authorized interview with Mr. J. P. Smith, the editor of the "Wine and Spirit Gazette," the position of the former Police Board—and of Senator Hill and his political allies as well—toward the enforcement of the excise law has been set forth with such clearness that I cannot do better than quote it. Mr. Smith's statement appeared on July 18 last. No attempt whatever has been made to controvert its truth, and it may be accepted as absolute. What makes it all the more important is that it was evidently made, not at all as an attack upon the persons implicated, but as a mere statement of fact to explain certain actions of the liquor-sellers in the past. The interview runs in part as follows:

"Governor Flower, as well as the Legislature of 1892, was elected upon distinct pledges that relief would be given by the Democratic party to the liquor-dealers, especially of the cities of the State. In accordance with this promise a Sunday-opening clause was inserted in the excise bill of 1892. Governor Flower then said that he could not approve the Sunday-opening clause; whereupon the Liquor Dealers' Association, which had charge of the bill, struck the Sunday-opening clause out. After Governor Hill had been elected for the second term I had several interviews with him on that very subject. He told me, 'Do you know, I am the friend of the liquor-dealers and will go to almost any length to help them and give them relief; but do not ask me to recommend to the Legislature the passage of the law opening the saloons on Sunday. I cannot do it, for it will ruin the Democratic party in the State.' He gave the same interview to various members of the State Liquor Dealers' Association, who waited upon him for the purpose of getting relief from the blackmail of the police, stating that the lack of having the Sunday question properly regulated was at the bottom of the trouble. Blackmail had been brought to such a state of perfection, and had become so oppressive to the liquor-dealers themselves, that they communicated first with Governor Hill and then with Mr. Croker. The 'Wine and Spirit Gazette' had taken up the subject because of gross discrimination made by the police in the enforcement of the Sunday-closing law. The paper again and again called upon the Police Commissioners to either uniformly enforce the law or uniformly disregard it. A committee of the Central Association of Liquor Dealers of this city then took up the matter and called upon Police Commissioner Martin. An agreement was then made between the leaders of Tammany Hall and the liquor-dealers, according to which the monthly blackmail paid to the police should be discontinued in return for political support. In other words, the retail dealers should bind themselves to solidly support the Tammany ticket in consideration of the discontinuance of the monthly blackmail by the police. This agreement was carried out. Now what was the consequence? If the liquor-dealer, after *the monthly blackmail ceased, showed any signs of independence, the Tammany Hall district leader would give the tip to the police captain, and that man would be pulled and arrested on the following Sunday."*

Continuing, Mr. Smith inveighs against the law, but says:—

"The Police Commissioners (the present Police Commissioners) are honestly endeavoring to have the law impartially carried out. They are no respecters of persons. And our information from all classes of liquor-dealers is that the rich and the poor, the influential and the uninfluential, are required equally to obey the law."

I call particular attention to the portion of the interview which I have italicized above. It shows conclusively that the Sunday-closing feature was deliberately left in by Senator Hill and his aides because they did not believe they could afford to strike it out. It is idle to talk of a provision thus embodied in statute law as being a dead letter. Still more idle is it to talk of a law as "antiquated" when it was enacted only three years ago.

Mr. Smith's statement shows moreover that Tammany heartily approved of keeping the law in its present condition because, by so doing, they kept a sword suspended over the neck of every recalcitrant saloon-keeper. The law was never dead at all. It was very much alive. We revived it only in the sense that we revived the forgotten habit of administering it with decency and impartiality.

To show the nonsense of the talk that it was obsolete or a dead letter, I call attention to the following figures. In the year 1893, 4,063 arrests were made in New York City for violation of the excise law on Sunday. This represented a falling off from previous years. In 1888, for instance, the arrests had numbered 5,880. In 1894, the year before we took office, when the Tammany Board still had absolute power, the arrests rose to 8,464. On Sunday, September 30 of that year, they numbered 233; on October 14, 230; on the following January 13, they rose to 254. During the time that the present Board has been enforcing the law the top number of arrests which we have reached was but 223, a much smaller number than was reached again and again under the old *régime*. Nevertheless by our arrests we actually closed the saloons, for we arrested men indiscriminately, and indeed paid particular attention to the worst offenders—the rich saloon-keepers with a pull; whereas under the old system the worst men were never touched at all, and all of them understood well that any display of energy by the police was merely spasmodic and done with some special purpose; so that always, after one or two dry Sundays, affairs were allowed to go back to their former condition. The real difference, the immense, the immeasurable difference between the old and the new methods of enforcing the law, is not one of severity, but of honesty. The old Tammany Board was as ruthless in closing the saloons where the owners had no pull, as we are in closing all saloons whether the owners have or have not a pull.

The corrupt and partial enforcement of the law under Tammany turned it into a gigantic implement for blackmailing a portion of the liquor-sellers, and for the wholesale corruption of the Police Department. The high Tammany officials, and the police captains and patrolmen, blackmailed and bullied the small liquor-sellers without a pull and turned them into abject slaves of Tammany Hall. On the other hand, the wealthy and politically influential liquor-sellers absolutely controlled the police, and made or marred captains, sergeants, and patrolmen at their pleasure. Many causes have tended to corrupt the police administration of New York, but no one cause was so potent as this.

In the foregoing interview the really startling feature is the matter-of-fact way in which Mr. Smith records his conference with the President of the Police Board, and the agreement by which the system of blackmail was commuted in view of faithful political service to be hereafter tendered to Tammany Hall. It is hard seriously to discuss the arguments of people who wish us to stop enforcing the law, when they must know, if they are capable of thinking and willing to think, that only by the rigid and impartial enforcement of the law is it possible to cut out from the body politic this festering sore of political corruption. It was not a case for the use of salves and ointments. There was need of merciless use of the knife.

When we entered office the law was really enforced at the will of the police officials. In some precincts most of the saloons were closed; in others almost all were open. In general, the poor man without political influence and without money had to shut up, while his rich rival who possessed a "pull" was never molested. Half of the liquor-sellers were allowed to violate the law. Half of them were not allowed to violate it. Under the circumstances we had one of two courses to follow. We could either instruct the police to allow all the saloon-keepers to become law-breakers, or else we could instruct them to stop all law-breaking. It is unnecessary to say that the latter course was the only one possible to officials who had respect for their oaths of office.

The clamor that followed our action was deafening; and it was also rather amusing in view of the fact that all we had done was to perform our obvious duty. At the outset the one invariable statement with which we were met was that we could not enforce the law. A hundred—aye, a thousand—times we were told by big politicians, by newspapers, by private individuals, that the excise law could not be enforced; that Mayor Hewitt had tried it and failed; that Superintendent Byrnes had tried it and failed; that nobody could succeed in such a task. Well, the answer is simple. We *have* enforced the law, so far. It is very badly drawn, so as to make it extremely difficult of enforcement; and some of the officials outside the Police Department hamper instead of aiding the police in their efforts to enforce it. However, we understand well that we must do the best we can with the tools actually at hand, if we cannot have the tools we wish. We cannot stop all illegal drinking on Sunday, any more than we can stop all theft; but so far we have succeeded in securing a substantial compliance with the law.

The next move of our opponents was to adopt the opposite tack, and to shriek that, in devoting our attention to enforcing the excise Law, we were neglecting all other laws; and that in consequence crime was on the increase. We met this by publishing the comparative statistics of the felonies committed, and of the felons arrested, under our administration and under the previous administration. These showed that for a like period of time about one felony less a day occurred under our administration, while the number of arrests for felonies increased at the rate of nearly one a day. During our term of service fewer crimes were committed and more criminals were arrested. In the Sunday arrests for intoxication, and for disorderly conduct resulting from intoxication, the difference was more striking. Thus in the four Sundays of April, 1895, the last month of the old *régime*, there were 341 arrests on charges of intoxication and of being drunk and disorderly. For the four Sundays beginning with June 30—the first day that we were able to rigidly enforce our policy of closing the saloons—the corresponding number of arrests was but 196. We put a stop to nearly half the violent drunkenness of the city.

The next argument advanced was that Americans of German origin demanded beer on Sundays, and that the popular sentiment was with them and must be heeded. To this we could only answer that we recognized popular sentiment only when embodied in law. To their discredit be it said, many men, who were themselves public officials, actually advocated our conniving at the violation of the law on this ground—of the alleged hostility of local sentiment. They took the view that as the law was passed by the State, for the entire State including the city, and was not (as they contended) upheld by public sentiment in the city, the officers of the law who are sworn to enforce it should connive at its violation. Such reasoning would justify any community in ignoring any law to which it objected. The income-tax law was passed through Congress by the votes of the Southerners and Westerners, but it was collected (prior to the time it was declared to be unconstitutional) mainly in the Northeast. Any argument which would justify us in refusing to obey the excise law in New York would justify the whole Northeast in refusing to obey the income-tax law.

The spirit shown by the men and the newspapers who denounce us for enforcing the law is simply one manifestation of the feeling which brings about and is responsible for lynchings, and for all the varieties of Whitecap outrages. The men who head a lynching party, and the officers who fail to protect criminals threatened with lynching, always advance, as their excuse, that public sentiment sanctions their action. The chief offenders often insist that they have taken such summary action because they fear lest the law be not enforced against the offender. In other words, they put public sentiment ahead of law in the first place; and in the second they offer, as a partial excuse for so doing, the fact that too often laws are not enforced by the men elected or appointed to enforce them. The only possible outcome of such an attitude is lawlessness, which gradually grows until it becomes mere anarchy. The one all-important element in good citizenship in our country is obedience to law. The greatest crimes that can be committed against our government are to put on the statute books, or to allow to remain there, laws that are not meant to be enforced, and to fail to enforce the laws that exist.

Mr. Jacob A. Riis, in a recent article, has put this in words so excellent that I cannot refrain from quoting them:

"That laws are made to break, not to obey, is a fact of which the street takes early notice, and shapes its conduct accordingly. Respect for the law is not going to spring from disregard of it. The boy who smokes his cigarette openly in defiance of one law, carries the growler early and late on week-days in defiance of another, and on Sunday of a third; observes fourteen saloons clustering about the door of his school in contempt of a fourth which expressly forbids their being there; plays hookey secure from arrest because nobody thinks of enforcing the compulsory education law; or slaves in the sweat-shop under a perjured age-certificate bought for a quarter of a perjured notary; and so on to the end of the long register, while a shoal of offensive ordinances prohibit him from flying a kite, tossing a ball, or romping on the grass, where there is any—cannot be expected to grow up with a very exalted idea of law and order. The indifference or hypocrisy that makes dead letters of so many of our laws is one of the constantly active feeders of our jails. . . . The one breaks the law, the other has it broken for him. . . . The saloon is their ally, and the saloon is the boy's club as he grows into early manhood. It is not altogether his fault that he has no other. From it he takes his politics and gets his backing in his disputes with the police. That he knows it to be despised and denounced by the sentiment responsible for the laws he broke with impunity all his days, while to him it represents the one potent, practical force of life, is well calculated to add to his mental confusion as to the relationship of things, but hardly to increase his respect for the law or for the sentiment behind it. We need an era of enforcement of law—less of pretence—more of purpose."

The Police Board is doing its best to bring about precisely such an era. The worst possible lesson to teach any citizen is contempt for the law. Laws should not be left on the statute books, still less put on the statute books, unless they are meant to be enforced. No man should take a public office unless he is willing to obey his oath and to enforce the law.

Many of the demagogues who have denounced us have reproached us especially because we took away "the poor man's beer," and have announced that, law or no law, the poor man had a right to his beer on Sunday if he wished it. These gentry, when they preach such doctrine, are simply preaching lawlessness. If the poor man has a right to break the law so as to get beer on Sunday, he has a right to break the law so as to get bread on any day. It is a good deal more important to the poor man that he should get fed on week-days than that he should get drunk on Sundays. The people who try to teach him that he has a right to break the law on one day to take beer are doing their best to prepare him for breaking the law some other day to take bread.

But as a matter of fact all the talk about the law being enforced chiefly at the expense of the poor man is the veriest nonsense and hypocrisy. We took especial care to close the bars of the big hotels. We shut every bar-room on Fifth Avenue as carefully as we shut every bar-room on Avenue A. We did not hurt the poor man at all. The people whom we hurt were the rich brewers and liquor-sellers, who had hitherto made money hand over fist by violating the Sunday law with the corrupt connivance of the police. There is small cause for wonder that they should grow hot with anger when they found that we had taken away the hundreds of thousands of dollars which they had made by violation of the law. There is small cause for wonder that their newspaper allies should have raved, and that Senator Hill should eagerly have run to their support. But it is a wonder that any citizen wishing well to his country should have been misled for one moment by what they have said. The fight they have waged was not a fight for the poor man; it was a fight in the interest of the rich and unscrupulous man who had been accustomed to buy immunity from justice. As a matter of fact we have helped the poor man and notably we have helped the poor man's wife and children. Many a man who before was accustomed to spend his week's wages getting drunk in a saloon now either puts them up or takes his wife and children for a day's outing. The hospitals found that their Monday labors were lessened by nearly half, owing to the startling diminution in cases of injury due to drunken brawls. The work of the magistrates who sat in the city courts for the trial of small offenders was correspondingly decreased. All this was brought about by our honest enforcement of the law.

To sum up, then, Senator Hill, and his allies of every grade, berate us because we have in good faith enforced an act which they, when they had complete control of the legislature and the government, put on the statute books with the full belief that it would be enforced with corrupt partiality. They are responsible for the law. We are responsible for having executed it honestly—the first time it ever has been executed honestly. We are responsible for the fact that we refused to continue the old dishonest methods, and that we broke up the gigantic system of blackmail and corruption to which these methods had given rise; a system which was the most potent of all the causes that have combined to debase public life in New York and to eat the very heart out of the New York police force. Senator Hill and his allies passed a law which was designed to serve as the most potent of weapons for keeping the saloon-keepers bound hand and foot in the power of Tammany Hall and of the State Democratic organization which followed Tammany's lead. We have undone their work by the simple process of administering the law in accordance with the elementary rules of decency and morality. I am far too good an American to believe that in the long run a majority of our people will declare in favor of the dishonest enforcement of law; though I readily admit the possibility that at some given election they may be hopelessly misled by demagogues, and may for the moment make a selfish and cowardly surrender of principle. The men who last fall won the fight for municipal reform, for decent government in our cities, cannot afford to borrow from their defeated antagonists the old methods of connivance at law-breaking.

In the end we shall win, in spite of the open opposition of the forces of evil, in spite of the timid surrender of the weakly good, if only we stand squarely and fairly on the platform of the honest enforcement of the law of the land. But if we were to face defeat instead of victory, that would not alter our convictions, and would not cause us to flinch one hand's breadth from the course we have been pursuing. There are prices too dear to be paid even for victory. We would rather face defeat as a consequence of honestly enforcing the law than win a suicidal triumph by a corrupt connivance at its violation.

"At Laying of Cornerstone of Gateway to Yellowstone National Park, Gardiner, Montana" (1903)

This short speech is engaging because of the way Roosevelt character-
izes the political and cultural implications of conservation. In laying this
access road to the great new national park, the country is underlining its
commitment both to the present and the future, says Roosevelt, because
"scrupulous" preservation is essentially democratic. The protection of this
"veritable wonderland" is thereby safeguarded for the "betterment and
enjoyment of the people," not just the wealthy who can afford to hire
their own tours. The "geysers, the extraordinary hot springs, the lakes,
the mountains, the canyons, and cataracts" create an atmosphere unparalleled anywhere else in the world, and every citizen should know that it
belongs to "all of us." Roosevelt explains that the preservation of forests
is crucial to our national interests, since it also means the protection of
our waterways and the potential of waterpower. But beyond such "utilitarian" purposes, the park is foremost a "beautiful natural playground" whose
preservation will ensure that the "old-time pleasure of the hardy life of the
wilderness" will be communicated to successive generations of Americans.

At Laying of Cornerstone of Gateway to Yellowstone National Park, Gardiner, Montana, April 24, 1903

Mr. Mayor, Mr. Superintendent, and my fellow citizens:

I wish to thank the people of Montana generally, those of Gardiner and Cinnabar especially, and more especially still all those employed in the Park, whether in civil or military capacity, for my very enjoyable two weeks' holiday.

It is a pleasure now to say a few words to you at the laying of the cornerstone of the beautiful road which is to mark the entrance to this Park. The Yellowstone Park is something absolutely unique in the world, so far as I know. Nowhere else in any civilized country is there to be found such a tract of veritable wonderland made accessible to all visitors, where at the same time not only the scenery of the wilderness, but the wild creatures of the Park are scrupulously preserved; the only change being that these same wild creatures have been so carefully protected as to show a literally astounding tameness. The creation and preservation of such a great natural playground in the interest of our people as a whole is a credit to the nation; but above all a credit to Montana, Wyoming, and Idaho. It has been preserved with wise foresight. The scheme of its preservation is noteworthy in its essential democracy. Private game preserves, though they may be handled in such a way as to be not only good things for themselves, but good things for the surrounding community, can yet never be more than poor substitutes, from the standpoint of the public, for great national playgrounds such as this Yellowstone Park. This Park was created, and is now administered, for the benefit and enjoyment of the people. The government must continue to appropriate for it especially in the direction of completing and perfecting an excellent system of driveways. But already its beauties can be seen with great comfort in a short space of time and at an astoundingly small cost, and with the sense on the part of every visitor that it is in part his property, that it is the property of Uncle Sam and therefore of all of us. The only way that the people as a whole can secure to themselves and their children the enjoyment in perpetuity of what the Yellowstone Park has to give is by assuming the ownership in the name of the nation and by jealously safeguarding and preserving the scenery, the forests, and the wild creatures. When we have a good system of carriage roads throughout the Park—for of course it would be very unwise to allow either steam or electric roads in the Park—we shall have a region as easy and accessible to travel in as it is already every whit as interesting as any similar territory of the Alps or the Italian Riviera. The geysers, the extraordinary hot springs, the lakes, the mountains, the canyons, and cataracts unite to make this region something not wholly to be paralleled elsewhere on the globe. It must be kept for the benefit and enjoyment of all of us; and I hope to see a steadily increasing number of our people take advantage of its attractions. At present it is rather singular that a greater number of people come from Europe to see it than come from our own Eastern States. The people nearby seem awake to its beauties; and I hope that more and more of our people who dwell far off will appreciate its really marvelous character. Incidentally I should like to point out that some time people will surely awake to the fact that the Park has special beauties to be seen in winter; and any hardy man who can go through it in that season on skis will enjoy himself as he scarcely could elsewhere.

I wish especially to congratulate the people of Montana, Wyoming, and Idaho, and notably you of Gardiner and Cinnabar and the immediate outskirts of the Park, for the way in which you heartily cooperate with the superintendent to prevent acts of vandalism and destruction. Major Pitcher has explained to me how much he owes to your co-operation and your lively appreciation of the fact that the Park is simply being kept in the interest of all of us, so that every one may have the chance to see its wonders with ease and comfort at the minimum of expense. I have always thought it was a liberal education to any man of the East to come West, and he can combine profit with pleasure if he will incidentally visit this Park, the Grand Canyon of the Colorado, and the Yosemite, and take the sea voyage to Alaska. Major Pitcher reports to me, by the way, that he has received invaluable assistance from the game wardens of Montana and Wyoming, and that the present game warden of Idaho has also promised his hearty aid.

The preservation of the forests is of course the matter of prime importance in every public reserve of this character. In this region of the Rocky Mountains and the Great Plains the problem of the water supply is the most important which the home-maker has to face. Congress has not of recent years done anything wiser than in passing the irrigation bill; and nothing is more essential to the preservation of the water supply than the preservation of the forests. Montana has in its water power a source of development which has hardly yet been touched. This water power will be seriously impaired if ample protection is not given the forests. Therefore this Park, like the forest reserves generally, is of the utmost advantage to the country around from the merely utilitarian side. But of course this Park, also because of its peculiar features, is to be preserved as a beautiful natural playground. Here all the wild creatures of the old days are being preserved, and their overflow into the surrounding country means that the people of the surrounding country, so long as they see that the laws are observed by all, will be able to insure to themselves and to their children and to their children's children much of the old-time pleasure of the hardy life of the wilderness and of the hunter in the wilderness. This pleasure, moreover, can under such conditions be kept for all who have the love of adventure and the hardihood to take advantage of it, with small regard for what their fortune may be. I can not too often repeat that the essential feature in the present management of the Yellowstone Park, as in all similar places, is its essential democracy—it is the preservation of the scenery, of the forests, of the wilderness life and the wilderness game for the people as a whole, instead of leaving the enjoyment thereof to be confined to the very rich who can control private reserves. I have been literally astounded at the enormous quantities of elk and at the number of deer, antelope, and mountain sheep which I have seen on their wintering grounds; and the deer and sheep in particular are quite as tame as range stock. A few buffalo are being preserved. I wish very much that the government could somewhere provide for an experimental breeding station of cross-breeds between buffalo and the common cattle. If these cross-breeds could be successfully perpetuated we should have animals which would produce a robe quite as good as the old buffalo robe with which twenty years ago every one was familiar, and animals moreover which would be so hardy that I think they would have a distinct commercial importance. They would, for instance, be admirably suited for Alaska, a territory which I look to see develop astoundingly within the next decade or two, not only because of its furs and fisheries, but because of its agricultural and pastoral possibilities.

"Natural Resources—
Their Wise Use or Their Waste" (1908)

This speech to the nation's governors, made near the end of his presidency, drawn from "Conservation as a National Duty," the longer address with which he convened a governors' meeting on the subject, expresses Roosevelt's passionate commitment to preserving natural resources and bears his characteristic stamp. In calling these executives together, Roosevelt is mindful of the historical conditions in which the states can and should act in concert, and he invokes no less an authority than George Washington to persuade the governors that the wise use of our resources, their conservation and the planning for their future, is a project in which the whole nation needs to share. The United States' greatness has been drawn on our seemingly "illimitable" resources, but the "rapid development" of our "civilization" through the nineteenth century has also led to the "rapid destruction" of those resources and thus threatens the basis on which our preeminence has been built. He closes the speech with a summation situating the ecological imperative within the context of national well-being. "Finally, let us remember that the conservation of our natural resources, though the gravest problem of today, is yet but part of another and greater problem to which this Nation is not yet awake, but to which it will awake in time, and with which it must hereafter grapple if it is to live . . . the patriotic duty of insuring the safety and continuance of the Nation."

Natural Resources—
Their Wise Use or Their Waste[†]

Governors of the several States, and gentlemen:

I welcome you to this conference at the White House. You have come hither at my request so that we may join together to consider the question of the conservation and use of the great fundamental sources of wealth of this nation. So vital is this question, that for the first time in our history the chief executive officers of the States separately, and of the States together forming the nation, have met to consider it.

With the governors come men from each State chosen for their special acquaintance with the terms of the problem that is before us. Among them are experts in natural resources and representatives of national organizations concerned in the development and use of these resources; the senators and representatives in Congress; the Supreme Court, the Cabinet, and the Inland Waterways Commission have likewise been invited to the conference, which is therefore national in a peculiar sense.

This conference on the conservation of natural resources is in effect a meeting of the representatives of all the people of the United States called to consider the weightiest problem now before the nation; and the occasion for the meeting lies in the fact that the natural resources of our country are in danger of exhaustion if we permit the old wasteful methods of exploiting them longer to continue.

With the rise of peoples from savagery to civilization, and with the consequent growth in the extent and variety of the needs of the average man, there comes a steadily increasing growth of the amount demanded

---

[†] Address at the opening of the conference on the Conservation of Natural Resources, at the White House, May 13, 1908.

by this average man from the actual resources of the country. Yet, rather curiously, at the same time the average man is apt to lose his realization of this dependence upon nature.

Savages, and very primitive peoples generally, concern themselves only with superficial natural resources; with those which they obtain from the actual surface of the ground. As peoples become a little less primitive, their industries, although in a rude manner, are extended to resources below the surface; then, with what we call civilization and the extension of knowledge, more resources come into use, industries are multiplied, and foresight begins to become a necessary and prominent factor in life. Crops are cultivated; animals are domesticated; and metals are mastered.

Every step of the progress of mankind is marked by the discovery and use of natural resources previously unused. Without such progressive knowledge and utilization of natural resources population could not grow, nor industries multiply, nor the hidden wealth of the earth be developed for the benefit of mankind.

From the first beginnings of civilization, on the banks of the Nile and the Euphrates, the industrial progress of the world has gone on slowly, with occasional setbacks, but on the whole steadily, through tens of centuries to the present day. But of late the rapidity of the process has increased at such a rate that more space has been actually covered during the century and a quarter occupied by our national life than during the preceding six thousand years that take us back to the earliest monuments of Egypt, to the earliest cities of the Babylonian plain.

When the founders of this nation met at Independence Hall in Philadelphia the conditions of commerce had not fundamentally changed from what they were when the Phœnician keels first furrowed the lonely waters of the Mediterranean. The differences were those of degree, not of kind, and they were not in all cases even those of degree. Mining was carried on fundamentally as it had been carried on by the Pharaohs in the countries adjacent to the Red Sea.

The wares of the merchants of Boston, of Charleston, like the wares of the merchants of Nineveh and Sidon, if they went by water, were carried by boats propelled by sails or oars; if they went by land they were carried in wagons drawn by beasts of draft or in packs on the backs of beasts of burden. The ships that crossed the high seas were better than the ships that had once crossed the Ægean, but they were of the same type, after all—they were wooden ships propelled by sails; and on land, the roads were not as good as the roads of the Roman Empire, while the service of the posts was probably inferior.

In Washington's time anthracite coal was known only as a useless black stone; and the great fields of bituminous coal were undiscovered. As steam was unknown, the use of coal for power production was undreamed of. Water was practically the only source of power, save the labor of men and animals; and this power was used only in the most primitive fashion. But a few small iron deposits had been found in this country, and the use of iron by our countrymen was very small. Wood was practically the only fuel, and what lumber was sawed was consumed locally, while the forests were regarded chiefly as obstructions to settlement and cultivation.

Such was the degree of progress to which civilized mankind had attained when this nation began its career. It is almost impossible for us in this day to realize how little our Revolutionary ancestors knew of the great store of natural resources whose discovery and use have been such vital factors in the growth and greatness of this nation, and how little they required to take from this store in order to satisfy their needs.

Since then our knowledge and use of the resources of the present territory of the United States have increased a hundredfold. Indeed, the growth of this nation by leaps and bounds makes one of the most striking and important chapters in the history of the world. Its growth has been due to the rapid development, and alas! that it should be said, to the rapid destruction of our natural resources. Nature has supplied to us in the United States, and still supplies to us, more kinds of resources in a more lavish degree than has ever been the case at any other time or with any other people. Our position in the world has been attained by the extent and thoroughness of the control we have achieved over nature; but we are more, and not less, dependent upon what she furnishes than at any previous time of history since the days of primitive man.

Yet our fathers, though they knew so little of the resources of the country, exercised a wise forethought in reference thereto. Washington clearly saw that the perpetuity of the States could only be secured by union, and that the only feasible basis of union was an economic one; in other words, that it must be based on the development and use of their natural resources. Accordingly, he helped to outline a scheme of commercial development, and by his influence an interstate waterways commission was appointed by Virginia and Maryland.

It met near where we are now meeting, in Alexandria, adjourned to Mount Vernon, and took up the consideration of interstate commerce by the only means then available, that of water. Further conferences were arranged, first at Annapolis, and then at Philadelphia. It was in Philadelphia that the representatives of all the States met for what was in its original conception merely a waterways conference; but when they had closed their deliberations the outcome was the Constitution which made the States into a nation.

The Constitution of the United States thus grew in large part out of the necessity for united action in the wise use of one of our natural resources. The wise use of all of our natural resources, which are our national resources as well, is the great material question of today. I have asked you to come together now because the enormous consumption of these resources, and the threat of imminent exhaustion of some of them, due to reckless and wasteful use, once more calls for common effort, common action.

Since the days when the Constitution was adopted, steam and electricity have revolutionized the industrial world. Nowhere has the revolution been so great as in our own country. The discovery and utilization of mineral fuels and alloys have given us the lead over all other nations in the production of steel. The discovery and utilization of coal and iron have given us our railways, and have led to such industrial development as has never before been seen. The vast wealth of lumber in our forests, the riches of our soils and mines, the discovery of gold and mineral oils, combined with the efficiency of our transportation, have made the conditions of our life unparalleled in comfort and convenience.

The steadily increasing drain on these natural resources has promoted to an extraordinary degree the complexity of our industrial and social life. Moreover, this unexampled development has had a determining effect upon the character and opinions of our people. The demand for efficiency in the great task has given us vigor, effectiveness, decision, and power, and a capacity for achievement which in its own lines has never yet been matched. So great and so rapid has been our material growth that there has been a tendency to lag behind in spiritual and moral growth; but that is not the subject upon which I speak to you today. Disregarding for the moment the question of moral purpose, it is safe to say that the prosperity of our people depends directly on the energy and intelligence with which our natural resources are used. It is equally clear that these resources are the final basis of national power and perpetuity. Finally, it is ominously evident that these resources are in the course of rapid exhaustion.

This nation began with the belief that its landed possessions were illimitable and capable of supporting all the people who might care to make our country their home; but already the next generation shall see the timber increased instead of diminished. Moreover, we can add enormous tracts of the most valuable possible agricultural land to the national domain by irrigation in the arid and semiarid regions and by drainage of great tracts of swamp-land in the humid regions. We can enormously increase our transportation facilities by the canalization of our rivers so as to complete a great system of waterways on the Pacific, Atlantic, and Gulf coasts and in the Mississippi valley, from the great plains to the Alleghenies and from the northern lakes to the mouth of the mighty Father of Waters. But all these various uses of our natural resources are so closely connected that they should be co-ordinated and should be treated as part of one coherent plan and not in haphazard and piecemeal fashion.

It is largely because of this that I appointed the Waterways Commission last year and that I have sought to perpetuate its work. I wish to take this opportunity to express in heartiest fashion my acknowledgment to all the members of the commission. At great personal sacrifice of time and effort they have rendered a service to the public for which we cannot be too grateful. Especial credit is due to the initiative, the energy, the devotion to duty, and the far-sightedness of Gifford Pinchot, to whom we owe so much of the progress we have already made in handling this matter of the co-ordination and conservation of natural resources. If it had not been for him this convention neither would nor could have been called.

"How I Became a Progressive" (1912)

During his campaign as a third-party candidate for the presidency, Roosevelt paused to spell out in an editorial for *Outlook*, an opinion and news magazine for which he also served as associate editor, his emergence as a Progressive politician. Indeed, over the course of the preceding few years, he had written dozens of editorials in its pages, on a host of subjects. Yet this one had a very definite occasion: it gave Roosevelt an opportunity to articulate what he saw as the Progressive point of view on a whole range of campaign issues. Interestingly, the most resonant word in this short piece is not "progressive" or "progress," as one might expect. Instead, the word Roosevelt comes back to again and again is "justice," so often that one can scarcely doubt the sincerity of Roosevelt's sense of himself learning to identify with working men and women, not just seeing their case and dispensing justice from above, as had been his earlier perspective. It is a passion for "social and industrial justice" underlying his commitments to labor reform, both in the city and in the country, an inclination he discovers as "a man doing his share of the work." Conservation too seems to Roosevelt an issue of justice, since it meant not only to preserve resources but also to protect them from monopolization. Finally, progressivism is a set of policies, derived from history that views the United States from an international perspective and thus can best ensure that the nation has both the "spirit and strength to repel injustice from abroad."

How I Became a Progressive

I suppose I had a natural tendency to become a Progressive, anyhow. That is, I was naturally a democrat, in believing in fair play for everybody. But I grew toward my present position, not so much as the result of study in the library or the reading of books—although I have been very much helped by such study and by such reading—as by actually living and working with men under many different conditions and seeing their needs from many different points of view.

The first set of our people with whom I associated so intimately as to get on thoroughly sympathetic terms with them were cow-punchers, then on the ranges in the West. I was so impressed with them that in doing them justice I did injustice to equally good citizens elsewhere whom I did not know; and it was a number of years before I grew to understand, first by associating with railway men, then with farmers, then with mechanics, and so on, that the things that I specially liked about my cow-puncher friends were; after all, to be found fundamentally in railway men, in farmers, in blacksmiths, carpenters—in fact, generally among my fellow American citizens.

Before I began to go with the cow-punchers, I had already, as the result of experience in the legislature at Albany, begun rather timidly to strive for social and industrial justice. But at that time my attitude was that of giving justice from above. It was the experience on the range that first taught me to try to get justice for all of us by working on the same level with the rest of my fellow citizens.

It was the conviction that there was much social and industrial injustice and the effort to secure social and industrial justice that first led me to taking so keen an interest in popular rule.

For years I accepted the theory, as most of the rest of us then accepted it, that we already had popular government; that this was a government by the people. I believed the power of the boss was due only to the indifference and short-sightedness of the average decent citizen. Gradually it came over me that while this was half the truth, it was only half the truth, and that while the boss owed part of his power to the fact that the average man did not do his duty, yet that there was the further fact to be considered, that for the average man it had already been made very difficult instead of very easy for him to do his duty. I grew to feel a keen interest in the machinery for getting adequate and genuine popular rule, chiefly because I found that we could not get social and industrial justice without popular rule, and that it was immensely easier to get such popular rule by the means of machinery of the type of direct nominations at primaries, the short ballot, the initiative, referendum, and the like.

I usually found that my interest in any given side of a question of justice was aroused by some concrete case. It was the examination I made into the miseries attendant upon the manufacture of cigars in tenement-houses that first opened my eyes to the need of legislation on such subjects. My friends come from many walks of life. The need for a workmen's compensation act was driven home to me by my knowing a brakeman who had lost his legs in an accident, and whose family was thereby at once reduced from self-respecting comfort to conditions that at one time became very dreadful. Of course, after coming across various concrete instances of this kind, I would begin to read up on the subject, and then I would get in touch with social workers and others who were experts and could acquaint me with what was vital in the matter. Looking back, it seems to me that I made my greatest strides forward while I was police commissioner, and this largely through my intimacy with Jacob Riis, for he opened all kinds of windows into the matter for me.

The conservation movement I approached from slightly different lines. I have always been fond of history and of science, and what has occurred to Spain, to Palestine, to China, and to North Africa from the destruction of natural resources is familiar to me. I have always been deeply impressed with Liebig's statement that it was the decrease of soil fertility, and not either peace or war, which was fundamental in bringing about the decadence of nations. While unquestionably nations have been destroyed by other causes, I have become convinced that it was the destruction of the soil itself which was perhaps the most fatal of all causes. But when, at the beginning of my term of service as President, under the influence of Mr. Pinchot and Mr. Newell, I took up the cause of conservation, I was already fairly well awake to the need of social and industrial justice; and from the outset we had in view, not only the preservation of natural resources, but the prevention of monopoly in natural resources, so that they should inhere in the people as a whole. There were plenty of newspapers, the New York *Times*, *Sun*, and *Evening Post*, for instance, which cordially supported our policy of conservation as long as we did not try to combine it with a movement against monopolization of resources, and which promptly abandoned us when it became evident that we wished to conserve the resources not for a part of the people but for all of the people.

The country-life movement was simply another side of this movement for a better and juster life. From Mary E. Wilkins to Sarah O. Jewett, in story after story which I would read for mere enjoyment, I would come upon things that not merely pleased me but gave me instruction—I have always thought that a good novel or a good story could teach quite as much as a more solemnly pretentious work, if it was written in the right way and read in the right way—and then my experience on farms, my knowledge of farmers, the way I followed what happened to the sons and daughters of the farmers I knew, all joined to make me feel the need of arousing the public interest and the public conscience as regards the conditions of life in the country.

Here again I have been fortunate enough to live with my own people, and not to live as an outsider, but as a man doing his share of the work. I know what the work and what the loneliness of a farmer's life too often are. I do not want to help the farmer or to help his wife in ways that will soften either, but I do want to join with both, and try to help them and help myself and help all of us, not by doing away with the need of work, but by trying to create a situation in which work will be more fruitful, and in which the work shall produce and go hand in hand with opportunities for self-development.

Very early I learned through my reading of history, and I found through my association with reformers, that one of the prime difficulties was to get the man who wished reform within a nation also to pay heed to the needs of the nation from the international standpoint. Every little city or republic of antiquity was continually torn between factions which wished to do justice at home but were weak abroad, and other factions which secured justice abroad by the loss of personal liberty at home. So here at home I too often found that men who were ardent for social and industrial reform would be ignorant of the needs of this nation as a nation, would be ignorant of what the navy meant to the nation, of what it meant to the nation to have and to fortify and protect the Panama Canal, of what it meant to the nation to get from the other nations of mankind the respect which comes only to the just, and which is denied to the weaker nation far more quickly than it is denied to the stronger.

It ought not to be necessary to insist upon a point like this, with China before our very eyes offering the most woful example of the ruin that comes to a nation which cannot defend itself against aggression—and China, by the way, offers the further proof that centuries of complete absence of militarism may yet result in the development of all the worst vices and all the deepest misery that grow up in nations that suffer from overmuch militarism. Here again I learn from books, I learn from study, and I learn most by dealing with men.

I feel that the Progressive party owes no small part of its strength to the fact that it not only stands for the most far-reaching measures of social and industrial reform, but in sane and temperate fashion stands also for the right and duty of this nation to take a position of self-respecting strength among the nations of the world, to take such a position as will do injustice to no foreign power, strong or weak, and yet will show that it has both the spirit and the strength to repel injustice from abroad.

"The Case Against the Reactionaries" (1912)

Roosevelt's address to the Republican National Convention in Chicago is very likely the most memorable speech an unsuccessful presidential candidate ever made at a nominating convention. The drama of the evening was high; the audience aroused; the stakes momentous. Having abjured a run for reelection in 1908, and ceding the field to William Howard Taft whom he warmly supported, Roosevelt decided to return to presidential politics in 1912, partly out of fear that his Republican successor had done so badly for the Progressive cause and partly out of disrespect for the Democratic alternative, Woodrow Wilson. Other selections in this volume detail his commitment to the new Progressive politics; here he addresses the faithful on pragmatic concerns, such as the way party bosses pursue power rather than the "war on privilege," which he and his supporters were waging. A large part of the address turns on Roosevelt's assessment of how the national committee was stealing the nomination from him by forbidding (wherever it could) primaries in states where Roosevelt was stronger than Taft. After handily winning those primaries where he could compete, he refused to yield to the newspaper owners or powerful capitalists who pulled the committee members' strings. Since their opposition galvanized his impending defeat at the nominating convention, Roosevelt means to expose the chicanery of these political foes. From his perspective, the great offense of the party bosses was their denial of the "common right of humanity" to choose its leaders and their appointment of some flunky of "privilege." He puts the conflict in terms of a battle for the future: a choice that Americans a century later may also recognize. At the end, he fuses both martial and biblical rhetoric in an unforgettably stirring image evoking a Christian vision of the apocalypse: "We fight in honorable fashion for the good of mankind; fearless of the future; unheeding of our individual fates; with unflinching hearts and undimmed eyes; we stand at Armageddon, and we battle for the Lord."

The Case Against the Reactionaries

My Friends and Fellow Citizens:

I address you as my fellow Republicans, but I also and primarily address you as fellow Americans, fellow citizens, for this has now become much more than an ordinary party fight. The issue is both simpler and larger than that involved in the personality of any man, or than that involved in any factional or in any ordinary party contest. We are standing for the great fundamental rights upon which all successful free government must be based. We are standing for elementary decency in politics. We are fighting for honesty against naked robbery; and where robbery is concerned the all-important question is not the identity of the man robbed, but the crime itself.

As far as Mr. Taft and I are personally concerned it little matters what the fate of either may be. But with Mr. Taft's acquiescence or by his direction, and in his interest, his followers have raised an issue which is all-important to this country. It is not a partisan issue; it is more than a political issue; it is a great moral issue. If we condone political theft, if we do not resent the kinds of wrong and injustice that injuriously affect the whole nation, not merely our Democratic form of government but our civilization itself cannot endure. If the methods adopted by the national committee are approved by the convention which is about to assemble, a great crime will have been committed. The triumph of such proceedings at the moment would mean the wreck of the Republican party; and if such proceedings became habitual, it would mean the wreck of popular government. The actions of the Taft leaders in the national committee, taken with the active aid of Mr. Taft's private secretary and of one of Mr. Taft's Cabinet officers, are monstrous, and they should be indignantly condemned by the moral sentiment of the whole country.

Tonight we come together to protest against a crime which strikes straight at the heart of every principle of political decency and honesty, a crime which represents treason to the people, and the usurpation of the sovereignty of the people by irresponsible political bosses, inspired by the sinister influences of moneyed privilege. We here in this hall are engaged not only in a fight for the rights of every decent Republican, we are engaged in a fight for the rights of every decent American whatsoever his party may be. And, oh, my friends, for one thing at least we should be profoundly grateful. We are more fortunate than our fathers in that there is no slightest tinge of sectionalism in the fight we are now waging. The principles for which we stand are as vital for the South as for the North, for the East as for the West. We make our appeal to all honest, far-sighted, and patriotic Americans, no matter where they may dwell.

When in February last I made up my mind that it was my duty to enter this fight, it was after long and careful deliberation. I had become convinced that Mr. Taft had definitely and completely abandoned the cause of the people and had surrendered himself wholly to the biddings of the professional political bosses and of the great privileged interests standing behind them. I had also become convinced that unless I did make the fight it could not be made at all, and that Mr. Taft's nomination would come to him without serious opposition. The event has justified both my beliefs. I very earnestly ask our fellow Progressives who have supported other candidates to remember that one of the cardinal principles of the doctrines which we hold in common is our duty normally, loyally, and in good faith to abide by the well-thought-out and honestly expressed action of a majority. The overwhelming majority of the Republican Progressives have declared for me. It has become clear beyond shadow of doubt that if I had not made the Progressive fight it would have completely broken down, and there would have been no substantial opposition to the forces of reaction and of political crookedness. Let those Progressives who stand for principle and who are concerned with the fortunes of any particular man only as a means for securing the triumph of principle, ponder these facts and refrain in this crisis from playing into the hands of our enemies.

Mr. Taft at first denied that he represented the bosses. His denial was of little consequence, for his deeds belied his words. But I doubt if at present he would venture to repeat the denial. As it has become constantly more and more evident that the people are against him, he has more and more undisguisedly thrown himself into the arms of the bosses. Here in Chicago at this moment he has never had one chance of success save what was given him by the action of Messrs. Crane, Barnes, Brooker, Penrose, Murphy, Guggenheim, Mulvane, Smoot, New, and their associates in cheating the people out of their rights. He was beaten so overwhelmingly by the people themselves in the States where primaries were held that in the last State in which he spoke, in New Jersey, he permitted himself to be betrayed into the frank admission that he expected to be nominated because he believed the national committee would stand by him. One member of his own Cabinet, representing a State that has just repudiated him, has been working hand in glove with the other Taft members of the national committee, under the lead of Mr. Crane, of Massachusetts, Mr. Penrose, of Pennsylvania, of Mr. Mulvane, of Kansas, of Mr. Murphy, of New Jersey, and Mr. Scott, of West Virginia—all of whom have just been repudiated by their own States—to steal from the people the victory which the people have won. Last February it was evident that Mr. Taft was the accepted representative of the bosses, of the men who upheld the combination of crooked politics and crooked business which has been the chief source not only of our political but of our social and industrial corruption. It has now, alas, become evident that Mr. Taft is willing to acquiesce in and to condone and to accept the fruits of any course of action on which these men embark, even though such action represent treason, as well as destruction, to the Republican party to which they nominally belong, and also treason to the cause of the American people as a whole.

Among the national committeemen who have taken part in this conspiracy there are a number of men who in the ordinary relations of life are doubtless decent and reputable. Probably these men excuse themselves to themselves for what they are now doing on the ground that they are not committing what the law recognizes as a crime. It may well be doubted whether on the whole our country does not suffer more from the misdeeds of men who recognize as binding on their consciences only the obligations of law-honesty, than it suffers from the misdeeds of actual criminals. Men like Messrs. Crane, of Massachusetts, Brooker, of Connecticut, and Nagel, of Missouri, who trail behind their bolder associates such as Messrs. Penrose, Murphy, and Mulvane, are doubtless genuinely shocked at the misconduct of a defaulting bank cashier or at the action of some small election official who on election day falsifies the returns. Yet the wrong to the American people, the damage to the country, by such action as these national committeemen have taken in deliberately seeking to nullify and overthrow the will of the people legitimately expressed as to their choice for President is infinitely greater than the wrong done by the tempted cashier or the bribed election official.

It has to me been both a sad and a strange thing to see men hitherto esteemed reputable take part in such action and to see it sustained by similar men outside. I suppose the explanation must be found in the fact that in the slow but general moral advance certain men lag a little behind the rate of progress of the community as a whole; and where their own real or fancied interests are concerned, such men fail to recognize generally accepted standards of right and wrong until long after they have been recognized by the majority of their fellows. There was a period when piracy and wrecking were esteemed honorable occupations, and long after the community as a whole had grown to reprehend them there were still backward persons who failed to regard them as improper. In the same way, as late as thirty years ago, there were many men in public life who while they would refuse to receive a bribe did not think it objectionable to give a bribe; although now the sentiment in the community has grown so strong that it is no longer possible to excuse the bribe-giver any more than the bribe-taker.

In the same way there are still in certain parts of this country representatives of a class far from uncommon a quarter of a century ago, a class which regards an election as a game without rules in which it is merely a sign of cleverness to swindle and cheat. Evidently the majority of the men whose actions we complain of on the national committee still hold this attitude toward nominations, although some of them may have passed beyond it as regards elections. But on the committee, and associated with the men who assume to be respectable, there are certain representatives of Mr. Taft whose presence gives us cause to wonder whether there are not far worse influences behind the action of the committee than any at which I have guessed. Mr. Stevenson, of Colorado, has appeared on the committee, now holding the proxy of one of Mr. Taft's delegates, now that of another. Judge Ben B. Lindsey, in his book "The Beast and the Jungle," has given a very graphic account of Mr. Stevenson's political activities in Denver. I very greatly wish that every decent man in this country, every plain right-thinking citizen who is in doubt as to what the representatives of Mr. Taft have done on the national committee, would read this book of Judge Lindsey's. In especial, let him study the part in which Judge Lindsey refers to Mr. Stevenson, and then let him think for himself just what it means when Mr. Taft and his associates accept the help of Mr. Stevenson, and import him from his own State of Colorado, to act for other States on the national committee, as one of the ablest men engaged in the movement to rob the people of their right to rule themselves. . . .

When I undertook this contest I was well aware of the intense bitterness which my re-entry into politics would cause, I knew that the powers that prey would oppose me, with tenfold the bitterness they would show in opposing any other Progressive candidate, simply because they do not fear any other Progressive candidate, whereas they very greatly fear me. I knew also that they would directly or indirectly influence very many men who pride themselves upon belonging to and indeed typifying what they regard as the educated and respectable classes. But it has been to me a matter of melancholy concern to see the effect that these influences have produced upon so many men in the Northeast, and in cities like New York, Boston, and Philadelphia, who lead lives that are on the whole rather pleasant, rather soft, and who are free from all possibility of the pressure of actual want. It has been a matter of concern to me to see how bitter and irrational has been the opposition to us among a very large proportion of these men, the men who are to be found in the most noted clubs, in the centres of big business, and in the places especially resorted to by those whose chief desires are for ease and pleasure. We have with us a small percentage of the heads of great corporations and of great corporation lawyers, including I believe almost every man of either class sufficiently high-minded and far-sighted to see that in the long run privilege spells destruction, not only to the class harmed by it but the class possessing it. We welcome the presence of these men. Every honest man, whatever his fortune, should be our ally. The great majority of capitalists, however, and of the big corporation lawyers so intimately connected with them, are naturally hostile to us. Their hostility did not surprise me. The men who are most benefited by privilege unless they are exceptionally disinterested and far-sighted, cannot be expected to feel friendly toward those who assail privilege. But associated with them are many men whose selfish interest in privilege is far less obvious. I genuinely regret that we have had with us so small a percentage of the men for whom life has been easy, who belong to or are intimately associated with the leisured and monied classes; so small a proportion of the class which furnishes the bulk of the membership in the larger social business and professional clubs, and which supplies the majority of the heads of our great educational institutions and of the men generally who take the lead in upholding the cause of virtue when only the minor moralities and the elegancies of life are at issue. My concern and regret are primarily for these men themselves. They could do us good by joining with us, for it is earnestly to be wished that this movement for social justice shall number among its leaders at least a goodly proportion of men whose leadership is obviously disinterested, who will themselves receive no material benefit from the changes which as a matter of justice they advocate. Yet the good to the people would be small compared to the good which these men would do to their own class by casting in their lot with us as we battle for the rights of humanity, as we battle for social and industrial justice, as we champion the cause of those who most need champions and for whom champions have been too few. I have been puzzled at the attitude of the men in question. They are often the men who in the past have been very severe in their condemnation of corruption, in their condemnation of bossism, and in railing at injustice and demanding higher ideals of public service and private life. Yet when the supreme test comes they prove false to all their professions of the past. They fear the people so intensely that they pardon and uphold every species of political and business crookedness in the panic-struck hope of strengthening the boss and special privilege and thereby raising a powerful shield to protect their own soft personalities from the public. They are foolish creatures; the people would never harm them; yet they still dread the people. They stand with servile acquiescence behind the worst representatives of crooked business and crooked politics in the country, and by speech or by silence they now encourage or condone the efforts of our opponents to steal from the people the victory they have won and to substitute boss rule for popular rule. Some of these men have in the past assumed to be teachers of their fellow men in political matters. Never again can they speak in favor of a high ideal of honesty and decency in political life, or of the duty to oppose political corruption and business wrong-doing; for to do so would expose them to the derision of all who abhor hypocrisy and who condemn fine words that are not translated into honorable deeds.

Apparently these men are influenced by a class consciousness which I had not supposed existed in any such strength. They live softly. Circumstances for which they are not responsible have removed their lives from the fears and anxieties of the ordinary men who toil. When a movement is undertaken to make life a little easier, a little better, for the ordinary man, to give him a better chance, these men of soft life seem cast into panic lest something that is not rightly theirs may be taken from them. In unmanly fear they stand against all change, no matter how urgent such change may be. They not only come far short of their duty when they thus act, but they show a lamentable short-sightedness. In this country of ours no man can permanently leave to his descendants the right to live softly; and if he could leave such a right it would in the end prove to be a right not worth having. The inheritance really worthwhile which we can transmit to our children and to our children's children is the ability to do work that counts, not the means of avoiding work—the ability for efficient effort, not the opportunity for the slothful avoidance of all effort. The leaders in the fight for industrial and social justice today should be the men to whom much has been given and from whom we have a right to expect in return much of honesty and of courage, much of disinterested and valorous effort for the common good. The multimillionaire who opposes us is the worst foe of his own children and children's children, and, little though he knows it, we are their benefactors when we strive to make this country one in which justice shall prevail; for it is they themselves who would in the end suffer most if in this country we permitted the average man gradually to grow to feel that fair play was denied him, that justice was denied to the many and privilege accorded to the few.

We who in this contest are fighting for the rights of the plain people, we who are fighting for the right of the people to rule themselves, need offer no better proof of the fact that we are fighting for all citizens, no matter what their politics, than that which is afforded by the action of that portion of the press which is controlled by privilege, by the great special interests in business. Newspapers of this type are found in every part of the country, in San Francisco, in Cincinnati, in Chicago and St. Louis, in Boston and Philadelphia. But they are strongest in New York. Some of these newspapers are nominally Democratic, some nominally Republican, some nominally independent. But in reality they are true only to the real or fancied interests of the great capitalist class by certain of whose members they are controlled. Sometimes the interests of this capitalist class are identical with those of the country as a whole, and in that case these papers serve the interests of the commonwealth. Sometimes the interests of the capitalist class are against the interests of the people as a whole, and in that case these papers are hostile to the interests of the common-wealth. But neither their acting favorably to nor their acting adversely to the interests of the commonwealth is anything more than an incident to their support of the interests to which they are bound. The great and far-reaching evil of their action is that they choke and foul the only chan-nels of information open to so many honest and well-meaning citizens. The most prominent representatives of these papers in New York and Massachusetts supported Mr. Parker against me in 1904. Mr. Parker was a Democrat, but he was entirely satisfactory to their masters, and for the time being they ardently did all they could to overthrow the Republican party and to elect a Democratic President. But when I began to be seri-ously talked about for the Republican nomination this year, these papers one and all turned Republican to the extent of becoming my furious oppo-nents and the furious champions of Mr. Taft. There is an element of pure comedy in reading in these papers continual lamentations about the like-lihood of my candidacy breaking up the Republican party. They them-selves did all they could to beat the Republican party when they thought they could elect Mr. Parker. Now these papers would eagerly champion the Republican party if they could keep Mr. Taft as its nominee for Presi-dent. In the past they have not concealed their contempt for Mr. Taft, and none of them regard him in any way as a leader.

The difference between us and our present-day opponents is as old as civilized history. In every great crisis of the kind we face today, we find arrayed on one side the men who with fervor and broad sympathy and lofty idealism stand for the forward movement, the men who stand for the uplift and betterment of mankind, and who have faith in the people; and over against them the men of restricted vision and contracted sympathy, whose souls are not stirred by the wrongs of others. Side by side with the latter, appear the other men who lack all intensity of conviction, who care only for the pleasure of the day; and also those other men who distrust the people, who if dishonest wish to keep the people helpless so as to exploit them, and who if honest so disbelieve in the power of the people to bring about wholesome reform that every appeal to popular conscience and popular intelligence fills them with an angry terror. According to their own lights, these men are often very respectable, very worthy, but they live on a plane of low ideals. In the atmosphere they create impostors flourish, and leadership comes to be thought of only as success in making money, and the vision of heaven becomes a sordid vision, and all that is highest and purest in human nature is laughed at, and honesty is bought and sold in the market-place.

Opposed undyingly to these men are the men of faith and vision, the men in whom love of righteousness burns like a flaming fire, who spurn lives of soft and selfish ease, of slothful self-indulgence, who scorn to think only of pleasure for themselves, who feel for and believe in their fellows, whose high fealty is reserved for all that is good, that is just, that is honorable. By their very nature these men are bound to battle for the truth and the right. They do not address themselves only to the cultured and exclusive few. They prize character even more than intellect. They know well that conscience is not the privilege merely of the men of wealth and cultivation, and they make their appeal to all men alike in the name of the great fundamental qualities, and qualities that every man should have, the qualities of generosity and unselfishness, of fearless honesty and high courage.

We who war against privilege pay heed to no outworn system of philosophy. We demand of our leaders today understanding of and sympathy with the living and the vital needs of those in the community whose needs are greatest. We are against privilege in every form. We believe in striking down every bulwark of privilege. Above all we are against the evil alliance of special privilege in business with special business in politics. We believe in giving the people a free hand to work in efficient fashion for true justice. To the big man and to the little man, in all the relations of life, we pledge justice and fair dealing.

A period of change is upon us. Our opponents, the men of reaction, ask us to stand still. But we could not stand still if we would; we must either go forward or go backward. Never was the need more imperative than now for men of vision who are also men of action. Disaster is ahead of us if we trust to the leadership of men whose souls are seared and whose eyes are blinded, men of cold heart and narrow mind, who believe we can find safety in dull timidity and dull inaction. The unrest cannot be quieted by ingenious trickery of those who profess to advance by merely marking time, or who seek to drown the cry for justice by loud and insincere clamor about issues that are false and issues that are dead. The trumpets sound the advance, and their peal cannot be drowned by repeating the war-cries of bygone battles, the victory shouts of vanished hosts. Here in this city of the State of Lincoln I can set forth the principles for which we stand today in the words which Lincoln used fifty-four years ago, when in speaking of the then phase of the eternal struggles between privilege and justice, between the rights of the many and the special interest of the few, he said:

"That is the real issue. That is the issue which will continue in this country when these poor tongues of Judge Douglas and myself shall be silent. It is the eternal struggle between two principles—right and wrong—throughout the world. They are the two principles that have stood face to face from the beginning of time. The one is the common right of humanity, the other the divine right of kings. It is the same principle in whatever shape it develops itself. It is the same spirit that says: 'You toil and work and earn bread, and I will eat it.' No matter in what shape it comes, whether from the mouth of a king who bestrides the people of his own nation and lives from the fruit of their labor, or from one race of men as an apology for enslaving another race, it is the same tyrannical principle."

Were Lincoln alive today he would add that it is also the same principle which is now at stake when we fight on behalf of the many against the oppressor in modern industry whether the abuse of special privilege be by a man whose wealth is great or is little, whether by the multimillionaire owner of railways and mines and factories who forgets his duties to those who earn his bread while earning their own, or by the owner of the foul little sweat-shop who coins dollars from the excessive and underpaid labor of haggard women. We who stand for the cause of progress are fighting to make this country a better place to live in for those who have been harshly treated by fate; and if we succeed it will also really be a better place for those who are already well off. None of us can really prosper permanently if masses of our fellows are debased and degraded, if they are ground down and forced to live starved and sordid lives, so that their souls are crippled like their bodies and the fine edge of their every feeling blunted. We ask that those of our people to whom fate has been kind shall remember that each is his brother's keeper, and that all of us whose veins thrill with abounding vigor shall feel our obligation to the less fortunate who work wearily beside us in the strain and stress of our eager modern life.

Friends, here in Chicago at this time you have a great task before you. I wish you to realize deep in your hearts that you are not merely facing a crisis in the history of a party. You are facing a crisis in the history of a nation and what you do will have an appreciable effect throughout the world at large. Here in America we the people have a continent on which to work out our destiny, and our faith is great that our men and women are fit to face the mighty days. Nowhere else in all the world is there such a chance for the triumph on a gigantic scale of the great cause of Democratic and popular government. If we fail, the failure will be lamentable, and our heads will be bowed with shame; for not only shall we fail for ourselves, but our failure will wreck the fond desires of all throughout the world who look toward us with the fond hope that here in this great Republic it shall be proved from ocean to ocean that the people can rule themselves, and thus ruling can gain liberty for and do justice both to themselves and to others. We who stand for the cause of the uplift of humanity and the betterment of mankind are pledged to eternal war against wrong whether by the few or by the many, by a plutocracy or by a mob. We believe that this country will not be a permanently good place for any of us to live in unless we make it a reasonably good place for all of us to live in. The sons of all of us will pay in the future if we of the present do not do justice to all in the present. Our cause is the cause of justice for all in the interest of all. The present contest is but a phase of the larger struggle. Assuredly the fight will go on whether we win or lose; but it will be a sore disaster to lose. What happens to me is not of the slightest consequence; I am to be used, as in a doubtful battle any man is used, to his hurt or not, so long as he is useful, and is then cast aside or left to die. I wish you to feel this. I mean it; and I shall need no sympathy when you are through with me, for this fight is far too great to permit us to concern ourselves about any one man's welfare. If we are true to ourselves by putting far above our own interests the triumph of the high cause for which we battle we shall not lose. It would be far better to fail honorably for the cause we champion than it would be to win by foul methods the foul victory for which our opponents hope. But the victory shall be ours, and it shall be won as we have already won so many victories, by clean and honest fighting for the loftiest of causes. We fight in honorable fashion for the good of mankind; fearless of the future; unheeding of our individual fates; with unflinching hearts and undimmed eyes; we stand at Armageddon, and we battle for the Lord.

"The Leader and the Cause" (1912)

As an example of Roosevelt's resilience, in Milwaukee, Wisconsin, on October 14, 1912, he delivered this stem-winder after he was shot by a would-be assassin, a disgruntled partisan who meant to make himself a martyr to the two-party system that he saw Roosevelt's Bull Moose campaign as undermining. The bullet lodged in his ribs, having ripped through the candidate's overcoat, his suit-jacket and the text of the speech itself. Incredibly, Roosevelt went on with the speech, which focused on the urgency of Americans' turn toward a new Progressive Party, not the reactionary parties, as Roosevelt described both Democratic and Republican organizations. Much is made of Roosevelt's self-possession, and indeed virtually the first association he makes is having been under fire in the Battle of San Juan Hill. He's then reminded of his true purpose that evening, in laying out an ecumenical vision of the potential for American heroism, the need to make his audience understand the egalitarian basis of the Bull Moose Party and his vision of a truly progressive United States and his faith in "making life a little easier for all our people," "a movement for justice now." For Roosevelt, this vision could only attain if Progressives would "enroll rich or poor" to stand united for the "most elementary rights of good citizenship." Notable in the speech is Roosevelt's recurring absence of self-concern, his avowal of having had a "jolly" life. As if to prove that point, only after an hour's oration does he finally sit down.

The Leader and the Cause

Friends, I shall ask you to be as quiet as possible. I don't know whether you fully understand that I have just been shot; but it takes more than that to kill a Bull Moose. But fortunately I had my manuscript, so you see I was going to make a long speech, and there is a bullet—there is where the bullet went through—and it probably saved me from it going into my heart. The bullet is in me now, so that I cannot make a very long speech, but I will try my best.

And now, friends, I want to take advantage of this incident and say a word of solemn warning to my fellow countrymen. First of all, I want to say this about myself: I have altogether too important things to think of to feel any concern over my own death; and now I cannot speak to you insincerely within five minutes of being shot. I am telling you the literal truth when I say that my concern is for many other things. It is not in the least for my own life. I want you to understand that I am ahead of the game, anyway. No man has had a happier life than I have led; a happier life in every way. I have been able to do certain things that I greatly wished to do, and I am interested in doing other things. I can tell you with absolute truthfulness that I am very much uninterested in whether I am shot or not. It was just as when I was colonel of my regiment. I always felt that a private was to be excused for feeling at times some pangs of anxiety about his personal safety, but I cannot understand a man fit to be a colonel who can pay any heed to his personal safety when he is occupied as he ought to be occupied with the absorbing desire to do his duty.

I am in this cause with my whole heart and soul. I believe that the Progressive movement is for making life a little easier for all our people; a movement to try to take the burdens off the men and especially the women and children of this country. I am absorbed in the success of that movement.

Friends, I ask you now this evening to accept what I am saying as absolutely true, when I tell you I am not thinking of my own success. I am not thinking of my life or of anything connected with me personally. I am thinking of the movement. I say this by way of introduction, because I want to say something very serious to our people and especially to the newspapers. I don't know anything about who the man was who shot me tonight. He was seized at once by one of the stenographers in my party, Mr. Martin, and I suppose is now in the hands of the police. He shot to kill. He shot—the shot, the bullet went in here—I will show you.

I am going to ask you to be as quiet as possible for I am not able to give the challenge of the bull moose quite as loudly. Now, I do not know who he was or what party he represented. He was a coward. He stood in the darkness in the crowd around the automobile and when they cheered me, and I got up to bow, he stepped forward and shot me in the darkness.

Now, friends, of course, I do not know, as I say, anything about him; but it is a very natural thing that weak and vicious minds should be inflamed to acts of violence by the kind of awful mendacity and abuse that have been heaped upon me for the last three months by the papers in the interest of not only Mr. Debs but of Mr. Wilson and Mr. Taft.

Friends, I will disown and repudiate any man of my party who attacks with such foul slander and abuse any opponent of any other party; and now I wish to say seriously to all the daily newspapers, to the Republican, the Democratic, and the Socialist parties, that they cannot, month in and month out and year in and year out, make the kind of untruthful, bitter assault that they have made and not expect that brutal, violent natures, or brutal and violent characters, especially when the brutality is accompanied by a not very strong mind; they cannot expect that such natures will be unaffected by it.

Now, friends, I am not speaking for myself at all. I give you my word, I do not care a rap about being shot; not a rap.

I have had a good many experiences in my time and this is one of them. What I care for is my country. I wish I were able to impress upon my people—our people, the duty to feel strongly but to speak the truth of their opponents. I say now, I have never said one word on the stump against any opponent that I cannot defend. I have said nothing that I could not substantiate and nothing that I ought not to have said—nothing that I—nothing that, looking back at, I would not say again.

Now, friends, it ought not to be too much to ask that our opponents— (*speaking to some one on the stage*)—I am not sick at all. I am all right. I cannot tell you of what infinitesimal importance I regard this incident as compared with the great issues at stake in this campaign, and I ask it not for my sake, not the least in the world, but for the sake of our common country, that they make up their minds to speak only the truth, and not to use the kind of slander and mendacity which if taken seriously must incite weak and violent natures to crimes of violence. Don't you make any mistake. Don't you pity me. I am all right. I am all right and you cannot escape listening to the speech either.

And now, friends, this incident that has just occurred—this effort to assassinate me—emphasizes to a peculiar degree the need of this Progressive movement. Friends, every good citizen ought to do everything in his or her power to prevent the coming of the day when we shall see in this country two recognized creeds fighting one another, when we shall see the creed of the "Havenots" arraigned against the creed of the "Haves." When that day comes then such incidents as this tonight will be commonplace in our history. When you make poor men—when you permit the conditions to grow such that the poor man as such will be swayed by his sense of injury against the men who try to hold what they improperly have won, when that day comes, the most awful passions will be let loose and it will be an ill day for our country.

Now, friends, what we who are in this movement are endeavoring to do is to forestall any such movement by making this a movement for justice now—a movement in which we ask all just men of generous hearts to join with the men who feel in their souls that lift upward which bids them to refuse to be satisfied themselves while their countrymen and countrywomen suffer from avoidable misery. Now, friends, what we Progressives are trying to do is to enroll rich or poor, whatever their social or industrial position, to stand together for the most elementary rights of good citizenship, those elementary rights which are the foundation of good citizenship in this great Republic of ours.

(*At this point a renewed effort was made to persuade Mr. Roosevelt to conclude his speech.*)

My friends are a little more nervous than I am. Don't you waste any sympathy on me. I have had an A-1 time in life and I am having it now.

I never in my life was in any movement in which I was able to serve with such whole-hearted devotion as in this; in which I was able to feel as I do in this that common weal. I have fought for the good of our common country.

And now, friends, I shall have to cut short much of the speech that I meant to give you, but I want to touch on just two or three of the points.

In the first place, speaking to you here in Milwaukee, I wish to say that the Progressive party is making its appeal to all our fellow citizens without any regard to their creed or to their birthplace. We do not regard as essential the way in which a man worships his God or as being affected by where he was born. We regard it as a matter of spirit and purpose. In New York, while I was police commissioner, the two men from whom I got the most assistance were Jacob Riis, who was born in Denmark, and Arthur von Briesen, who was born in Germany—both of them as fine examples of the best and highest American citizenship as you could find in any part of this country.

I have just been introduced by one of your own men here—Henry Cochems. His grandfather, his father, and that father's seven brothers, all served in the United States army, and they entered it four years after they had come to this country from Germany. Two of them left their lives, spent their lives, on the field of battle. I am all right—I am a little sore. Anybody has a right to be sore with a bullet in him. You would find that if I was in battle now I would be leading my men just the same. Just the same way I am going to make this speech.

At one time I promoted five men for gallantry on the field of battle. Afterward in making some inquiries about them I found it happened that two of them were Protestants, two Catholics, and one a Jew. One Protestant came from Germany and one was born in Ireland. I did not promote them because of their religion. It just happened that way. If all five of them had been Jews I would have promoted them, or if all five had been Protestants I would have promoted them; or if they had been Catholics. In that regiment I had a man born in Italy who distinguished himself by gallantry; there was a young fellow, a son of Polish parents, and another who came here when he was a child from Bohemia, who likewise distinguished themselves; and friends, I assure you, that I was incapable of considering any question whatever, but the worth of each individual as a fighting man. If he was a good fighting man, then I saw that Uncle Sam got the benefit from it. That is all.

I make the same appeal in our citizenship. I ask in our civic life that we in the same way pay heed only to the man's quality of citizenship, to repudiate as the worst enemy that we can have whoever tries to get us to discriminate for or against any man because of his creed or his birthplace.

Now, friends, in the same way I want our people to stand by one another without regard to differences or class or occupation. I have always stood by the labor-unions. I am going to make one omission tonight. I have prepared my speech because Mr. Wilson had seen fit to attack me by showing up his record in comparison with mine. But I am not going to do that tonight. I am going to simply speak of what I myself have done and of what I think ought to be done in this country of ours.

It is essential that there should be organizations of labor. This is an era of organization. Capital organizes and therefore labor must organize. My appeal for organized labor is twofold; to the outsider and the capitalist I make my appeal to treat the laborer fairly, to recognize the fact that he must organize, that there must be such organization, that the laboring man must organize for his own protection, and that it is the duty of the rest of us to help him and not hinder him in organizing. That is one-half of the appeal that I make.

Now, the other half is to the labor man himself. My appeal to him is to remember that as he wants justice, so he must do justice. I want every labor man, every labor leader, every organized union man, to take the lead in denouncing crime or violence. I want them to take the lead in denouncing disorder and in denouncing the inciting of riot; that in this country we shall proceed under the protection of our laws and with all respect to the laws, and I want the labor men to feel in their turn that exactly as justice must be done them so they must do justice. That they must bear their duty as citizens, their duty to this great country of ours, and that they must not rest content unless they do that duty to the fullest degree.

I know these doctors, when they get hold of me, will never let me go back, and there are just a few things more that I want to say to you.

And here I have got to make one comparison between Mr. Wilson and myself, simply because he has invited it and I cannot shrink from it. Mr. Wilson has seen fit to attack me, to say that I did not do much against the trusts when I was President. I have got two answers to make to that. In the first place what I did, and then I want to compare what I did while I was President with what Mr. Wilson did not do while he was governor.

When I took office the antitrust law was practically a dead letter and the interstate commerce law in as poor a condition. I had to revive both laws. I did. I enforced both. It will be easy enough to do now what I did then, but the reason that it is easy now is because I did it when it was hard.

Nobody was doing anything. I found speedily that the interstate commerce law by being made more perfect could be made a most useful instrument for helping solve some of our industrial problems. So with the antitrust law. I speedily found that almost the only positive good achieved by such a successful lawsuit as the Northern Securities suit, for instance, was in establishing the principle that the government was supreme over the big corporation, but that by itself that law did not accomplish any of the things that we ought to have accomplished; and so I began to fight for the amendment of the law along the lines of the interstate commerce law, and now we propose, we Progressives, to establish an interstate commission having the same power over industrial concerns that the Interstate Commerce Commission has over railroads, so that whenever there is in the future a decision rendered in such important matters as the recent suits against the Standard Oil, the Sugar—no, not that—Tobacco—Tobacco Trust—we will have a commission which will see that the decree of the court is really made effective; that it is not made a merely nominal decree.

Our opponents have said that we intend to legalize monopoly. Nonsense. They have legalized monopoly. At this moment the Standard Oil and Tobacco Trust monopolies are legalized; they are being carried on under the decree of the Supreme Court. Our proposal is really to break up monopoly. Our proposal is to lay down certain requirements, and then require the commerce commission—the industrial commission—to see that the trusts live up to those requirements. Our opponents have spoken as if we were going to let the commission declare what the requirements should be. Not at all. We are going to put the requirements in the law and then see that the commission requires them to obey that law.

And now, friends, as Mr. Wilson has invited the comparison, I only want to say this: Mr. Wilson has said that the States are the proper authorities to deal with the trusts. Well, about eighty per cent of the trusts are organized in New Jersey. The Standard Oil, the Tobacco, the Sugar, the Beef, all those trusts are organized in New Jersey and the laws of New Jersey say that their charters can at any time be amended or repealed if they misbehave themselves and give the government ample power to act about those laws, and Mr. Wilson has been governor a year and nine months and he has not opened his lips. The chapter describing what Mr. Wilson has done about the trusts in New Jersey would read precisely like a chapter describing the snakes in Ireland, which ran: "There are no snakes in Ireland." Mr. Wilson has done precisely and exactly nothing about the trusts.

I tell you, and I told you at the beginning, I do not say anything on the stump that I do not believe. I do not say anything I do not know. Let any of Mr. Wilson's friends on Tuesday point out one thing or let Mr. Wilson point out one thing he has done about the trusts as governor of New Jersey.

And now, friends, there is one thing I want to say especially to you people here in Wisconsin. All that I have said so far is what I would say in any part of this Union. I have a peculiar right to ask that in this great contest you men and women of Wisconsin shall stand with us. You have taken the lead in progressive movements here in Wisconsin. You have taught the rest of us to look to you for inspiration and leadership. Now, friends, you have made that movement here locally. You will be doing a dreadful injustice to yourselves; you will be doing a dreadful injustice to the rest of us throughout this Union, if you fail to stand with us now that we are making this national movement. What I am about to say now I want you to understand. If I speak of Mr. Wilson I speak with no mind of bitterness. I merely want to discuss the difference of policy between the Progressive and the Democratic party and to ask you to think for yourselves which party you will follow. I will say that, friends, because the Republican party is beaten. Nobody needs to have any idea that anything can be done with the Republican party.

When the Republican party—not the Republican party—when the bosses in the control of the Republican party, the Barneses and Penroses, last June stole the nomination and wrecked the Republican party for good and all—I want to point out to you nominally they stole that nomination from me, but really it was from you. They did not like me, and the longer they live the less cause they will have to like me. But while they do not like me, they dread you. You are the people that they dread. They dread the people themselves, and those bosses and the big special interests behind them made up their mind that they would rather see the Republican party wrecked than see it come under the control of the people themselves. So I am not dealing with the Republican party. There are only two ways you can vote this year. You can be progressive or reactionary. Whether you vote Republican or Democratic it does not make any difference, you are voting reactionary.

Now, the Democratic party in its platform and through the utterances of Mr. Wilson has distinctly committed itself to the old flintlock, muzzle-loaded doctrine of States' rights, and I have said distinctly that we are for the people's rights. We are for the rights of the people. If they can be obtained best through the National Government, then we are for national rights. We are for the people's rights however it is necessary to secure them.

Mr. Wilson has made a long essay against Senator Beveridge's bill to abolish child labor. It is the same kind of an argument that would be made against our bill to prohibit women from working more than eight hours a day in industry. It is the same kind of argument that would have to be made; if it is true, it would apply equally against our proposal to insist that in continuous industries there shall be by law one day's rest in seven and a three-shift eight-hour day. You have labor laws here in Wisconsin, and any chamber of commerce will tell you that because of that fact there are industries that will not come into Wisconsin. They prefer to stay outside where they can work children of tender years, where they can work women fourteen and sixteen hours a day, where, if it is a continuous industry, they can work men twelve hours a day and seven days a week.

Now, friends, I know that you of Wisconsin would never repeal those laws even if they are to your commercial hurt, just as I am trying to get New York to adopt such laws even though it will be to New York's commercial hurt. But if possible I want to arrange it so that we can have justice without commercial hurt, and you can only get that if you have justice enforced nationally. You won't be burdened in Wisconsin with industries not coming to the State if the same good laws are extended all over the other States. Do you see what I mean? The States all compete in a common market; and it is not justice to the employers of a State that has enforced just and proper laws to have them exposed to the competition of another State where no such laws are enforced. Now, the Democratic platform, and their speakers, declare that we shall not have such laws. Mr. Wilson has distinctly declared that you shall not have a national law to prohibit the labor of children, to prohibit child labor. He has distinctly declared that we shall not have a law to establish a minimum wage for women.

I ask you to look at our declaration and hear and read our platform about social and industrial justice and then, friends, vote for the Progressive ticket without regard to me, without regard to my personality, for only by voting for that platform can you be true to the cause of progress throughout this Union.

Observations
and
Travels

———————◆◆◆———————

"Hunting the Grisly" (1893)

Roosevelt prided himself on the cultivation of his woodcraft and his skills as an outdoorsman, especially as a hunter, an activity he pursued for most of his adulthood. He also might have prided himself on his ability to write about his adventures, for his accounts are unfailingly vivid. In this section from his successful book by the same title, he describes three encounters with his foe during his trips to the Far West. With each encounter, Roosevelt also stalks the reader by increasing the level of tension and of danger. He renders each scene with a spare diction that neither sentimentalizes nor sensationalizes, rarely lapsing into abstraction but recounting in concrete detail the sights, sounds, and smells of his pursuit. (He even pauses to indulge his special love of birding and registers the ones he sees while waiting out his prey. The account reads in part like a how-to, a field guide to grizzly hunting that might instruct readers in the steps one must take in pitting oneself against such a quarry. Nor does Roosevelt exaggerate the bears' fearsomeness; instead, he is at pains to describe how the bears have learned to try to evade rather than confront their pursuers.

Hunting the Grisly

If out in the late fall or early spring, it is often possible to follow a bear's trail in the snow; having come upon it either by chance or hard hunting, or else having found where it leads from some carcass on which the beast has been feeding. In the pursuit one must exercise great caution, as at such times the hunter is easily seen a long way off, and game is always especially watchful for any foe that may follow its trail.

Once I killed a grisly in this manner. It was early in the fall, but snow lay on the ground, while the gray weather boded a storm. My camp was in a bleak, wind-swept valley, high among the mountains which form the divide between the head-waters of the Salmon and Clarke's Fork of the Columbia. All night I had lain in my buffalo-bag, under the lea of a wind-break of branches, in the clump of fir-trees, where I had halted the preceding evening. At my feet ran a rapid mountain torrent, its bed choked with ice-covered rocks; I had been lulled to sleep by the stream's splashing murmur, and the loud moaning of the wind along the naked cliffs. At dawn I rose and shook myself free of the buffalo robe, coated with hoar-frost. The ashes of the fire were lifeless; in the dim morning the air was bitter cold. I did not linger a moment, but snatched up my rifle, pulled on my fur cap and gloves, and strode off up a side ravine; as I walked I ate some mouthfuls of venison, left over from supper.

Two hours of toil up the steep mountain brought me to the top of a spur. The sun had risen, but was hidden behind a bank of sullen clouds. On the divide I halted, and gazed out over a vast landscape, inconceivably wild and dismal. Around me towered the stupendous mountain masses which make up the backbone of the Rockies. From my feet, as far as I could see, stretched a rugged and barren chaos of ridges and detached rock masses. Behind me, far below, the stream wound like a silver ribbon, fringed with dark conifers and the changing, dying foliage of poplar and quaking aspen. In front the bottoms of the valleys were filled with the sombre evergreen forest, dotted here and there with black, ice-skimmed tarns; and the dark spruces clustered also in the higher gorges, and were scattered thinly along the mountain sides. The snow which had fallen lay in drifts and streaks, while, where the wind had scope it was blown off, and the ground left bare.

For two hours I walked onwards across the ridges and valleys. Then among some scattered spruces, where the snow lay to the depth of half a foot, I suddenly came on the fresh, broad trail of a grisly. The brute was evidently roaming restlessly about in search of a winter den, but willing, in passing, to pick up any food that lay handy. At once I took the trail, travelling above and to one side, and keeping a sharp look-out ahead. The bear was going across wind, and this made my task easy. I walked rapidly, though cautiously; and it was only in crossing the large patches of bare ground that I had to fear making a noise. Elsewhere the snow muffled my footsteps, and made the trail so plain that I scarcely had to waste a glance upon it, bending my eyes always to the front.

At last, peering cautiously over a ridge crowned with broken rocks, I saw my quarry, a big, burly bear, with silvered fur. He had halted on an open hill-side, and was busily digging up the caches of some rock gophers or squirrels. He seemed absorbed in his work, and the stalk was easy. Slipping quietly back, I ran towards the end of the spur, and in ten minutes struck a ravine, of which one branch ran past within seventy yards of where the bear was working. In this ravine was a rather close growth of stunted evergreens, affording good cover, although in one or two places I had to lie down and crawl through the snow. When I reached the point for which I was aiming, the bear had just finished rooting, and was starting off. A slight whistle brought him to a standstill, and I drew a bead behind his shoulder, and low down, resting the rifle across the crooked branch of a dwarf spruce. At the crack he ran off at speed, making no sound, but the thick spatter of blood splashes, showing clear on the white snow, betrayed the mortal nature of the wound. For some minutes I followed the trail; and then, topping a ridge, I saw the dark bulk lying motionless in a snow drift at the foot of a low rock-wall, down which he had tumbled.

The usual practice of the still-hunter who is after grisly is to toll it to baits. The hunter either lies in ambush near the carcass, or approaches it stealthily when he thinks the bear is at its meal.

One day while camped near the Bitter Root Mountains in Montana I found that a bear had been feeding on the carcass of a moose which lay some five miles from the little open glade in which my tent was pitched, and I made up my mind to try to get a shot at it that afternoon. I stayed in camp till about three o'clock, lying lazily back on the bed of sweet-smelling evergreen boughs, watching the pack ponies as they stood under the pines on the edge of the open, stamping now and then, and switching their tails. The air was still, the sky a glorious blue; at that hour in the afternoon even the September sun was hot. The smoke from the smouldering logs of the camp fire curled thinly upwards. Little chipmunks scuttled out from their holes to the packs, which lay in a heap on the ground, and then scuttled madly back again. A couple of drab-colored whisky-jacks, with bold mien and fearless bright eyes, hopped and fluttered round, picking up the scraps, and uttering an extraordinary variety of notes, mostly discordant; so tame were they that one of them lit on my outstretched arm as I half dozed, basking in the sunshine.

When the shadows began to lengthen, I shouldered my rifle and plunged into the woods. At first my route lay along a mountain side; then for half a mile over a windfall, the dead timber piled about in crazy confusion. After that I went up the bottom of a valley by a little brook, the ground being carpeted with a sponge of soaked moss. At the head of this brook was a pond covered with water-lilies; and a scramble through a rocky pass took me into a high, wet valley, where the thick growth of spruce was broken by occasional strips of meadow. In this valley the moose carcass lay, well at the upper end.

In moccasined feet I trod softly through the soundless woods. Under the dark branches it was already dusk, and the air had the cool chill of evening. As I neared the clump where the body lay, I walked with redoubled caution, watching and listening with strained alertness. Then I heard a twig snap; and my blood leaped, for I knew the bear was at his supper. In another moment I saw his shaggy, brown form. He was working with all his awkward giant strength, trying to bury the carcass, twisting it to one side and the other with wonderful ease. Once he got angry and suddenly gave it a tremendous cuff with his paw; in his bearing he had something half humorous, half devilish. I crept up within forty yards; but for several minutes he would not keep his head still. Then something attracted his attention in the forest, and he stood motionless looking towards it, broadside to me, with his fore-paws planted on the carcass. This gave me my chance. I drew a very fine bead between his eye and ear, and pulled trigger. He dropped like a steer when struck with a pole-axe.

If there is a good hiding-place handy it is better to lie in wait at the carcass. One day on the head-waters of the Madison, I found that a bear was coming to an elk I had shot some days before; and I at once determined to ambush the beast when he came back that evening. The carcass lay in the middle of a valley a quarter of a mile broad. The bottom of this valley was covered by an open forest of tall pines; a thick jungle of smaller evergreens marked where the mountains rose on either hand. There were a number of large rocks scattered here and there, one, of very convenient shape, being only some seventy or eighty yards from the carcass. Up this I clambered. It hid me perfectly, and on its top was a carpet of soft pine needles, on which I could lie at my ease.

Hour after hour passed by. A little black woodpecker with a yellow crest ran nimbly up and down the tree-trunks for some time and then flitted away with a party of chickadees and nut-hatches. Occasionally a Clarke's crow soared about overhead or clung in any position to the swaying end of a pine branch, chattering and screaming. Flocks of cross-bills, with wavy flight and plaintive calls, flew to a small mineral lick near by, where they scraped the clay with their queer little beaks.

As the westering sun sank out of sight beyond the mountains these sounds of bird-life gradually died away. Under the great pines the evening was still with the silence of primeval desolation. The sense of sadness and loneliness, the melancholy of the wilderness, came over me like a spell. Every slight noise made my pulses throb as I lay motionless on the rock gazing intently into the gathering gloom. I began to fear that it would grow too dark to shoot before the grisly came.

Suddenly and without warning, the great bear stepped out of the bushes and trod across the pine needles with such swift and silent footsteps that its bulk seemed unreal. It was very cautious, continually halting to peer around; and once it stood up on its hind legs and looked long down the valley towards the red west. As it reached the carcass I put a bullet between its shoulders. It rolled over, while the woods resounded with its savage roaring. Immediately it struggled to its feet and staggered off; and fell again to the next shot, squalling and yelling. Twice this was repeated; the brute being one of those bears which greet every wound with a great outcry, and sometimes seem to lose their feet when hit—although they will occasionally fight as savagely as their more silent brethren. In this case the wounds were mortal, and the bear died before reaching the edge of the thicket.

I spent much of the fall of 1889 hunting on the head-waters of the Salmon and Snake in Idaho, and along the Montana boundary line from the Big Hole Basin and the head of the Wisdom River to the neighborhood of Red Rock Pass and to the north and west of Henry's Lake. . . .

The country was for the most part fairly open, as I kept near the foothills where glades and little prairies broke the pine forest. The trees were of small size. There was no regular trail, but the course was easy to keep, and I had no trouble of any kind save on the second day. That afternoon I was following a stream which at last "canyoned up," that is, sank to the bottom of a canyon-like ravine impassable for a horse. I started up a side valley, intending to cross from its head coulies to those of another valley which would lead in below the canyon.

However, I got enmeshed in the tangle of winding valleys at the foot of the steep mountains, and as dusk was coming on I halted and camped in a little open spot by the side of a small, noisy brook, with crystal water. The place was carpeted with soft, wet, green moss, dotted red with the kinnikinnic berries, and at its edge, under the trees where the ground was dry, I threw down the buffalo bed on the mat of sweet-smelling pine needles. Making camp took but a moment. I opened the pack, tossed the bedding on a smooth spot, knee-haltered the little mare, dragged up a few dry logs, and then strolled off, rifle on shoulder, through the frosty gloaming, to see if I could pick up a grouse for supper.

For half a mile I walked quickly and silently over the pine needles, across a succession of slight ridges separated by narrow, shallow valleys. The forest here was composed of lodge-pole pines, which on the ridges grew close together, with tall slender trunks, while in the valleys the growth was more open. Though the sun was behind the mountains there was yet plenty of light by which to shoot, but it was fading rapidly.

At last, as I was thinking of turning towards camp, I stole up to the crest of one of the ridges, and looked over into the valley some sixty yards off. Immediately I caught the loom of some large, dark object; and another glance showed me a big grisly walking slowly off with his head down. He was quartering to me, and I fired into his flank, the bullet, as I afterwards found, ranging forward and piercing one lung. At the shot he uttered a loud, moaning grunt and plunged forward at a heavy gallop, while I raced obliquely down the hill to cut him off. After going a few hundred feet he reached a laurel thicket, some thirty yards broad, and two or three times as long which he did not leave. I ran up to the edge and there halted, not liking to venture into the mass of twisted, close-growing stems and glossy foliage. Moreover, as I halted, I heard him utter a peculiar, savage kind of whine from the heart of the brush. Accordingly, I began to skirt the edge, standing on tiptoe and gazing earnestly to see if I could not catch a glimpse of his hide. When I was at the narrowest part of the thicket, he suddenly left it directly opposite, and then wheeled and stood broadside to me on the hill-side, a little above. He turned his head stiffly towards me; scarlet strings of froth hung from his lips; his eyes burned like embers in the gloom.

I held true, aiming behind the shoulder, and my bullet shattered the point or lower end of his heart, taking out a big nick. Instantly the great bear turned with a harsh roar of fury and challenge, blowing the bloody foam from his mouth, so that I saw the gleam of his white fangs; and then he charged straight at me, crashing and bounding through the laurel bushes, so that it was hard to aim. I waited until he came to a fallen tree, raking him as he topped it with a ball, which entered his chest and went through the cavity of his body, but he neither swerved nor flinched, and at the moment I did not know that I had struck him. He came steadily on, and in another second was almost upon me. I fired for his forehead, but my bullet went low, entering his open mouth, smashing his lower jaw and going into the neck. I leaped to one side almost as I pulled trigger; and through the hanging smoke the first thing I saw was his paw as he made a vicious side blow at me. The rush of his charge carried him past. As he struck he lurched forward, leaving a pool of bright blood where his muzzle hit the ground; but he recovered himself and made two or three jumps onwards, while I hurriedly jammed a couple of cartridges into the magazine, my rifle holding only four, all of which I had fired. Then he tried to pull up, but as he did so his muscles seemed suddenly to give way, his head drooped, and he rolled over and over like a shot rabbit. Each of my first three bullets had inflicted a mortal wound.

It was already twilight, and I merely opened the carcass, and then trotted back to camp. Next morning I returned and with much labor took off the skin. The fur was very fine, the animal being in excellent trim, and unusually bright-colored. Unfortunately, in packing it out I lost the skull, and had to supply its place with one of plaster. The beauty of the trophy, and the memory of the circumstances under which I procured it, make me value it perhaps more highly than any other in my house.

This is the only instance in which I have been regularly charged by a grisly. On the whole, the danger of hunting these great bears has been much exaggerated. At the beginning of the present century, when white hunters first encountered the grisly, he was doubtless an exceedingly savage beast, prone to attack without provocation, and a redoubtable foe to persons armed with the clumsy, small-bore, muzzle-loading rifles of the day. But at present bitter experience has taught him caution. He has been hunted for sport, and hunted for his pelt, and hunted for the bounty, and hunted as a dangerous enemy to stock, until, save in the very wildest districts, he has learned to be more wary than a deer, and to avoid man's presence almost as carefully as the most timid kind of game. Except in rare cases he will not attack of his own accord, and, as a rule, even when wounded his object is escape rather than battle.

Still, when fairly brought to bay, or when moved by a sudden fit of ungovernable anger, the grisly is beyond peradventure a very dangerous antagonist. The first shot, if taken at a bear a good distance off and previously unwounded and unharried, is not usually fraught with much danger, the startled animal being at the outset bent merely on flight. It is always hazardous, however, to track a wounded and worried grisly into thick cover, and the man who habitually follows and kills this chief of American game in dense timber, never abandoning the bloody trail whithersoever it leads, must show no small degree of skill and hardihood, and must not too closely count the risk to life or limb. Bears differ widely in temper, and occasionally one may be found who will not show fight, no matter how much he is bullied; but, as a rule, a hunter must be cautious in meddling with a wounded animal which has retreated into a dense thicket, and has been once or twice roused; and such a beast, when it does turn, will usually charge again and again, and fight to the last with unconquerable ferocity. The short distance at which the bear can be seen through the underbrush, the fury of his charge, and his tenacity of life make it necessary for the hunter on such occasions to have steady nerves and a fairly quick and accurate aim. It is always well to have two men in following a wounded bear under such conditions. This is not necessary, however, and a good hunter, rather than lose his quarry, will, under ordinary circumstances, follow and attack it, no matter how tangled the fastness in which it has sought refuge; but he must act warily and with the utmost caution and resolution, if he wishes to escape a terrible and probably fatal mauling. An experienced hunter is rarely rash, and never heedless; he will not, when alone, follow a wounded bear into a thicket, if by the exercise of patience, skill, and knowledge of the game's habits he can avoid the necessity; but it is idle to talk of the feat as something which ought in no case to be attempted. While danger ought never to be needlessly incurred, it is yet true that the keenest zest in sport comes from its presence, and from the consequent exercise of the qualities necessary to overcome it. The most thrilling moments of an American hunter's life are those in which, with every sense on the alert, and with nerves strung to the highest point, he is following alone into the heart of its forest fastness the fresh and bloody footprints of an angered grisly; and no other triumph of American hunting can compare with the victory to be thus gained. . . .

"A Chilean Rondeo" from
A Book-Lover's Holiday in the Open (1913)

Perhaps the earliest of Theodore Roosevelt's writings were his travel letters when, as a youth, he visited Europe and Egypt. During that time, he learned to appreciate new sights and register the impression of new stimuli. That youthful pleasure of testing himself amid new circumstances never left him and ultimately formed the basis of a key feature of his writing: his recording of new experiences. He wrote very often about his hunting trips, but also about the sights he observed and people he encountered. In his later African writings, which cover a trip partly sponsored by the Smithsonian, Roosevelt returned to his very first intellectual curiosity, in his detailing of the flora and fauna he found there. Even more dramatically, his great adventure along the Amazon was the stuff of a terrifying adventure tale, a Rooseveltian journey into the heart of darkness. Once he embarked on a public career, however, he had little time to engage in conventional tourism or the exotic kind that was so much more to his liking, such as we see in his sketch of a rodeo (*rondeo*) in Chile during a visit to South America following his unsuccessful presidential campaign of 1912. Those travel adventures were often much more momentous than his observations of the likenesses and differences between the sport of cowboys or, in this case, the *huasos*, but readers can see the vivid, concrete details that impress Roosevelt, his sense of both the historical and social underpinnings of the folkways he observes.

A Chilean Rondeo

On November 21, 1913, we crossed the Andes into Chile by rail. The railway led up the pass which, used from time immemorial by the Indians, afterward marked the course of traffic for their Spanish successors, and was traversed by the army of San Martin in the hazardous march that enabled him to strike the decisive blows in the war for South American independence. The valleys were gray and barren, the sides of the towering mountains were bare, the landscape was one of desolate grandeur. To the north the stupendous peak of Aconquija rose in its snows.

On the Chilean side, as we descended, we passed a lovely lake, and went through wonderful narrow gorges; and farther down were trees, and huge cactus, and flowers of many colors. Then we reached the lower valleys and the plains; and the change was like magic. Suddenly we were in a rich fairy-land of teeming plenty and beauty, a land of fertile fields and shady groves, a land of grain and, above all, of many kinds of luscious fruits.

As in the Argentine and Brazil, every courtesy and hospitality was shown us in Chile. We enjoyed every experience throughout our stay. One of the pleasantest and most interesting days we passed was at a great ranch, a great cattle-farm and country place twenty-five or thirty miles from Santiago. It was some fifteen miles from the railway station. The road led through a rich, fertile country largely under tillage, but also largely consisting of great fenced pastures.

The owners of the ranch, our kind and courteous hosts, had summoned all the riders of the neighborhood to attend the *rondeo* (round-up and sports), and several hundred, perhaps a thousand, came. With the growth of cultivation of the soil and the introduction of improved methods of stock-breeding in Chile, the old rude life of the wild cow-herders is passing rapidly away. But in many places it remains in modified form, and the country folk whose business is pastoral form a striking and distinctive class. These countrymen live their lives in the saddle. All these men, whose industries are connected with cattle, are known as *huasos*. They are kin to the Argentine *gauchos*, and more remotely to our own cowboys.

As we neared the ranch, slipping down broad, dusty, tree-bordered roads beside which irrigation streams ran, we began to come across the *huasos* gathering for the sports. They rode singly and by twos and threes, or in parties of fifteen or twenty. They were on native Chilean horses—stocky, well-built beasts, hardy and enduring, and on the whole docile. Almost all the men wore the light *manta*, less heavy than the *serapi*, but like it in shape, the head of the rider being thrust through a hole in the middle. It would seem as though it might interfere with the free use of their arms, but it does not, and at the subsequent cattle sports many of the participants never took off their *mantas*. The riders wore straw hats of various types, but none of them with the sugar-loaf cones of the Mexicans. Their long spurs bore huge rowels. The *mantas* were not only picturesque, but gave the company a look of diversified and gaudy brilliancy, for they were of all possible colors, green, red, brown, and blue, solid and patterned. The saddles were far forward, and the shoe-shaped wooden stirrups were elaborately carved.

The men were fine-looking fellows, some with smooth faces or mustaches, some with beards, some of them light, most of them dark. They rode their horses with the utter ease found only in those who are born to the saddle. Now and then there were family parties, mother and children, all, down to the smallest, riding their own horses or perhaps all going in a wagon. Once or twice we passed horsemen who were coming out of the yards of their tumble-down houses, women and children crowding round. Generally the women had something in the dress that reminded one more or less of our Southwestern semicivilized Indians, and the strain of Indian blood in both men and women was evident. Some of the men were poorly clad, others had paid much attention to their get-up and looked like very efficient dandies; but in its essentials the dress was always the same.

When we reached the ranch we first drove to a mass of buildings, which included the barns, branding-pens, corrals, and the like. It was here that the horsemen had gathered, and one of the pens was filled with an uneasy mass of cattle. Not far from this pen was a big hitching rail or bar, very stout, consisting of tree trunks at least a foot in diameter, the total length of the rail being forty or fifty feet. Beside it was a very large and stout corral. The inside of this corral was well padded with poles, making a somewhat springy wall, a feature I have never seen in any corrals in our own ranch country, but essential where the horses are trained to jam the cattle against the corral side.

Most of the sports took place inside this big corral. Gates led into it from opposite ends. Some thirty or forty feet in front of one of the gates, and just about that distance from the middle of the corral, was a short, crescent-shaped fence which served to keep the stock that had yet to be worked separate from those that had been worked. Proceedings were begun by some thirty riders and a mob of cattle coming through one of the doors of the corral. A glance at the cattle was enough to show that the old days of the wild ranches had passed. These were not longhorns, staring, vicious creatures, shy and fleet as deer; they were graded stock, domestic in their ways, and rather reluctant to run. Among the riders, however, there was not the slightest falling off from the old dash and skill, and their very air, as they rode quietly in, and the way they sat every sudden, quick move of their horses showed their complete ease and self-confidence.

In addition to the *huasos*, the peasants-on-horseback, the riders included several of the gentry, the great landed proprietors. These took part in the sports, precisely as in our own land men of the corresponding class follow the hounds or play polo. Two of the most skilful and daring riders, who always worked together, were a wealthy neighboring ranchman and his son.

The first feat began by two of the horsemen, acting together, cutting out an animal from the bunch. This was done with skill and precision, but differed in no way from the work I used formerly to see and take part in on the Little Missouri. What followed, however, was totally different. The animal was raced by the two men out from the herd and from behind the little semicircular fence, and was taken at full speed round the edge of the great corral past the closed gate on the other side, and almost back to the starting-point. One horseman rode behind the animal, a little on its inner side. The other rode outside it, the horse's head abreast of the steer's flank. As they galloped the riders uttered strange, long-drawn cries, evidently of Indian origin. Round the corral rushed the steer, and, after it passed the door on the opposite side and began to return toward its starting-point and saw the other cattle ahead, it put on speed. Then the outside rider raced forward and at the same moment wheeled inward, pinning the steer behind the horns and either by the neck or shoulder against the rough, yielding boughs with which the corral was lined. Instantly the other horseman pressed the steer's hind quarters outward, so that it found itself not only checked, but turned in the opposite direction. Again it was urged into a gallop, the calling horsemen following and repeating their performance. The steer was thus turned three times. After the third turning the gate which it had passed was opened and it trotted out.

A dozen times different pairs of riders performed the feat with different steers. It was a fine exhibition of daring prowess and of good training in both the horses and the riders. Of course, if it had not been for the lining of the inner fence with limber poles the steer would have been killed or crippled—we saw one of them injured, as it was. The horse, which entered heartily into the spirit of the chase, had to crash straight into the fence, nailing the steer and bringing it to a standstill in the midst of its headlong gallop. Once or twice at the critical moment the rider was not able to charge quickly enough; and when the steer was caught too far back it usually made its escape and rejoined the huddle of cattle from which it had been cut out. The men were riders of such skill that shaking them in their seats was impossible, no matter how quickly the horse turned or how violent the shocks were; nor was a single horse hurt in the rough play. It was a wild scene, and an exhibition of prowess well worth witnessing.

Other exhibitions of horsemanship followed, including the old feat of riding a bull. The bull, a vicious one, was left alone in the ring, and his temper soon showed signs of extreme shortness as he pawed the dirt, tossing it above his shoulders. Watching the chance when the bull's attention was fixed elsewhere, a man ran in and got to the little fence before the bull could charge him. Then, while the bull was still angrily endeavoring to get at the man, the corral gate opposite was thrown open and six or eight horsemen entered, riding with quiet unconcern. The bull was obviously not in the least afraid of the footman, whereas he had a certain feeling of respect for the horsemen. Two of the latter approached him. One got his rope over the bull's horns, and the other then dexterously roped the hind legs. The footman rushed in and seized the tail, and the bull was speedily on his side. Then a lean, slab-sided, rather frowzy-looking man, outwardly differing in no essential respect from the professional bronco-buster of the Southwest, slipped from the spectators' seats into the ring. A saddle was girthed tight on the bull, and a rope ring placed round his broad chest so as to give the rider something by which to hang. The lassos upon him were cast loose, and he rose, snorting with rage and terror. If he had thrown the man, the horsemen would have had to work with instantaneous swiftness to save his life. But all the bull's furious bucking and jumping could not unseat the rider. The horsemen began to tease the animal, flapping red blankets in his face, and luring him to charges which they easily evaded. Finally they threw him again, took off his saddle and turned him loose, and at the same time some steers were driven into the corral to serve as company for him. A couple of the horsemen took him out of the bunch and raced him round the corral, turning him when they wished by pressing him against the pole corral lining, thus repeating the game that had already been played with so many of the steers. In his case it was, of course, more dangerous. But they showed complete mastery, and the horses had not the slightest fear, nailing him flat against the wall with their chests, and spinning him round when they struck him on occasions when he was trying to make up his mind to resist.

Meanwhile the bull-rider passed his hat among the spectators, who tossed silver pieces into it—thus marking the fundamental difference between the life we were witnessing and our own Western ranch life. In Chile, with its aristocratic social structure, there is a wide gulf between the gentry and the ranch-hands; whereas in the democratic life of our own cow country the ranch-owner has, more often than not, at one time been himself a ranch-hand.

After the sports in the corral were finished eight or ten of the *huasos* appeared on big horses at the bar of which I have spoken, and took part in a sport which was entirely new to me. Two champions would appear side by side or half-facing each other, at the bar. Each would turn his horse's head until it hung over the bar as they half-fronted each other, on the same side of the bar. The object was for each man to try to push his opponent away from the bar and then shove past him, usually carry-ing his opponent with him. Sometimes it was a contest of man against man. Sometimes each would have two or three backers. No one could touch any other man's horse, and each drove his animal right against his opponent. The two men fronting each other at the bar kept their horses head-on against the bar; the others strove each to get his horse's head between the body of one of his opponents and the head of that opponent's horse. They then remained in a knot for some minutes, the riders cheering the horses with their strange, wild, Indian-like cries, while the horses pushed and strained. Usually there was almost no progress on either side at first. It would look as though not an inch was gained. Gradually, however, the horses on one side or the other got an inch or two or three inches advantage of position by straining and shoving. Suddenly the right vantage-point was attained. There was an outburst of furious shouting from the riders. The horses of one side with straining quarters thrust their way through the press, whirling round or half upsetting their opponents, and rushed down alongside the bar. Why the men's legs were not broken I could not say. On this occasion all the men were good-natured. But it was a rough sport, and I could well credit the statement that, if there were bad blood to gratify, the chances were excellent for a fight.

After the sports we motored down to a great pasture on one side of a lake, beyond which rose lofty mountains. Then we returned to the ranch-house itself—a huge, white, single-storied house with a great courtyard in the middle and wings extending toward the stable, the saddle-rooms, and the like. It was a house of charm and distinction; the low building—or rather group of buildings, with galleries and colonnades connecting them—being in the old native style, an outgrowth of the life and the land. After a siesta our hosts led us out across a wide garden brilliant and fragrant with flowers, to the deep, cool shade of a row of lofty trees, where stood a long table spread with white linen and laden with silver and glass; and here, we were served with a delicious and elaborate breakfast—the Chilean breakfast, that of Latin Europe, for in most ways the life of South America is a development of that of Latin Europe, and much more closely kin to it than it is to the life of the English-speaking peoples north of the Rio Grande.

In the afternoon we drove back to the railroad. At one point of our drive we were joined by a rider who had taken part in the morning's sports. He galloped at full speed beside the rushing motor-car, waving his hat to us and shouting good-by. He was a tall, powerfully built, middle-aged man, with fine, clean-cut features; his brightly colored mantle streamed in the wind, and he sat in the saddle with utter ease while his horse tore over the ground alongside us. He was a noble figure, and his farewell to us was our last glimpse of the wild, oldtime *huaso* life.

BIOGRAPHY

"The Struggle with the Nullifiers" from *Thomas Hart Benton* (1887)

Roosevelt found Missouri Senator Thomas Hart Benton an especially appealing subject for a biography none the least for the westerner's famous obstinacy and integrity. Although once tolerant of slavery, Benton ultimately came to oppose it, even if that meant losing his backing at home and his seat in the Senate. In this brief excerpt, Roosevelt chronicles Benton's dealings, during what may well have been his finest hour, the crucial period of political negotiation in the 1830s when South Carolina's Ordinance of Nullification endangered the Union by voiding the Tariff of 1832, which had insufficiently relieved the burden of the Tariff of 1828, known in the South as the Tariff of Abominations. In response President Andrew Jackson offered the "force bill," empowering the federal government to take arms to collect the tariff and presumably against any potential insurrection, what Roosevelt calls a "collision" between separatists and unionists. The compromise struck was to find a way to remove the inducement to secede by lowering hostility toward the high tariff that the North favored and that the South found untenable. As a western anti-tariff legislator, Benton was in the position to do so and collaborated with Senator Daniel Webster of Massachusetts to build the necessary support. The result was to accept the right to exact tariffs but to reduce their value, a compromise both Democratic senators Calhoun and Benton could accept, although the South Carolina legislature promptly nullified the Force Bill.

The Struggle with the Nullifiers

It must always be kept in mind in describing the attitude of the Jacksonian Democrats towards the Nullifiers that they were all along, especially in the West, hostile to a very high tariff. Jackson and Benton had always favored a much lower tariff than that established in 1828 and hardly changed in 1832. It was no change of front on their part now to advocate a reduction of duties. Jackson and Benton both felt that there was much ground for South Carolina's original complaint, although as strongly opposed to her nullification attitude as any Northerner. Most of the Southern senators and representatives, though opposed to nullification, were almost equally hostile to the high tariff; and very many others were at heart in sympathy with nullification itself. The intensely national and anti-separatist tone of Jackson's declaration—a document that might well have come from Washington or Lincoln, and that would have reflected high honor on either—though warmly approved by Benton, was very repugnant to many of the Southern Democrats, and was too much even for certain of the Whigs. In fact, it reads like the utterance of some great Federalist or Republican leader. The feeling in Congress, as a whole, was as strong against the tariff as it was against nullification; and Jackson had to take this into account, all the more because not only was he in some degree of the same way of thinking, but also many of his followers entertained the sentiment even more earnestly.

Calhoun introduced a series of nullification resolutions into the Senate, and defended them strongly in the prolonged constitutional debate that followed. South Carolina meanwhile put off the date at which her decrees were to take effect, so that she might see what Congress would do. Beyond question, Jackson's firmness, and the way in which he was backed up by Benton, Webster, and their followers, was having some effect. He had openly avowed his intention, if matters went too far, of hanging Calhoun "higher than Haman." He unquestionably meant to imprison him, as well as the other South Carolina leaders, the instant that state came into actual collision with the Union; and to the end of his life regretted, and with reason, that he had not done so without waiting for an overt act of resistance. Some historians have treated this as if it were an idle threat; but such it certainly was not. Jackson undoubtedly fully meant what he said, and would have acted promptly had the provocation occurred, and, moreover, he would have been sustained by the country. He was not the man to weigh minutely what would and what would not fall just on one side or the other of the line defining treason; nor was it the time for too scrupulous adherence to precise wording. Had a collision occurred, neither Calhoun nor his colleague would ever have been permitted to leave Washington; and brave though they were, the fact unquestionably had much influence with them.

Webster was now acting heartily with Benton. He introduced a set of resolutions which showed that in the matters both of the tariff and of nullification his position was much the same as was that of the Missourian. Unfortunately Congress, as a whole, was by no means so stiff-kneed. A certain number of Whigs followed Webster, and a certain number of Democrats clung to Benton; but most Southerners were very reluctant to allow pressure to be brought to bear on South Carolina, and many Northerners were as willing to compromise as Henry Clay himself. In accordance with Jackson's recommendations two bills were introduced: one the so-called "Force bill," to allow the president to take steps to defend the federal authority in the event of actual collision; and the other a moderate, and, on the whole, proper tariff bill, to reduce protective duties. Both were introduced by administration supporters. Benton and Webster warmly sustained the "Force bill," which was bitterly attacked by the Nullifiers and by most of the Southerners, who really hardly knew what stand to take, the leading opponent being Tyler of Virginia, whose disunion attitude was almost as clearly marked as that of Calhoun himself. The measure was eminently just, and was precisely what the crisis demanded; and the Senate finally passed it and sent it to the House.

All this time an obstinate struggle was going on over the tariff bill. Calhoun and his sympathizers were beginning to see that there was real danger ahead, alike to themselves, their constituents, and their principles, if they followed unswervingly the course they had laid down; and the weak-kneed brethren on the other side, headed by Clay, were becoming even more uneasy. Calhoun wished to avert collision with the federal government; Clay was quite as anxious to avoid an outbreak in the South and to save what he could of the protective system, which was evidently doomed. Calhoun was willing to sacrifice some of his constitutional theories in regard to protection; Clay was ready greatly to reduce protection itself. Each of them, but especially Clay, was prepared to shift his stand somewhat from that of abstract moral right to that of expediency. Benton and Webster were too resolute and determined in their hostility to any form of yielding to South Carolina's insolent defiance to admit any hope of getting them to accept a compromise; but the majority of the members were known to be only too ready to jump at any half-way measure which would patch up the affair for the present, no matter what the sacrifice of principle or how great the risk incurred for the future. Accordingly, Clay and Calhoun met and agreed on a curious bill, in reality recognizing the protective system, but making a great although gradual reduction of duties; and Clay introduced this as a "compromise measure." It was substituted in the House for the administration tariff bill, was passed and sent to the Senate. It gave South Carolina much, but not all, that she demanded. Her representatives announced themselves satisfied, and supported it, together with all their Southern sympathizers. Webster and Benton fought it stoutly to the last, but it was passed by a great majority; a few Northerners followed Webster, and Benton received fair support from his Missouri colleagues and the Maryland senators; the other senators, Whigs and Democrats alike, voted for the measure. Many of the Southerners were imbued with separatist principles, although not yet to the extent that Calhoun was; others, though Union men, did not possess the unflinching will and stern strength of character that enabled Benton to stand out against any section of the country, even his own, if it was wrong. Silas Wright, of New York, a typical Northern "dough-face" politician, gave exact expression to the "dough-face" sentiment, which induced Northern members to vote for the compromise, when he stated that he was unalterably opposed to the principle of the bill, but that on account of the attitude of South Carolina, and of the extreme desire which he had to remove all cause of discontent in that state, and in order to enable her again to become an affectionate member of the Union, he would vote for what was satisfactory to her, although repugnant to himself. Wright, Marcy, and their successors in New York politics, almost up to the present day, certainly carried cringing subserviency to the South to a pitch that was fairly sublime.

The "Force bill" and the compromise tariff bill passed both houses nearly simultaneously, and were sent up to the president, who signed both on the same day. His signing the compromise bill was a piece of weakness out of keeping with his whole character, and especially out of keeping with his previous course towards the Nullifiers. The position assumed by Benton and Webster, that South Carolina should be made to submit first and should have the justice of her claims examined into afterwards, was unquestionably the only proper attitude.

Benton wrote:—

> My objections to this bill, and to its mode of being passed, were deep and abiding, and went far beyond its own obnoxious provisions, and all the transient and temporary considerations connected with it. . . . A compromise made with a state in arms is a capitulation to that state. . . . The injury was great then, and a permanent evil example. It remitted the government to the condition of the old confederation, acting upon sovereignties instead of individuals. It violated the feature of our Union which discriminated it from all confederacies that ever existed, and which was wisely and patriotically put into the Constitution to save it from the fate which had attended all confederacies, ancient and modern. . . . The framers of our Constitution established a Union instead of a League—to be sovereign and independent within its sphere, acting upon persons through its own laws and courts, instead of acting on communities through persuasion or force. The effect of this compromise legislation was to destroy this great feature of our Union—to bring the general and state governments into conflict—and to substitute a sovereign state for an offending individual as often as a state chose to make the cause of that individual her own.

Not only was Benton's interpretation of the Constitution sound, and one that by the course of events has now come to be universally accepted, but his criticisms on the wisdom of the compromise bill were perfectly just. Had the Anti-Nullifiers stood firm, the Nullifiers would probably have given way, and if not, would certainly have been crushed. Against a solid North and West, with a divided South, even her own people not being unanimous, and with Jackson as chief executive, South Carolina could not have made even a respectable resistance. A salutary lesson then might very possibly have saved infinite trouble and bloodshed thereafter. But in Jackson's case it must be remembered that, so far as his acts depended purely upon his own will and judgment, no fault can be found with him; he erred only in ratifying a compromise agreed to by the vast majority of the representatives of the people in both houses of Congress.

The battle did not result in a decisive victory for either side. This was shown by the very fact that each party insisted that it had won a signal triumph. Calhoun and Clay afterwards quarreled in the senate chamber as to which had given up the more in the compromise. South Carolina had declared, first, that the tariff was unconstitutional, and therefore to be opposed upon principle; second, that it worked injustice to her interests, and must be abolished forthwith; thirdly, that, if it were not so abolished, she would assert her power to nullify a federal law, and, if necessary, would secede from the Union. When her representatives agreed to the compromise bill, they abandoned the first point; the second was decided largely in her favor, though protection was not by any means entirely given up; the third she was allowed to insist upon with impunity, although the other side, by passing the "Force bill," showed that in case matters did proceed to extremities they were prepared to act upon the opposite conviction. Still, she gained most of that for which she contended, and the victory, as a whole, rested with her. Calhoun's purposes seem to have been, in the main, pure; but few criminals have worked as much harm to their country as he did. The plea of good intentions is not one that can be allowed to have much weight in passing historical judgment upon a man whose wrong-headedness and distorted way of looking at things produced, or helped to produce, such incalculable evil; there is a wide political applicability in the remark attributed to a famous Texan, to the effect that he might, in the end, pardon a man who shot him on purpose, but that he would surely never forgive one who did so accidentally.

Without doubt, the honors of the nullification dispute were borne off by Benton and Webster. The latter's reply to Hayne is, perhaps, the greatest single speech of the nineteenth century, and he deserves the highest credit for the stubbornness with which he stood by his colors to the last. There never was any question of Webster's courage; on the occasions when he changed front he was actuated by self-interest and ambition, not by timidity. Usually he appears as an advocate rather than an earnest believer in the cause he represents; but when it came to be a question of the Union, he felt what he said with the whole strength of his nature.

An even greater meed of praise attaches to Benton for the unswerving fidelity which he showed to the Union in this crisis. Webster was a high-tariff man, and was backed up by all the sectional antipathies of the Northeast in his opposition to the Nullifiers; Benton, on the contrary, was a believer in a low tariff, or in one for revenue merely, and his sectional antipathies were the other way. Yet, even when deserted by his chief, and when he was opposed to every senator from south of the Potomac and the Ohio, he did not flinch for a moment from his attitude of aggressive loyalty to the national Union. He had a singularly strong and upright character; this country has never had a statesman more fearlessly true to his convictions, when great questions were at stake, no matter what might be the cost to himself, or the pressure from outside—even when, as happened later, his own state was against him. Intellectually he cannot for a moment be compared to the great Massachusetts senator; but morally he towers much higher.

Yet, while praising Jackson and Benton for their behavior towards South Carolina, we cannot forget that but a couple of years previously they had not raised their voices even in the mildest rebuke of Georgia for conduct which, though not nearly so bad in degree as that of South Carolina, was of much the same kind. Towards the close of Adams's term, Georgia had bid defiance to the mandates of the Supreme Court, and proceeded to settle the Indian question within her borders without regard to the authority of the United States, and these matters were still unsettled when Jackson became president. Unfortunately he let his personal feelings bias him; and, as he took the Western and Georgian view of the Indian question, and, moreover, hated the Supreme Court because it was largely Federalist in its composition, he declined to interfere. David Crockett, himself a Union man and a nationalist to the back-bone, rated

Jackson savagely, and with justice, for the inconsistency of his conduct in the two cases, accusing him of having, by his harmful leniency to Georgia, encouraged South Carolina to act as she did, and ridiculing him because, while he smiled at the deeds of the one state, when the like acts were done by the other, "he took up the rod of correction and shook it over her."

"Minister to France"
from *Gouverneur Morris* (1888)

During the brief period when Roosevelt was trying to make his living as a writer, he turned to a biography of this lesser-known founding father. *Gouverneur Morris*, however, represented more than a nice check from the Macmillan Co., giving Roosevelt the occasion to meditate on the contours of a career for a man of political and of business affairs. Morris first came to prominence in the New York State Committee on Public Safety, after establishing himself against his family's Tory interests (in ways that might have reminded Roosevelt of his own struggle to establish himself as a reformer). Morris later served in the Continental Congress and participated in drawing up the Articles of Confederation. The apogee of his political activity came later, in the Constitutional Congress, in which his Federalist conviction in a strong central government established him among the most vocal debaters and where he vigorously advanced the cause of religious freedom. We hear echoes of his experiences when Roosevelt makes clear Morris's consternation over the seemingly indiscriminate violence he witnessed during the French Revolution. Morris was indeed more skeptical about democracy than Thomas Jefferson, his predecessor as ambassador to France, but as much as he might have sympathized with Louis XVI and his queen (he even tried to broker a deal for their escape from Paris), he valued an effective democratic movement, not the chaos he witnessed in the summer of 1792. During a season of intense unrest, Morris exhibited considerable bravery in refusing to leave Paris and in giving shelter to Americans. Also in evidence here is Roosevelt's skillful rendering of a dramatic scene.

Minister to France

The rest of his two years' history as minister forms one of the most brilliant chapters in our diplomatic annals. His boldness, and the frankness with which he expressed his opinions, though they at times irritated beyond measure the factions of the revolutionists who successively grasped a brief but tremendous power, yet awed them, in spite of themselves. He soon learned to combine courage and caution, and his readiness, wit, and dash always gave him a certain hold over the fiery nation to which he was accredited. He was firm and dignified in insisting on proper respect being shown our flag, while he did all he could to hasten the payment of our obligations to France. A very large share of his time, also, was taken up with protesting against the French decrees aimed at neutral—which meant American—commerce, and with interfering to save American shipmasters, who had got into trouble by unwittingly violating them. Like his successor, Mr. Washburne, in the time of the commune, Morris was the only foreign minister who remained in Paris during the terror. He stayed at the risk of his life; and yet, while fully aware of his danger, he carried himself as coolly as if in a time of profound peace, and never flinched for a moment when he was obliged for his country's sake to call to account the rulers of France for the time being—men whose power was as absolute as it was ephemeral and bloody, who had indulged their desire for slaughter with the unchecked ferocity of madmen, and who could by a word have had him slain as thousands had been slain before him. Few foreign ministers have faced such difficulties, and not one has ever come near to facing such dangers as Morris did during his two years' term of service. His feat stands by itself in diplomatic history; and, as a minor incident, the letters and dispatches he sent home give a very striking view of the French Revolution.

As soon as he was appointed he went to see the French minister of foreign affairs; and, in answer to an observation of the latter, stated with his customary straightforwardness that it was true that, while a mere private individual, sincerely friendly to France, and desirous of helping her, and whose own nation could not be compromised by his acts, he had freely taken part in passing events, had criticised the Constitution, and advised the king and his ministers; but he added that, now that he was a public man, he would no longer meddle with their affairs. To this resolution he kept, save that, as already described, sheer humanity induced him to make an effort to save the king's life. He had predicted what would ensue as the result of the exaggerated decentralization into which the opponents of absolutism had rushed; when they had split the state up into more than forty thousand sovereignties, each district the sole executor of the law, and the only judge of its propriety, and therefore obedient to it only so long as it listed, and until rendered hostile by the ignorant whim or ferocious impulse of the moment; and now he was to see his predictions come true. In that brilliant and able state paper, the address he had drawn up for Louis to deliver when in 1791 the latter accepted the Constitution, the keynote of the situation was struck in the opening words: "It is no longer a king who addresses you, Louis XVI is a private individual"; and he had then scored off, point by point, the faults in a document that created an unwieldy assembly of men unaccustomed to govern, that destroyed the principle of authority, though no other could appeal to a people helpless in their new-born liberty, and that created out of one whole a jarring multitude of fractional sovereignties. Now he was to see one of these same sovereignties rise up in successful rebellion against the government that represented the whole, destroy it and usurp its power, and establish over all France the rule of an anarchic despotism which, by what seems to a free American a gross misnomer, they called a democracy.

All through June, at the beginning of which month Morris had been formally presented at court, the excitement and tumult kept increasing. When, on the 20th, the mob forced the gates of the château, and made the king put on the red cap, Morris wrote in his diary that the Constitution had given its last groan. A few days afterwards he told Lafayette that in six weeks everything would be over, and tried to persuade him that his only chance was to make up his mind instantly to fight either for a good constitution or for the wretched piece of paper which bore the name.

Just six weeks to a day from the date of this prediction came the 10th of August to verify it.

Throughout July the fevered pulses of the people beat with always greater heat. Looking at the maddened mob, the American minister thanked God from his heart that in his own country there was no such populace, and prayed with unwonted earnestness that our education and morality should forever stave off such an evil. At court even the most purblind dimly saw their doom. Calling there one morning, he chronicles with a matter-of-fact brevity, impressive from its very baldness, that nothing of note had occurred except that they had stayed up all night expecting to be murdered. He wrote home that he could not tell "whether the king would live through the storm; for it blew hard."

His horror of the base mob, composed of people whose kind was absolutely unknown in America, increased continually, as he saw them going on from crimes that were great to crimes that were greater, incited by the demagogues who flattered them and roused their passions and appetites, and blindly raging because they were of necessity disappointed in the golden prospects held out to them. He scorned the folly of the enthusiasts and doctrinaires who had made a constitution all sail and no ballast, that overset at the first gust; who had freed from all restraint a mass of men as savage and licentious as they were wayward; who had put the executive in the power of the legislature, and this latter at the mercy of the leaders who could most strongly influence and inflame the mob. But his contempt for the victims almost exceeded his anger at their assailants. The king, who could suffer with firmness, and who could act either not at all, or else with the worst possible effect, had the head and heart that might have suited the monkish idea of a female saint, but which were hopelessly out of place in any rational being supposed to be fitted for doing good in the world. Morris wrote home that he knew his friend Hamilton had no particular aversion to kings, and would not believe them to be tigers, but that if Hamilton came to Europe to see for himself, he would surely believe them to be monkeys; the Empress of Russia was the only reigning sovereign whose talents were not "considerably below par." At the moment of the final shock, the court was involved in a set of paltry intrigues "unworthy of anything above the rank of a footman or a chambermaid. Every one had his or her little project, and every little project had some abettors. Strong, manly counsels frightened the weak, alarmed the envious, and wounded the enervated minds of the lazy and luxurious." The few such counsels that appeared were always approved, rarely adopted, and never followed out.

Then, in the sweltering heat of August, the end came. A raving, furious horde stormed the château, and murdered, one by one, the brave mountaineers who gave their lives for a sovereign too weak to be worthy of such gallant bloodshed. King and queen fled to the National Assembly, and the monarchy was over. Immediately after the awful catastrophe Morris wrote to a friend: "The voracity of the court, the haughtiness of the nobles, the sensuality of the church, have met their punishment in the road of their transgressions. The oppressor has been squeezed by the hands of the oppressed; but there remains yet to be acted an awful scene in this great tragedy, played on the theatre of the universe for the instruction of mankind."

Not the less did he dare everything, and jeopardize his own life in trying to save some at least among the innocent who had been overthrown in the crash of the common ruin. When on the 10th of August the whole city lay abject at the mercy of the mob, hunted men and women, bereft of all they had, and fleeing from a terrible death, with no hiding-place, no friend who could shield them, turned in their terror-struck despair to the one man in whose fearlessness and generous gallantry they could trust. The shelter of Morris's house and flag was sought from early morning till past midnight by people who had nowhere else to go, and who felt that within his walls they were sure of at least a brief safety from the maddened savages in the streets. As far as possible they were sent off to places of greater security; but some had to stay with him till the storm lulled for a moment. An American gentleman who was in Paris on that memorable day, after viewing the sack of the Tuileries, thought it right to go to the house of the American minister. He found him surrounded by a score of people, of both sexes, among them the old Count d'Estaing, and other men of note, who had fought side by side with us in our war for independence, and whom now our flag protected in their hour of direst need. Silence reigned, only broken occasionally by the weeping of the women and children. As his visitor was leaving, Morris took him to one side, and told him that he had no doubt there were persons on the watch who would find fault with his conduct as a minister in receiving and protecting these people; that they had come of their own accord, uninvited. "Whether my house will be a protection to them or to me, God only knows; but I will not turn them out of it, let what will happen to me; you see, sir, they are all persons to whom our country is more or less indebted, and, had they no such claim upon me, it would be inhuman to force them into the hands of the assassins." No one of Morris's countrymen can read his words even now without feeling a throb of pride in the dead statesman who, a century ago, held up so high the honor of his nation's name in the times when the souls of all but the very bravest were tried and found wanting.

Soon after this he ceased writing in his diary, for fear it might fall into the hands of men who would use it to incriminate his friends; and for the same reason he had also to be rather wary in what he wrote home, as his letters frequently bore marks of being opened, thanks to what he laughingly called "patriotic curiosity." He was, however, perfectly fearless as regards any ill that might befall himself; his circumspection was only exercised on behalf of others, and his own opinions were given as frankly as ever.

He pictured the French as huddled together, in an unreasoning panic, like cattle before a thunderstorm. Their every act increased his distrust of their capacity for self-government. They were for the time agog with their republic, and ready to adopt any form of government with a huzza; but that they would adopt a good form, or, having adopted it, keep it, he did not believe; and he saw that the great mass of the population were already veering round, under the pressure of accumulating horrors, until they would soon be ready to welcome as a blessing even a despotism, if so they could gain security to life and property. They had made the common mistake of believing that to enjoy liberty they had only to abolish authority; and the equally common consequence was that they were now, through anarchy, on the high road to absolutism. Said Morris: "Since I have been in this country I have seen the worship of many idols, and but little of the true God. I have seen many of these idols broken, and some of them beaten to the dust. I have seen the late constitution in one short year admired as a stupendous monument of human wisdom, and ridiculed as an egregious production of folly and vice. I wish much, very much, the happiness of this inconstant people. I love them, I feel grateful for their efforts in our cause, and I consider the establishment of a good constitution here as the principal means, under Divine Providence, of extending the blessings of freedom to the many millions of my fellow men who groan in bondage on the continent of Europe. But I do not greatly indulge the flattering illusions of hope, because I do not yet perceive that reformation of morals without which liberty is but an empty sound." These words are such as could only come from a genuine friend of France, and champion of freedom; from a strong, earnest man, saddened by the follies of dreamers, and roused to stern anger by the licentious wickedness of scoundrels who used the name of liberty to cloak the worst abuses of its substance.

His stay in Paris was now melancholy indeed. The city was shrouded in a gloom only relieved by the frenzied tumults that grew steadily more numerous. The ferocious craving once roused could not be sated; the thirst grew ever stronger as the draughts were deeper. The danger to Morris's own person merely quickened his pulses, and roused his strong, brave nature; he liked excitement, and the strain that would have been too tense for weaker nerves keyed his own up to a fierce, half-exultant thrilling. But the woes that befell those who had befriended him caused him the keenest grief. It was almost unbearable to be seated quietly at dinner, and hear by accident "that a friend was on his way to the place of execution," and to have to sit still and wonder which of the guests dining with him would be the next to go to the scaffold. The vilest criminals swarmed in the streets, and amused themselves by tearing the earrings from women's ears, and snatching away their watches. When the priests shut up in the *carnes* and the prisoners in the *abbaie* were murdered, the slaughter went on all day, and eight hundred men were engaged in it.

He wrote home that, to give a true picture of France, he would have to paint it like an Indian warrior, black and red. The scenes that passed were literally beyond the imagination of the American mind. The most hideous and nameless atrocities were so common as to be only alluded to incidentally, and to be recited in the most matter-of-fact way in connection with other events. For instance, a man applied to the Convention for a recompense for damage done to his quarry, a pit dug deep through the surface of the earth into the stone bed beneath: the damage consisted in such a number of dead bodies having been thrown into the pit as to choke it up so that he could no longer get men to work it. Hundreds, who had been the first in the land, were thus destroyed without form or trial, and their bodies thrown like dead dogs into the first hole that offered. Two hundred priests were killed for no other crime than having been conscientiously scrupulous about taking the prescribed oath. The guillotine went smartly on, watched with a devilish merriment by the fiends who were themselves to perish by the instrument their own hands had wrought. "Heaven only knew who was next to drink of the dreadful cup; as far as man could tell, there was to be no lack of liquor for some time to come."

HISTORY

"Champlain"
from *The Naval War of 1812* (1882)

Roosevelt's first book written as a professional writer will seem to most readers today a laborious historical study, aimed primarily at historians and military specialists. Indeed, the history quickly won an enthusiastic (and loyal) audience among the latter and enjoyed high standing among the former for many years. It is important to remember that Roosevelt was writing for a reading public that cared about such detailed and lucid accounting, while contemporary tastes prefer strong narratives infused with the psychology or the sociology of war. Yet reading it today yields a double source of edification. We are privy to an accurate, incisive chronicle of how early-nineteenth-century naval warfare was conducted and the lessons a late-century audience might draw from the right appreciation of tactical maneuvers. Moreover, we also see how Roosevelt initially formulated his identity as a writer: a detached observer who was also capable of strikingly subjective insight. His several biographies of famous men and his sweeping history of the settling of North America by the English-speaking peoples might not have outlived their time had they not been authored by a man who later became president, but *The Naval War of 1812* remained a work that commanded respect from students of the subject for years to come.

Champlain

This lake, which had hitherto played but an inconspicuous part, was now to become the scene of the greatest naval battle of the war. A British army of 11,000 men under Sir George Prevost undertook the invasion of New York by advancing up the western bank of Lake Champlain. This advance was impracticable unless there was a sufficiently strong British naval force to drive back the American squadron at the same time. Accordingly, the British began to construct a frigate, the *Confiance*, to be added to their already existing force, which consisted of a brig, two sloops, and 12 or 14 gun-boats. The Americans already possessed a heavy corvette, a schooner, a small sloop, and 10 gun-boats or row-galleys; they now began to build a large brig, the *Eagle*, which was launched about the 16th of August. Nine days later, on the 25th, the *Confiance* was launched. The two squadrons were equally deficient in stores, etc.; the *Confiance* having locks to her guns, some of which could not be used, while the American schooner *Ticonderoga* had to fire her guns by means of pistols flashed at the touch-holes (like Barclay on Lake Erie). Macdonough and Downie were hurried into action before they had time to prepare themselves thoroughly; but it was a disadvantage common to both, and arose from the nature of the case, which called for immediate action. The British army advanced slowly toward Plattsburg, which was held by General Macomb with less than 2,000 effective American troops. Captain Thomas Macdonough, the American commodore, took the lake a day or two before his antagonist, and came to anchor in Plattsburg harbor. The British fleet, under Captain George Downie, moved from Isle-aux-Noix on Sept. 8th, and on the morning of the 11th sailed into Plattsburg harbor.

The American force consisted of the ship *Saratoga*, Captain T. Macdonough, of about 734 tons,[‡] carrying eight long 24-pounders, six 42-pound and twelve 32-pound carronades; the brig *Eagle*, Captain Robert Henly, of about 500 tons, carrying eight long 18's and twelve 32-pound carronades; schooner *Ticonderoga*, Lieut.-Com. Stephen Cassin, of about 350 tons carrying eight long 12-pounders, four long 18-pounders, and five 32-pound carronades; sloop *Preble*, Lieutenant Charles Budd, of about 80 tons, mounting seven long 9's; the row-galleys *Borer, Centipede, Nettle, Allen, Viper,* and *Burrows*, each of about 70 tons, and mounting one long 24- and one short 18-pounder; and the row-galleys *Wilmer, Ludlow, Aylwin,* and *Ballard*, each of about 40 tons, and mounting one long 12. James puts down the number of men on board the squadron as 950—merely a guess, as he gives no authority. Cooper says "about 850 men, including officers, and a small detachment of soldiers to act as marines." Lossing says 882 in all. Vol. xiv of the "American State Papers" contains on p. 572 the prize-money list presented by the purser, George Beale, Jr. This numbers the men (the dead being represented by their heirs or executors) up to 915, including soldiers and seamen, but many of the numbers are omitted, probably owing to the fact that their owners, though belonging on board, happened to be absent on shore, or in the hospital; so that the actual number of names tallies very closely with that given by Lossing; and accordingly I shall take that.[§] The total number of men in the galleys (including a number of soldiers, as there were not enough sailors) was 350. The exact proportions in which this force was distributed among the gun-

‡   In the Naval Archives ("Masters'-Commandant Letters," 1814, 1, No. 134) is a letter from Macdonough in which he states that the *Saratoga* is intermediate in size between the *Pike*, of 875, and the *Madison*, of 593 tons; this would make her 734. The *Eagle* was very nearly the size of the *Lawrence* or *Niagara*, on Lake Erie. The *Ticonderoga* was originally a small steamer, but Commodore Macdonough had her schooner-rigged, because he found that her machinery got out of order on almost every trip that she took. Her tonnage is only approximately known, but she was of the same size as the *Linnet*.

§   In the Naval Archives are numerous letters from Macdonough, in which he states continually that, as fast as they arrive, he substitutes sailors for the soldiers with which the vessels were originally manned. Men were continually being sent ashore on account of sickness. In the Bureau of Navigation is the log-book of "sloop-of-war *Surprise*, Captain Robert Henly" (*Surprise* was the name the *Eagle* originally went by). It mentions from time to time that men were buried and sent ashore to the hospital (five being sent ashore on September 2d); and finally mentions that the places of the absent were partially filled by a draft of 21 soldiers, to act as marines. The notes on the day of battle are very brief.

boats can not be told, but it may be roughly said to be 41 in each large gal-ley and 26 in each small one. The complement of the *Saratoga* was 210, of the *Eagle*, 130, of the *Ticonderoga*, 100, and of the *Preble*, 30; but the first three had also a few soldiers distributed between them. The following list is probably pretty accurate as to the aggregate; but there may have been a score or two fewer men on the gun-boats, or more on the larger vessels.

Macdonough's Force

Name	Tons	Crew	Broadside	Metal, from long or short guns
Saratoga	734	240	414 LBS.	LONG, 96; SHORT, 318
Eagle	500	150	264 "	LONG, 72; SHORT, 192
Ticonderoga	350	112	180 "	LONG, 84; SHORT, 96
Preble	80	30	36 "	LONG, 36
Six gun-boats	420	246	252 "	LONG, 144; SHORT, 108
Four gun-boats	160	104	48 "	LONG, 48

In all, 14 vessels of 2,244 tons and 882 men, with 86 guns throwing at a broadside 1,194 lbs. of shot, 480 from long, and 714 from short guns.

The force of the British squadron in guns and ships is known accu-rately, as most of it was captured. The *Confiance* rated for years in our lists as a frigate of the class of the *Constellation*, *Congress*, and *Macedonian*; she was thus of over 1,200 tons. (Cooper says more, "nearly double the tonnage of the *Saratoga*.") She carried on her main-deck thirty long 24's, fifteen in each broadside. She did not have a complete spar-deck; on her poop, which came forward to the mizzen-mast, were two 32-pound (or possibly 42-pound) carronades and on her spacious top-gallant forecastle were four 32- (or 42-) pound carronades, and a long 24 on a pivot.¶ She had aboard her a furnace for heating shot; eight or ten of which heated shot were found with the furnace.** This was, of course, a perfectly legiti-mate advantage. The *Linnet*, Captain Daniel Pring, was a brig of the same

---

¶   This is her armament as given by Cooper, on the authority of Lieutenant E. A. F. Lavallette, who was in charge of her for three months, and went aboard her ten minutes after the *Linnet* struck.

**   James stigmatizes the statement of Commodore Macdonough about the furnace as "as gross a falsehood as ever was uttered"; but he gives no authority for the denial, and it appears to have been

size as the *Ticonderoga*, mounting 16 long 12's. The *Chubb* and *Finch*, Lieutenants James McGhie and William Hicks, were formerly the American
sloops *Growler* and *Eagle*, of 112 and 110 tons respectively. The former
mounted ten 18-pound carronades and one long 6; the latter, six 18-
pound carronades, four long 6's, and one short 18. There were twelve gun-
boats.[††] Five of these were large, of about 70 tons each; three mounted a
long 24 and a 32-pound carronade each; one mounted a long 18 and a
32-pound carronade; one a long 18 and a short 18. Seven were smaller, of
about 40 tons each; three of these carried each a long 18, and four carried
each a 32-pound carronade. There is greater difficulty in finding out the
number of men in the British fleet. American historians are unanimous in
stating it at from 1,000 to 1,100; British historians never do any thing but
copy James blindly. Midshipman Lea of the *Confiance*, in a letter (already
quoted) published in the "London Naval Chronicle," vol. xxxii, p. 292,
gives her crew as 300; but more than this amount of dead and prisoners were taken out of her. The number given her by Commander Ward
in his "Naval Tactics," is probably nearest right—325.[‡‡] The *Linnet* had
about 125 men, and the *Chubb* and *Finch* about 50 men each. According
to Admiral Paulding (given by Lossing, in his "Field Book of the War of
1812," p. 868) their gun-boats averaged 50 men each. This is probably
true, as they were manned largely by soldiers, any number of whom could
be spared from Sir George Prevost's great army; but it may be best to consider the large ones as having 41, and the small 26 men, which were the
complements of the American gun-boats of the same sizes.

Downie's Squadron

Name	Tonnage	Crew	Broadside	From what guns, long or short
Confiance	1200	325	480 LBS.	LONG, 384; SHORT, 96
Linnet	350	125	96 "	LONG, 96

merely an ebullition of spleen on his part. Every American officer who went aboard the *Confiance* saw
the furnace and the hot shot.

[††]   Letter of General George Prevost, Sept. 11, 1814. All the American accounts say 13; the British
official account had best be taken. James says only ten, but gives no authority; he appears to have been
entirely ignorant of all things connected with this action.

[‡‡]   James gives her but 270 men—without stating his authority.

Chubb	112	50	96 "	LONG, 6; SHORT, 90
Finch	110	50	84 "	LONG, 12; SHORT, 72
Five gun-boats	350	205	254 "	LONG, 12; SHORT, 72
Seven gun-boats	280	182	182 "	LONG, 54; SHORT, 128

In all, 16 vessels, of about 2,402 tons, with 937 men,[§§] and a total of 92 guns, throwing at a broadside 1,192 lbs., 660 from long and 532 from short pieces. . . .

Macdonough saw that the British would be forced to make the attack in order to get the control of the waters. On this long, narrow lake the winds usually blow pretty nearly north or south, and the set of the current is of course northward; all the vessels, being flat and shallow, could not beat to windward well, so there was little chance of the British making the attack when there was a southerly wind blowing. So late in the season there was danger of sudden and furious gales, which would make it risky for Downie to wait outside the bay till the wind suited him; and inside the bay the wind was pretty sure to be light and baffling. Young Macdonough (then but 28 years of age) calculated all these chances very coolly and decided to await the attack at anchor in Plattsburg Bay, with the head of his line so far to the north that it could hardly be turned; and then proceeded to make all the other preparations with the same foresight. Not only were his vessels provided with springs, but also with anchors to be used astern in any emergency. The *Saratoga* was further prepared for a change of wind, or for the necessity of winding ship, by having a kedge planted broad off on each of her bows, with a hawser and preventer hawser (hanging in bights under water) leading from each quarter to the kedge on that side. There had not been time to train the men thoroughly at the guns; and to make these produce their full effect the constant supervision of the officer had to be exerted. The British were laboring under this same disadvantage, but neither side felt the want very much, as the smooth water, stationary position of the ships, and fair range, made the fire of both sides very destructive.

Plattsburg Bay is deep and opens to the southward; so that a wind which would enable the British to sail up the lake would force them to beat when entering the bay. The east side of the mouth of the bay is formed by Cumberland Head; the entrance is about a mile and a half across, and

---

§§   About; there were probably more rather than less.

the other boundary, southwest from the Head, is an extensive shoal, and a small, low island. This is called Crab Island, and on it was a hospital and one six-pounder gun, which was to be manned in case of necessity by the strongest patients. Macdonough had anchored in a north-and-south line a little to the south of the outlet of the Saranac, and out of range of the shore batteries, being two miles from the western shore. The head of his line was so near Cumberland Head that an attempt to turn it would place the opponent under a very heavy fire, while to the south the shoal prevented a flank attack. The *Eagle* lay to the north, flanked on each side by a couple of gun-boats; then came the *Saratoga*, with three gun-boats between her and the *Ticonderoga*, the next in line; then came three gun-boats and the *Preble*. The four large vessels were at anchor; the galleys being under their sweeps and forming a second line about 40 yards back, some of them keeping their places and some not doing so. By this arrangement his line could not be doubled upon, there was not room to anchor on his broadside out of reach of his carronades, and the enemy was forced to attack him by standing in bows on.

The morning of September 11th opened with a light breeze from the northeast. Downie's fleet weighed anchor at daylight, and came down the lake with the wind nearly aft, the booms of the two sloops swinging out to starboard. At half-past seven,¶¶ the people in the ships could see their adversaries' upper sails across the narrow strip of land ending in Cumberland Head, before the British doubled the latter. Captain Downie hove to with his four large vessels when he had fairly opened the Bay, and waited for his galleys to overtake him. Then his four vessels filled on the starboard tack and headed for the American line, going abreast, the *Chubb* to the north, heading well to windward of the *Eagle*, for whose bows the *Linnet* was headed, while the *Confiance* was to be laid athwart the hawse of the *Saratoga*; the *Finch* was to leeward with the twelve gun-boats, and was to engage the rear of the American line.

As the English squadron stood bravely in, young Macdonough, who feared his foes not at all, but his God a great deal, knelt for a moment,

---

¶¶   The letters of the two commanders conflict a little as to time, both absolutely and relatively. Pring says the action lasted two hours and three quarters; the American accounts, two hours and twenty minutes. Pring says it began at 8.00; Macdonough says a few minutes before nine, etc. I take the mean time.

with his officers, on the quarter-deck; and then ensued a few minutes of perfect quiet, the men waiting with grim expectancy for the opening of the fight. The *Eagle* spoke first with her long 18's, but to no effect, for the shot fell short. Then, as the *Linnet* passed the *Saratoga*, she fired her broadside of long 12's, but her shot also fell short, except one that struck a hen-coop which happened to be aboard the *Saratoga*. There was a game cock inside, and, instead of being frightened at his sudden release, he jumped up on a gun-slide, clapped his wings, and crowed lustily. The men laughed and cheered; and immediately afterward Macdonough himself fired the first shot from one of the long guns. The 24-pound ball struck the *Confiance* near the hawse-hole and ranged the length of her deck, killing and wounding several men. All the American long guns now opened and were replied to by the British galleys.

The *Confiance* stood steadily on without replying. But she was baffled by shifting winds, and was soon so cut up, having both her port bow-anchors shot away, and suffering much loss, that she was obliged to port her helm and come to while still nearly a quarter of a mile distant from the *Saratoga*. Captain Downie came to anchor in grand style—securing every thing carefully before he fired a gun, and then opening with a terribly destructive broadside. The *Chubb* and *Linnet* stood farther in, and anchored forward the *Eagle's* beam. Meanwhile the *Finch* got abreast of the *Ticonderoga*, under her sweeps, supported by the gun-boats. The main fighting was thus to take place between the vans, where the *Eagle*, *Saratoga*, and six or seven gun-boats were engaged with the *Chubb*, *Linnet*, *Confiance*, and two or three gun-boats; while in the rear, the *Ticonderoga*, the *Preble*, and the other American galleys engaged the *Finch* and the remaining nine or ten English galleys. The battle at the foot of the line was fought on the part of the Americans to prevent their flank being turned, and on the part of the British to effect that object. At first the fighting was at long range, but gradually the British galleys closed up, firing very well. The American galleys at this end of the line were chiefly the small ones, armed with one 12-pounder apiece, and they by degrees drew back before the heavy fire of their opponents. About an hour after the discharge of the first gun had been fired the *Finch* closed up toward the *Ticonderoga*, and was completely crippled by a couple of broadsides from the latter. She drifted helplessly down the line and grounded near Crab Island; some of the convalescent patients manned the six-pounder and fired a shot or two at her, when she struck, nearly half of her crew being killed or wounded. About the same time the British gun-boats forced the *Preble* out of line, whereupon she cut her cable and drifted inshore out of the fight. Two or three of the British gun-boats had already been sufficiently damaged by some of the shot from the *Ticonderoga's* long guns to make them wary; and the contest at this part of the line narrowed down to one between the American schooner and the remaining British gun-boats, who combined to make a most determined attack upon her. So hastily had the squadron been fitted out that many of the matches for her guns were at the last moment found to be defective. The captain of one of the divisions was a midshipman, but sixteen years old, Hiram Paulding. When he found the matches to be bad he fired the guns of his section by having pistols flashed at them, and continued this through the whole fight. The *Ticonderoga's* commander, Lieut. Cassin, fought his schooner most nobly. He kept walking the taffrail amidst showers of musketry and grape, coolly watching the movements of the galleys and directing the guns to be loaded with canister and bags of bullets, when the enemy tried to board. The British galleys were handled with determined gallantry, under the command of Lieutenant Bell. Had they driven off the *Ticonderoga* they would have won the day for their side, and they pushed up till they were not a boat-hook's length distant, to try to carry her by boarding; but every attempt was repulsed and they were forced to draw off, some of them so crippled by the slaughter they had suffered that they could hardly man the oars.

Meanwhile the fighting at the head of the line had been even fiercer. The first broadside of the *Confiance*, fired from 16 long 24's, double shotted, coolly sighted, in smooth water, at point-blank range, produced the most terrible effect on the *Saratoga*. Her hull shivered all over with the shock, and when the crash subsided nearly half of her people were seen stretched on deck, for many had been knocked down who were not seriously hurt. Among the slain was her first lieutenant, Peter Gamble; he was kneeling down to sight the bow-gun, when a shot entered the port, split the quoin, and drove a portion of it against his side, killing him without breaking the skin. The survivors carried on the fight with undiminished energy. Macdonough himself worked like a common sailor, in pointing and handling a favorite gun. While bending over to sight it a round shot cut in two the spanker boom, which fell on his head and struck him senseless for two or three minutes; he then leaped to his feet and continued as before, when a shot took off the head of the captain of the gun and drove it in his face with such a force as to knock him to the other side of the deck. But after the first broadside not so much injury was done; the guns of the *Confiance* had been levelled to point-blank range, and as the quoins were loosened by the successive discharges they were not properly replaced, so that her broadsides kept going higher and higher and doing less and less damage. Very shortly after the beginning of the action her gallant captain was slain. He was standing behind one of the long guns when a shot from the *Saratoga* struck it and threw it completely off the carriage against his right groin, killing him almost instantly. His skin was not broken; a black mark, about the size of a small plate, was the only visible injury. His watch was found flattened, with its hands pointing to the very second at which he received the fatal blow. As the contest went on the fire gradually decreased in weight, the guns being disabled. The inexperience of both crews partly caused this. The American sailors overloaded their carronades so as to very much destroy the effect of their fire; when the officers became disabled, the men would cram the guns with shot till the last projected from the muzzle. Of course, this lessened the execution, and also gradually crippled the guns. On board the *Confiance* the confusion was even worse; after the battle the charges of the guns were drawn, and on the side she had fought one was found with a canvas bag containing two rounds of shot rammed home and wadded without any powder; another with two cartridges and no shot; and a third with a wad below the cartridge.

At the extreme head of the line the advantage had been with the British. The *Chubb* and *Linnet* had begun a brisk engagement with the *Eagle* and American gun-boats. In a short time the *Chubb* had her cable, bowsprit, and main-boom shot away, drifted within the American lines, and was taken possession of by one of the *Saratoga*'s midshipmen. The *Linnet* paid no attention to the American gun-boats, directing her whole fire against the *Eagle*, and the latter was, in addition, exposed to part of the fire of the *Confiance*. After keeping up a heavy fire for a long time her springs were shot away, and she came up into the wind, hanging so that she could not return a shot to the well-directed broadsides of the *Linnet*. Henly accordingly cut his cable, started home his top-sails, ran down, and anchored by the stern between and inshore of the *Confiance* and *Ticonderoga*, from which position he opened on the *Confiance*. The *Linnet* now directed her attention to the American gun-boats, which at this end of the line were very well fought, but she soon drove them off, and then sprung her broadside so as to rake the *Saratoga* on her bows.

Macdonough by this time had his hands full, and his fire was slackening; he was bearing the whole brunt of the action, with the frigate on his beam and the brig raking him. Twice his ship had been set on fire by the hot shot of the *Confiance*; one by one his long guns were disabled by shot, and his carronades were either treated the same way or else rendered useless by excessive overcharging. Finally but a single carronade was left in the starboard batteries, and on firing it the naval-bolt broke, the gun flew off the carriage and fell down the main hatch, leaving the Commodore without a single gun to oppose to the few the *Confiance* still presented. The battle would have been lost had not Macdonough's foresight provided the means of retrieving it. The anchor suspended astern of the *Saratoga* was let go, and the men hauled in on the hawser that led to the starboard quarter, bringing the ship's stern up over the kedge. The ship now rode by the kedge and by a line that had been bent to a bight in the stream cable, and she was raked badly by the accurate fire of the *Linnet*. By rousing on the line the ship was at length got so far round that the aftermost gun of the port broadside bore on the *Confiance*. The men had been sent forward to keep as much out of harm's way as possible, and now some were at once called back to man the piece, which then opened with effect. The next gun was treated in the same manner; but the ship now hung and would go no farther round. The hawser leading from the port quarter was then got forward under the bows and passed aft to the starboard quarter, and a minute afterward the ship's whole port battery opened with fatal effect. The *Confiance* meanwhile had also attempted to round. Her springs, like those of the *Linnet*, were on the starboard side, and so of course could not be shot away as the *Eagle*'s were; but, as she had nothing but springs to rely on, her efforts did little beyond forcing her forward, and she hung with her head to the wind. She had lost over half of her crew,*** most of her guns on the engaged side were dismounted, and her stout masts had been splintered till they looked like bundles of matches; her sails had been torn to rags, and she was forced to strike, about two hours after she had fired the first broadside. Without pausing a minute the *Saratoga* again hauled on her starboard hawser till her broadside was sprung to bear on the *Linnet*, and the ship and brig began a brisk fight, which the *Eagle* from her position could take no part in, while

---

*** Midshipman Lee, in his letter already quoted, says "not five men were left unhurt"; this would of course include bruises, etc., as hurts.

the *Ticonderoga* was just finishing up the British galleys. The shattered and disabled state of the *Linnet*'s masts, sails, and yards precluded the most distant hope of Capt. Pring's effecting his escape by cutting his cable; but he kept up a most gallant fight with his greatly superior foe, in hopes that some of the gun-boats would come and tow him off, and despatched a lieutenant to the *Confiance* to ascertain her state. The lieutenant returned with news of Capt. Downie's death, while the British gun-boats had been driven half a mile off; and, after having maintained the fight single-handed for fifteen minutes, until, from the number of shot between wind and water, the water had risen a foot above her lower deck, the plucky little brig hauled down her colors, and the fight ended, a little over two hours and a half after the first gun had been fired. Not one of the larger vessels had a mast that would bear canvas, and the prizes were in a sinking condition. The British galleys drifted to leeward, none with their colors up; but as the *Saratoga*'s boarding-officer passed along the deck of the *Confiance* he accidentally ran against a lock-string of one of her starboard guns,[†††] and it went off. This was apparently understood as a signal by the galleys, and they moved slowly off, pulling but a very few sweeps, and not one of them hoisting an ensign.

On both sides the ships had been cut up in the most extraordinary manner; the *Saratoga* had 55 shot-holes in her hull, and the *Confiance* 105 in hers, and the *Eagle* and *Linnet* had suffered in proportion. The number of killed and wounded can not be exactly stated; it was probably about 200 on the American side, and over 300 on the British.[‡‡‡]

Captain Macdonough at once returned the British officers their

---

[†††]   A sufficient commentary, by the way, on James's assertion that the guns of the *Confiance* had to be fired by matches, as the gun-locks did not fit!

[‡‡‡]   Macdonough returned his loss as follows:

	Killed	Wounded
Saratoga	28	29
Eagle	13	20
Ticonderoga	6	6
Preble	2	
Boxer	3	1
Centipede		1
Wilmer		1

swords. Captain Pring writes: "I have much satisfaction in making you acquainted with the humane treatment the wounded have received from Commodore Macdonough; they were immediately removed to his own hospital on Crab Island, and furnished with every requisite. His generous and polite attention to myself, the officers, and men, will ever hereafter be gratefully remembered." The effects of the victory were immediate and of the highest importance. Sir George Prevost and his army at once fled in great haste and confusion back to Canada, leaving our northern frontier clear for the remainder of the war; while the victory had a very great effect on the negotiations for peace.

In this battle the crews on both sides behaved with equal bravery, and left nothing to be desired in this respect; but from their rawness they of course showed far less skill than the crews of most of the American and some of the British ocean cruisers, such as the *Constitution*, *United States*, or *Shannon*, the *Hornet*, *Wasp*, or *Reindeer*. Lieut. Cassin handled the *Ticonderoga*, and Captain Pring the *Linnet*, with the utmost gallantry and skill, and, after Macdonough, they divide the honors of the day. But Macdonough in this battle won a higher fame than any other commander of the war, British or American. He had a decidedly superior force to contend against, the officers and men of the two sides being about on a par in every respect; and it was solely owing to his foresight and resource that we won the victory. He forced the British to engage at a disadvantage by his excellent choice of position; and he prepared beforehand for every possible contingency. His personal prowess had already been shown

---

A total of 52 killed and 58 wounded; but the latter head apparently only included those who had to go to the hospital. Probably about 90 additional were more or less slightly wounded. Captain Pring, in his letter of Sept. 12th, says the *Confiance* had 41 killed and 40 wounded; the *Linnet*, 10 killed and 14 wounded; the *Chubb*, 6 killed and 16 wounded; the *Finch*, 2 wounded; in all, 57 killed and 72 wounded. . . . The Americans took out 180 dead and wounded from the *Confiance*, 50 from the *Linnet*, and 40 from the *Chubb* and *Finch*; in all, 270. James ("Naval Occurrences," p. 412) says the *Confiance* had 83 wounded. As Captain Pring wrote his letter in Plattsburg Bay the day after the action, he of course could not give the loss aboard the British gun-boats; so James at once assumed that they suffered none. As well as could be found out they had between 50 and 100 killed and wounded. The total British loss was between 300 and 400, as nearly as can be ascertained. For this action, as already shown, James is of no use whatever. Compare his statements, for example, with those of Midshipman Lee, in the "Naval Chronicle." The comparative loss, as a means of testing the competitive prowess of the combatants, is not of much consequence in this case, as the weaker party in point of force conquered.

at the cost of the rovers of Tripoli, and in this action he helped fight the guns as ably as the best sailor. His skill, seamanship, quick eye, readiness of resource, and indomitable pluck, are beyond all praise. Down to the time of the Civil War he is the greatest figure in our naval history. A thoroughly religious man, he was as generous and humane as he was skilful and brave; one of the greatest of our sea-captains, he has left a stainless name behind him.

British Loss

Name	Tons	Guns	Remarks
Brig	100	10	BURNT BY LIEUT. GREGORY.
Magnet	187	12	" BY HER CREW.
Black Snake	30	1	CAPTURED.
Gun-boat	50	2	"
"	50	3	"
Confiance	1,200	37	"
Linnet	350	16	"
Chubb	112	11	"
Finch	110	11	"
9 VESSELS	2,189	103	

American Loss

Name	Tons	Guns	Remarks
Growler	81	7	CAPTURED.
Boat	50	2	"
Tigress	96	1	"
Scorpion	86	2	"
Ohio	94	1	"
Somers	98	2	"
6 VESSELS	505	15	

"The Spread of the English-Speaking Peoples" from *The Winning of the West* (1889)

Roosevelt would be both mystified and infuriated at the incredulity with which contemporary readers will likely greet his account of how the English-speaking peoples were formed more than a thousand years ago and how the experiences of Germanic tribes conquering Britain predicate the expansion of the United States a few hundred years later. We will find nearly incomprehensible Roosevelt's dizzying catalogue of those tribes' various ways of conquering Europe and the critical difference he finds in how the English themselves were assimilated rather than merely subjugated, how they learned as a conquered people to give rights, not abrogate them, when they themselves became conquerors. Moreover, his attribution of traits to different "races," and his generalizations of northern European ethnicities, strike us today as alternately repulsive and risible. Despite such resistance, Roosevelt's six-volume history of the continentalization of America must still be counted among his greatest achievements as a writer. Working within the sociological limits of his day, Roosevelt crafts a skillful narrative that explains how Americans subdued their antagonists—native resistance, foreign countries' claims, and an often unforgiving land and challenging climate—and shaped a nation. This history highlights key victories in battle as well as political negotiations, with a host of characters stepping forward to showcase their contributions to the expansion of America. Roosevelt pursues his subject as a professional historian might, weighing his evidence against the best possible sources, always aiming to be both animated and circumspect, sometimes claiming authority on the basis of personal experience, but much more often on sources like government documents or predecessors' trusted research. As much as we may mistrust the social premises out of which Roosevelt labored, one can still respect the scope and energy of the history he created.

The Spread of the English-Speaking Peoples

During the past three centuries the spread of the English-speaking peoples over the world's waste spaces has been not only the most striking feature in the world's history, but also the event of all others most far-reaching in its effects and its importance.

Spread of the Modern English Race.

The tongue which Bacon feared to use in his writings, lest they should remain forever unknown to all but the inhabitants of a relatively unimportant insular kingdom, is now the speech of two continents. The Common Law which Coke jealously upheld in the southern half of a single European island is now the law of the land throughout the vast regions of Australasia, and of America north of the Rio Grande. The names of the plays that Shakespeare wrote are household words in the mouths of mighty nations, whose wide domains were to him more unreal than the realm of Prester John. Over half the descendants of their fellow countrymen of that day now dwell in lands which, when these three Englishmen were born, held not a single white inhabitant; the race which, when they were in their prime, was hemmed in between the North and the Irish seas today holds sway over worlds, whose endless coasts are washed by the waves of the three great oceans.

There have been many other races that at one time or another had their great periods of race expansion—as distinguished from mere conquest—but there has never been another whose expansion has been either so broad or so rapid.

At one time, many centuries ago, it seemed as if the Germanic peoples, like their Celtic foes and neighbors, would be absorbed into the all-conquering Roman power, and, merging their identity in that of the victors, would accept their law, their speech, and their habits of thought. But this danger vanished forever on the day of the slaughter by the Teutoburger Wald, when the legions of Varus were broken by the rush of Hermann's wild warriors.

First Overflow of the Germanic Peoples.

Two or three hundred years later the Germans, no longer on the defensive, themselves went forth from their marshy forests conquering and to conquer. For century after century they swarmed out of the dark woodland east of the Rhine, and north of the Danube; and as their force spent itself, the movement was taken up by their brethren who dwelt along the coasts of the Baltic and the North Atlantic. From the Volga to the Pillars of Hercules, from Sicily to Britain, every land in turn bowed to the warlike prowess of the stalwart sons of Odin. Rome and Novgorod, the imperial city of Italy as well as the squalid capital of Muscovy, acknowledged the sway of kings of Teutonic or Scandinavian blood.

Fails Greatly to Extend Germany.

In most cases, however, the victorious invaders merely intruded themselves among the original and far more numerous owners of the land, ruled over them, and were absorbed by them. This happened to both Teuton and Scandinavian; to the descendants of Alaric, as well as to the children of Rurik. The Dane in Ireland became a Celt; the Goth of the Iberian peninsula became a Spaniard; Frank and Norwegian alike were merged into the mass of Romance-speaking Gauls, who themselves finally grew to be called by the names of their masters. Thus it came about that though the German tribes conquered Europe they did not extend the limits of Germany nor the sway of the German race. On the contrary, they strengthened the hands of the rivals of the people from whom they sprang. They gave rulers—kaisers, kings, barons, and knights—to all the lands they overran; here and there they imposed their own names on kingdoms and principalities—as in France, Normandy, Burgundy, and Lombardy; they grafted the feudal system on the Roman jurisprudence, and interpolated a few Teutonic words in the Latin dialects of the peoples they had conquered; but, hopelessly outnumbered, they were soon lost in the mass of their subjects, and adopted from them their laws, their culture, and their language. As a result, the mixed races of the south—the Latin nations as they are sometimes called—strengthened by the infusion of northern blood, sprang anew into vigorous life, and became for the time being the leaders of the European world.

The Winning of England Stands by Itself.

There was but one land whereof the winning made a lasting addition to Germanic soil; but this land was destined to be of more importance in the future of the Germanic peoples than all their continental possessions, original and acquired, put together. The day when the keels of the low-Dutch sea-thieves first grated on the British coast was big with the doom of many nations. There sprang up in conquered southern Britain, when its name had been significantly changed to England, that branch of the Germanic stock which was in the end to grasp almost literally world-wide power, and by its over-shadowing growth to dwarf into comparative insignificance all its kindred folk. At the time, in the general wreck of the civilized world, the making of England attracted but little attention. Men's eyes were riveted on the empires conquered by the hosts of Alaric, Theodoric, and Clovis, not on the swarm of little kingdoms and earldoms founded by the nameless chiefs who led each his band of hard-rowing, hard-fighting henchmen across the stormy waters of the German Ocean. Yet the rule and the race of Goth, Frank, and Burgund have vanished from off the earth; while the sons of the unknown Saxon, Anglian, and Friesic warriors now hold in their hands the fate of the coming years.

Formation of the Nations; Races of Mixed Blood.

After the great Teutonic wanderings were over, there came a long lull, until, with the discovery of America, a new period of even vaster race expansion began. During this lull the nations of Europe took on their present shapes. Indeed, the so-called Latin nations—the French and Spaniards, for instance—may be said to have been born after the first set of migrations ceased. Their national history, as such, does not really begin until about that time, whereas that of the Germanic peoples stretches back unbroken to the days when we first hear of their existence. It would be hard to say which one of half a dozen races that existed in Europe during the early centuries of the present era should be considered as especially the ancestor of the modern Frenchman or Spaniard. When the Romans conquered Gaul and Iberia they did not in any place drive out the ancient owners of the soil; they simply Romanized them, and left them as the base of the population. By the Frankish and Visigothic invasions another strain of blood was added, to be speedily absorbed; while the invaders took the language of the conquered people, and established themselves as the ruling class. Thus the modern nations who sprang from this mixture derive portions of their governmental system and general policy from one race, most of their blood from another, and their language, law, and culture from a third.

Peculiarity of English History.

The English race, on the contrary, has a perfectly continuous history. When Alfred reigned, the English already had a distinct national being; when Charlemagne reigned, the French, as we use the term today, had no national being whatever. The Germans of the mainland merely overran the countries that lay in their path; but the sea-rovers who won England to a great extent actually displaced the native Britons. The former were absorbed by the subject-races; the latter, on the contrary, slew or drove off or assimilated the original inhabitants. Unlike all the other Germanic swarms, the English took neither creed nor custom, neither law nor speech, from their beaten foes. At the time when the dynasty of the Capets had become firmly established at Paris, France was merely part of a country where Latinized Gauls and Basques were ruled by Latinized Franks, Goths, Burgunds, and Normans; but the people across the Channel then showed little trace of Celtic or Romance influence. It would be hard to say whether Vercingetorix or Cæsar, Clovis or Syagrius, has the better right to stand as the prototype of a modern French general. There is no such doubt in the other case. The average Englishman, American, or Australian of today who wishes to recall the feats of power with which his race should be credited in the shadowy dawn of its history, may go back to the half-mythical glories of Hengist and Horsa, perhaps to the deeds of

Civilis the Batavian, or to those of the hero of the Teutoburger fight, but certainly to the wars neither of the Silurian chief Caractacus nor of his conqueror, the after-time Emperor Vespasian.

England's Separate Position.

Nevertheless, when, in the sixteenth century, the European peoples began to extend their dominions beyond Europe, England had grown to differ profoundly from the Germanic countries of the mainland. A very large Celtic element had been introduced into the English blood, and, in addition, there had been a considerable Scandinavian admixture. More important still were the radical changes brought by the Norman conquest; chief among them the transformation of the old English tongue into the magnificent language which is now the common inheritance of so many widespread peoples. England's insular position, moreover, permitted it to work out its own fate comparatively unhampered by the presence of out-side powers; so that it developed a type of nationality totally distinct from the types of the European mainland.

All this is not foreign to American history. The vast movement by which this continent was conquered and peopled cannot be rightly understood if considered solely by itself. It was the crowning and greatest achievement of a series of mighty movements, and it must be taken in connection with them. Its true significance will be lost unless we grasp, however roughly, the past race-history of the nations who took part therein.

Period of Extra-European Colonization.

When, with the voyages of Columbus and his successors, the great period of extra-European colonization began, various nations strove to share in the work. Most of them had to plant their colonies in lands across the sea; Russia alone was by her geographical position enabled to extend her frontiers by land, and in consequence her comparatively recent colonization of Siberia bears some resemblance to our own work in the western United States. The other countries of Europe were forced to find their outlets for conquest and emigration beyond the ocean, and, until the colonists had taken firm root in their new homes the mastery of the seas thus became a matter of vital consequence.

Among the lands beyond the ocean America was the first reached and the most important. It was conquered by different European races, and shoals of European settlers were thrust forth upon its shores. These sometimes displaced and sometimes merely overcame and lived among the natives. They also, to their own lasting harm, committed a crime whose shortsighted folly was worse than its guilt, for they brought hordes of African slaves, whose descendants now form immense populations in certain portions of the land. Throughout the continent we therefore find the white, red, and black races in every stage of purity and intermixture. One result of this great turmoil of conquest and immigration has been that, in certain parts of America, the lines of cleavage of race are so far from coinciding with the lines of cleavage of speech that they run at right angles to them—as in the four communities of Ontario, Quebec, Hayti, and Jamaica.

Twofold Character of the Warfare.

Each intruding European power, in winning for itself new realms beyond the seas, had to wage a twofold war, overcoming the original inhabitants with one hand, and with the other warding off the assaults of the kindred nations that were bent on the same schemes. Generally the contests of the latter kind were much the most important. The victories by which the struggles between the European conquerors themselves were ended deserve lasting commemoration. Yet, sometimes, even the most important of them, sweeping though they were, were in parts less sweeping than they seemed. It would be impossible to overestimate the far-reaching effects of the overthrow of the French power in America; but Lower Canada, where the fatal blow was given, itself suffered nothing but a political conquest, which did not interfere in the least with the growth of a French state along both sides of the lower St. Lawrence. In a somewhat similar way Dutch communities have held their own, and indeed have sprung up in South Africa.

Spain's Share.

All the European nations touching on the Atlantic seaboard took part in the new work, with very varying success; Germany alone, then rent by many feuds, having no share therein. Portugal founded a single state,

Brazil. The Scandinavian nations did little; their chief colony fell under the control of the Dutch. The English and the Spaniards were the two nations to whom the bulk of the new lands fell; the former getting much the greater portion. The conquests of the Spaniards took place in the sixteenth century. The West Indies and Mexico, Peru and the limitless grass plains of what is now the Argentine Confederation—all these and the lands lying between them had been conquered and colonized by the Spaniards before there was a single English settlement in the New World, and while the fleets of the Catholic king still held for him the lordship of the ocean. Then the cumbrous Spanish vessels succumbed to the attacks of the swift war-ships of Holland and England, and the sun of the Spanish world-dominion set as quickly as it had risen. Spain at once came to a standstill; it was only here and there that she even extended her rule over a few neighboring Indian tribes, while she was utterly unable to take the offensive against the French, Dutch, and English. But it is a singular thing that these vigorous and powerful new-comers, who had so quickly put a stop to her further growth, yet wrested from her very little of what was already hers. They plundered a great many Spanish cities and captured a great many Spanish galleons, but they made no great or lasting conquests of Spanish territory. Their mutual jealousies, and the fear each felt of the others, were among the main causes of this state of things; and hence it came about that after the opening of the seventeenth century the wars they waged against one another were of far more ultimate consequence than the wars they waged against the former mistress of the western world. England in the end drove both France and Holland from the field; but it was under the banner of the American Republic, not under that of the British Monarchy, that the English-speaking people first won vast stretches of land from the descendants of the Spanish conquerors.

The French and the Dutch.

The three most powerful of Spain's rivals waged many a long war with one another to decide which should grasp the sceptre that had slipped from Spanish hands. The fleets of Holland fought with stubborn obstinacy to wrest from England her naval supremacy; but they failed, and in the end the greater portion of the Dutch domains fell to their foes. The French likewise began a course of conquest and colonization at the same time the

English did, and after a couple of centuries of rivalry, ending in prolonged warfare, they also succumbed. The close of the most important colonial contest ever waged left the French without a foot of soil on the North American mainland; while their victorious foes had not only obtained the lead in the race for supremacy on that continent, but had also won the command of the ocean. They thenceforth found themselves free to work their will in all seagirt lands, unchecked by hostile European influence.

Most fortunately, when England began her career as a colonizing power in America, Spain had already taken possession of the populous tropical and subtropical regions, and the northern power was thus forced to form her settlements in the sparsely peopled temperate zone.

Difference between the Spanish and the English Conquests.

It is of vital importance to remember that the English and Spanish conquests in America differed from each other very much as did the original conquests which gave rise to the English and the Spanish nations. The English had exterminated or assimilated the Celts of Britain, and they substantially repeated the process with the Indians of America; although of course in America there was very little, instead of very much, assimilation. The Germanic strain is dominant in the blood of the average Englishman, exactly as the English strain is dominant in the blood of the average American. Twice a portion of the race has shifted its home, in each case undergoing a marked change, due both to outside influence and to internal development; but in the main retaining, especially in the last instance, the general race characteristics.

It was quite otherwise in the countries conquered by Cortes, Pizarro, and their successors. Instead of killing or driving off the natives as the English did, the Spaniards simply sat down in the midst of a much more numerous aboriginal population. The process by which Central and South America became Spanish bore very close resemblance to the process by which the lands of southwestern Europe were turned into Romance-speaking countries. The bulk of the original inhabitants remained unchanged in each case. There was little displacement of population. Roman soldiers and magistrates, Roman merchants and handicraftsmen were thrust in among the Celtic and Iberian peoples, exactly as the Spanish military and civil rulers, priests, traders, land-owners, and mine-owners settled down among the Indians of Peru and Mexico. By degrees, in each case, the many learnt the language and adopted the laws, religion, and governmental system of the few, although keeping certain of their own customs and habits of thought. Though the ordinary Spaniard of today speaks a Romance dialect, he is mainly of Celto-Iberian blood; and though most Mexicans and Peruvians speak Spanish, yet the great majority of them trace their descent back to the subjects of Montezuma and the Incas. Moreover, exactly as in Europe little ethnic islands of Breton and Basque stock have remained unaffected by the Romance flood, so in America there are large communities where the inhabitants keep unchanged the speech and the customs of their Indian forefathers.

The English-speaking peoples now hold more and better land than any other American nationality or set of nationalities. They have in their veins less aboriginal American blood than any of their neighbors. Yet it is noteworthy that the latter have tacitly allowed them to arrogate to themselves the title of "Americans," whereby to designate their distinctive and individual nationality.

The English Settlements and Conquests.

So much for the difference between the way in which the English and the way in which other European nations have conquered and colonized. But there have been likewise very great differences in the methods and courses of the English-speaking peoples themselves, at different times and in different places.

The settlement of the United States and Canada, throughout most of their extent, bears much resemblance to the later settlement of Australia and New Zealand. The English conquest of India and even the English conquest of South Africa come in an entirely different category. The first was a mere political conquest, like the Dutch conquest of Java or the extension of the Roman Empire over parts of Asia. South Africa in some respects stands by itself, because there the English are confronted by another white race which it is as yet uncertain whether they can assimilate, and, what is infinitely more important, because they are there confronted by a very large native population with which they cannot mingle, and which neither dies out nor recedes before their advance. It is not likely, but it is at least within the bounds of possibility, that in the course of centuries the whites of South Africa will suffer a fate akin to that which befell the Greek colonists in the Tauric Chersonese, and be swallowed up in the overwhelming mass of black barbarism.

On the other hand, it may fairly be said that in America and Australia the English race has already entered into and begun the enjoyment of its great inheritance. When these continents were settled they contained the largest tracts of fertile, temperate, thinly peopled country on the face of the globe. We cannot rate too highly the importance of their acquisition. Their successful settlement was a feat which by comparison utterly dwarfs all the European wars of the last two centuries; just as the importance of the issues at stake in the wars of Rome and Carthage completely overshadowed the interests for which the various contemporary Greek kingdoms were at the same time striving.

Australia.

Australia, which was much less important than America, was also won and settled with far less difficulty. The natives were so few in number and of such a low type, that they practically offered no resistance at all, being but little more hindrance than an equal number of ferocious beasts. There was no rivalry whatever by any European power, because the actual settlement—not the mere expatriation of convicts—only began when England, as a result of her struggle with Republican and Imperial France, had won the absolute control of the seas. Unknown to themselves, Nelson and his fellow admirals settled the fate of Australia, upon which they probably never wasted a thought. Trafalgar decided much more than the mere question whether Great Britain should temporarily share the fate that so soon befell Prussia; for in all probability it decided the destiny of the island-continent that lay in the South Seas.

The history of the English-speaking race in America has been widely different. In Australia there was no fighting whatever, whether with natives or with other foreigners. In America for the past two centuries and a half there has been a constant succession of contests with powerful and warlike native tribes, with rival European nations, and with American nations of European origin. But even in America there have been wide differences in the way the work has had to be done in different parts of the country, since the close of the great colonial contests between England, France, and Spain.

Canada.

The extension of the English westward through Canada since the war of the Revolution has been in its essential features merely a less important repetition of what has gone on in the northern United States. The gold miner, the transcontinental railway, and the soldier have been the pioneers of civilization. The chief point of difference, which was but small, arose from the fact that the whole of western Canada was for a long time under the control of the most powerful of all the fur companies, in whose employ were very many French voyageurs and coureurs des bois. From these there sprang up in the valleys of the Red River and the Saskatchewan a singular race of half-breeds, with a unique semi-civilization of their own. It was with these half-breeds, and not, as in the United States, with the Indians, that the settlers of northwestern Canada had their main difficulties.

The United States.

In what now forms the United States, taking the country as a whole, the foes who had to be met and overcome were very much more formidable. The ground had to be not only settled but conquered, sometimes at the expense of the natives, often at the expense of rival European races. As already pointed out the Indians themselves formed one of the main factors in deciding the fate of the continent. They were never able in the end to avert the white conquest, but they could often delay its advance for a long spell of years. The Iroquois, for instance, held their own against all comers for two centuries. Many other tribes stayed for a time the oncoming white flood, or even drove it back; in Maine the settlers were for a hundred years confined to a narrow strip of sea-coast. Against the Spaniards, there were even here and there Indian nations who definitely recovered the ground they had lost.

When the whites first landed, the superiority and, above all, the novelty of their arms gave them a very great advantage. But the Indians soon became accustomed to the new-comers' weapons and style of warfare. By the time the English had consolidated the Atlantic colonies under their rule, the Indians had become what they have remained ever since, the most formidable savage foes ever encountered by colonists of European stock. Relatively to their numbers, they have shown themselves far more to be dreaded than the Zulus or even the Maoris.

Effect of the Indian upon our History.

Their presence has caused the process of settlement to go on at unequal rates of speed in different places; the flood has been hemmed in at one point, or has been forced to flow round an island of native population at another. Had the Indians been as helpless as the native Australians were, the continent of North America would have had an altogether different history. It would not only have been settled far more rapidly, but also on very different lines. Not only have the red men themselves kept back the settlements, but they have also had a very great effect upon the outcome of the struggles between the different intrusive European peoples. Had the original inhabitants of the Mississippi valley been as numerous and unwarlike as the Aztecs, de Soto would have repeated the work of Cortes, and we would very possibly have been barred out of the greater portion of our present domain. Had it not been for their Indian allies, it would have been impossible for the French to prolong, as they did, their struggle with their much more numerous English neighbors.

The Indians have shrunk back before our advance only after fierce and dogged resistance. They were never numerous in the land, but exactly what their numbers were when the whites first appeared is impossible to tell. Probably an estimate of half a million for those within the limits of the present United States is not far wrong; but in any such calculation there is of necessity a large element of mere rough guess-work. Formerly writers greatly over-estimated their original numbers, counting them by millions. Now it is the fashion to go to the other extreme, and even to maintain that they have not decreased at all. This last is a theory that can only be upheld on the supposition that the whole does not consist of the sum of the parts; for whereas we can check off on our fingers the tribes that have slightly increased, we can enumerate scores that have died out almost before our eyes. Speaking broadly, they have mixed but little with the English (as distinguished from the French and Spanish) invaders. They are driven back, or die out, or retire to their own reservations; but they are not often assimilated. Still, on every frontier, there is always a certain amount of assimilation going on, much more than is commonly admitted[§§§]; and whenever a French or Spanish community has been absorbed by the energetic Americans, a certain amount of Indian blood has been absorbed also. There seems to be a chance that in one part of our country, the Indian territory, the Indians, who are continually advancing in civilization, will remain as the ground element of the population, like the Creoles in Louisiana, or the Mexicans in New Mexico.

Territorial Advances of the People of the United States.

The Americans when they became a nation continued even more successfully the work which they had begun as citizens of the several English colonies. At the outbreak of the Revolution they still all dwelt on the seaboard, either on the coast itself or along the banks of the streams flowing into the Atlantic. When the fight at Lexington took place they had no settlements beyond the mountain chain on our western border. It had taken them over a century and a half to spread from the Atlantic to the Alleghenies. In the next three quarters of a century they spread from the Alleghenies to the Pacific. In doing this they not only dispossessed the Indian tribes, but they also won the land from its European owners. Britain had to yield the territory between the Ohio and the Great Lakes. By a purchase, of which we frankly announced that the alternative would be war, we acquired from France the vast, ill-defined region known as Louisiana. From the Spaniards, or from their descendants, we won the lands of Florida, Texas, New Mexico, and California.

The Americans a Distinct People from the British.

All these lands were conquered after we had become a power, independent of every other, and one within our own borders; when we were no

---

[§§§]   To this I can testify of my own knowledge as regards Montana, Dakota, and Minnesota. The mixture usually takes place in the ranks of the population where individuals lose all trace of their ancestry after two or three generations; so it is often honestly ignored, and sometimes mention of it is suppressed, the man regarding it as a taint. But I also know many very wealthy old frontiersmen whose half-breed children are now being educated, generally at convent schools, while in the Northwestern cities I could point out some very charming men and women, in the best society, with a strain of Indian blood in their veins.

longer a loose assemblage of petty seaboard communities, each with only such relationship to its neighbor as was implied in their common subjection to a foreign king and a foreign people. Moreover, it is well always to remember that at the day when we began our career as a nation we already differed from our kinsmen of Britain in blood as well as in name; the word American already had more than a merely geographical signification. Americans belong to the English race only in the sense in which Englishmen belong to the German. The fact that no change of language has accompanied the second wandering of our people, from Britain to America, as it accompanied their first, from Germany to Britain, is due to the further fact that when the second wandering took place the race possessed a fixed literary language, and, thanks to the ease of communication, was kept in touch with the parent stock. The change of blood was probably as great in one case as in the other. The modern Englishman is descended from a Low-Dutch stock, which, when it went to Britain, received into itself an enormous infusion of Celtic, a much smaller infusion of Norse and Danish, and also a certain infusion of Norman-French blood. When this new English stock came to America it mingled with and absorbed into itself immigrants from many European lands, and the process has gone on ever since. It is to be noted that, of the new blood thus acquired, the greatest proportion has come from Dutch and German sources, and the next greatest from Irish, while the Scandinavian element comes third, and the only other of much consequence is French Huguenot. Thus it appears that no new element of importance has been added to the blood. Additions have been made to the elemental race-strains in much the same proportion as these were originally combined.

Some latter-day writers deplore the enormous immigration to our shores as making us a heterogeneous instead of a homogeneous people; but as a matter of fact we are less heterogeneous at the present day than we were at the outbreak of the Revolution. Our blood was as much mixed a century ago as it is now. No State now has a smaller proportion of English blood than New York or Pennsylvania had in 1775. Even in New England, where the English stock was purest, there was a certain French and Irish mixture; in Virginia there were Germans in addition. In the other colonies, taken as a whole, it is not probable that much over half of the blood was English; Dutch, French, German, and Gaelic communities abounded.

Territorial Expansion.

But all were being rapidly fused into one people. As the Celt of Cornwall and the Saxon of Wessex are now alike Englishmen, so in 1775 Hollander and Huguenot, whether in New York or South Carolina, had become Americans, undistinguishable from the New Englanders and Virginians, the descendants of the men who followed Cromwell or charged behind Rupert. When the great western movement began we were already a people by ourselves. Moreover, the immense immigration from Europe that has taken place since, had little or no effect on the way in which we extended our boundaries; it only began to be important about the time that we acquired our present limits. These limits would in all probability be what they now are even if we had not received a single European colonist since the Revolution.

Thus the Americans began their work of western conquest as a separate and individual people, at the moment when they sprang into national life. It has been their great work ever since. All other questions save those of the preservation of the Union itself and of the emancipation of the blacks have been of subordinate importance when compared with the great question of how rapidly and how completely they were to subjugate that part of their continent lying between the eastern mountains and the Pacific. Yet the statesmen of the Atlantic seaboard were often unable to perceive this, and indeed frequently showed the same narrow jealousy of the communities beyond the Alleghanies that England felt for all America. Even if they were too broad-minded and far-seeing to feel thus, they yet were unable to fully appreciate the magnitude of the interests at stake in the west. They thought more of our right to the North Atlantic fisheries than of our ownership of the Mississippi valley; they were more interested in the fate of a bank or a tariff than in the settlement of the Oregon boundary. Most contemporary writers showed similar shortcomings in their sense of historic perspective. The names of Ethan Allen and Marion are probably better known than is that of George Rogers Clark; yet their deeds, as regards their effects, could no more be compared to his, than his could be compared to Washington's. So it was with Houston. During his lifetime there were probably fifty men who, east of the Mississippi, were deemed far greater than he was. Yet in most cases their names have already almost faded from remembrance, while his fame will grow steadily brighter as the importance of his deeds is more thoroughly realized. Fortunately, in the long run, the mass of easterners always backed up their western brethren.

The kind of colonizing conquest, whereby the people of the United States have extended their borders, has much in common with the similar movements in Canada and Australia, all of them standing in sharp contrast to what has gone on in Spanish-American lands. But of course each is marked out in addition by certain peculiarities of its own. Moreover, even in the United States, the movement falls naturally into two divisions, which on several points differ widely from each other.

The Northwest Acquired by the Nation.

The way in which the southern part of our western country—that is, all the land south of the Ohio, and from thence on to the Rio Grande and the Pacific—was won and settled, stands quite alone. The region north of it was filled up in a very different manner. The Southwest, including therein what was once called simply the West, and afterwards the Middle West, was won by the people themselves, acting as individuals, or as groups of individuals, who hewed out their own fortunes in advance of any governmental action. On the other hand, the Northwest, speaking broadly, was acquired by the government, the settlers merely taking possession of what the whole country guaranteed them. The Northwest is essentially a national domain; it is fitting that it should be, as it is, not only by position but by feeling, the heart of the nation.

North of the Ohio the regular army went first. The settlements grew up behind the shelter of the federal troops of Harmar, St. Claire, and Wayne, and of their successors even to our own day. The wars in which the borderers themselves bore any part were few and trifling compared to the contests waged by the adventurers who won Kentucky, Tennessee, and Texas.

In the Southwest the early settlers acted as their own army, and supplied both leaders and men. Sevier, Robertson, Clark, and Boone led their fellow pioneers to battle, as Jackson did afterwards, and as Houston did later still. Indeed the Southwesterners not only won their own soil for themselves, but they were the chief instruments in the original acquisition of the Northwest also. Had it not been for the conquest of the Illinois towns in 1779 we would probably never have had any Northwest to settle; and the huge tract between the upper Mississippi and the Columbia, then called Upper Louisiana, fell into our hands, only because the Kentuckians and Tennesseans were resolutely bent on taking possession of New Orleans, either by bargain or battle. All of our territory lying beyond the Alleghenies, north and south, was first won for us by the Southwesterners, fighting for their own hand. The northern part was afterwards filled up by the thrifty, vigorous men of the Northeast, whose sons became the real rulers as well as the preservers of the Union; but these settlements of Northerners were rendered possible only by the deeds of the nation as a whole. They entered on land that the Southerners had won, and they were kept there by the strong arm of the Federal Government; whereas the Southerners owed most of their victories only to themselves.

The first-comers around Marietta did, it is true, share to a certain extent in the dangers of the existing Indian wars; but their trials are not to be mentioned beside those endured by the early settlers of Tennessee and Kentucky, and whereas these latter themselves subdued and drove out their foes, the former took but an insignificant part in the contest by which the possession of their land was secured. Besides, the strongest and most numerous Indian tribes were in the Southwest.

The Southwest Won by Individual Settlers.

The Southwest developed its civilization on its own lines, for good and for ill; the Northwest was settled under the national ordinance of 1787, which absolutely determined its destiny, and thereby in the end also determined the destiny of the whole nation. Moreover, the gulf coast, as well as the interior, from the Mississippi to the Pacific, was held by foreign powers; while in the north this was only true of the country between the Ohio and the Great Lakes during the first years of the Revolution, until the Kentucky backwoodsmen conquered it. Our rivals of European race had dwelt for generations along the lower Mississippi and the Rio Grande, in Florida, and in California, when we made them ours. Detroit, Vincennes, St. Louis, and New Orleans, St. Augustine, San Antonio, Santa Fé, and San Francisco are cities that were built by Frenchmen or Spaniards; we did not found them, but conquered them. All but the first two are in the Southwest, and of these two one was first taken and governed by Southwesterners. On the other hand, the Northwestern cities, from Cincinnati and Chicago to Helena and Portland, were founded by our own people, by the people who now have possession of them.

The Winning of the West and Southwest.

The Southwest was conquered only after years of hard fighting with the original owners. The way in which this was done bears much less resemblance to the sudden filling up of Australia and California by the practically unopposed overflow from a teeming and civilized mother country, than it does to the original English conquest of Britain itself. The warlike borderers who thronged across the Alleghenies, the restless and reckless hunters, the hard, dogged, frontier farmers, by dint of grim tenacity overcame and displaced Indians, French, and Spaniards alike, exactly as, fourteen hundred years before, Saxon and Angle had overcome and displaced the Cymric and Gaelic Celts. They were led by no one commander; they acted under orders from neither king nor congress; they were not carrying out the plans of any far-sighted leader. In obedience to the instincts working half blindly within their breasts, spurred ever onwards by the fierce desires of their eager hearts, they made in the wilderness homes for their children, and by so doing wrought out the destinies of a continental nation. They warred and settled from the high hill-valleys of the French Broad and the Upper Cumberland to the half-tropical basin of the Rio Grande, and to where the Golden Gate lets through the long-heaving waters of the Pacific. The story of how this was done forms a compact and continuous whole. The fathers followed Boone or fought at King's Mountain; the sons marched south with Jackson to overcome the Creeks and beat back the British; the grandsons died at the Alamo or charged to victory at San Jacinto. They were doing their share of a work that began with the conquest of Britain, that entered on its second and wider period after the defeat of the Spanish Armada, that culminated in the marvellous growth of the United States. The winning of the West and Southwest is a stage in the conquest of a continent.

"The Cavalry at Santiago" (The Battle of San Juan Hill) from *The Rough Riders* (1899)

Roosevelt's part in the Spanish-American War contributed so decisively to his emerging public image that, without this experience, he might never have gone on to become president. Upon his return from the war, he was newly celebrated by war journalists throughout the country and thereby rose to a new level of renown for leading the charge up the strategically important San Juan Hill. The war exaggerated his virtues as well as his defects. Roosevelt went to Cuba as a public figure of some distinction and charm, who often nettled his opponents; he came back a hero, beloved for his personification of an ideal of American masculinity, whom his opponents feared. Almost immediately upon his return, he was elected governor of New York, where he served less than two years before William McKinley selected him as his running mate in the election of 1900. Partly facilitating his ascendancy was this account of the First U.S. Volunteer Cavalry under his command, the Rough Riders, a cohort of volunteers Roosevelt seemingly (and secretly) recruited single-handedly, a mélange of Ivy Leaguers, cowpokes, and high-spirited men from all walks of American life. In the famous battle described here, Roosevelt gives readers something of the "hurly-burly" of combat, even as he narrates the key logistical developments amid the haze of war. A strange reserve seems to preside over that report. As near to danger as he is and so arbitrary the toll of human life, Roosevelt refrains from giving his part the dramatic centrality a reader might expect from someone who had lamented his whole adulthood never having had such an occasion to test himself. Instead, Roosevelt seems restrained and, in places, abashed by the scene of the greatest achievement of his life. Readers can hear that reticence especially in his dignified, straightforward depiction of the way soldiers die.

The passage is marred only by the casual denigration of some perceived lack of initiative and leadership in the very same African American troops he otherwise praises for conducting themselves well. However conventional, it is a shame that Roosevelt felt obliged to condescend so inappropriately inasmuch as his general respect for these soldiers would ultimately help him to see their value as citizens and a base of political support. Be that as it may, the book sold extremely well, and Roosevelt's rise would thereafter seem unstoppable.

The Cavalry at Santiago

As the sun rose the men fell in, and at the same time a battery of field guns was brought up on the hill-crest just beyond, between us and toward Santiago. It was a fine sight to see the great horses straining under the lash as they whirled the guns up the hill and into position.

Our brigade was drawn up on the hither side of a kind of half basin, a big band of Cubans being off to the left. As yet we had received no orders, except that we were told that the main fighting was to be done by Lawton's infantry division, which was to take El Caney, several miles to our right, while we were simply to make a diversion. This diversion was to be made mainly with the artillery, and the battery which had taken position immediately in front of us was to begin when Lawton began.

It was about six o'clock that the first report of the cannon from El Caney came booming to us across the miles of still jungle. It was a very lovely morning, the sky of cloudless blue, while the level, shimmering rays from the just-risen sun brought into fine relief the splendid palms which here and there towered above the lower growth. The lofty and beautiful mountains hemmed in the Santiago plain, making it an amphitheatre for the battle.

Immediately our guns opened, and at the report great clouds of white smoke hung on the ridge crest. For a minute or two there was no response. Wood and I were sitting together, and Wood remarked to me that he wished our brigade could be moved somewhere else, for we were directly in line of any return fire aimed by the Spaniards at the battery. Hardly had he spoken when there was a peculiar whistling, singing sound in the air, and immediately afterward the noise of something exploding over our heads. It was shrapnel from the Spanish batteries. We sprung to our feet and leaped on our horses. Immediately afterward a second shot came which burst directly above us; and then a third. From the second shell one of the shrapnel bullets dropped on my wrist, hardly breaking the skin, but raising a bump about as big as a hickory-nut. The same shell wounded four of my regiment, one of them being Mason Mitchell, and two or three of the regulars were also hit, one losing his leg by a great fragment of shell. Another shell exploded right in the middle of the Cubans, killing and wounding a good many, while the remainder scattered like guinea-hens. Wood's led horse was also shot through the lungs. I at once hustled my regiment over the crest of the hill into the thick underbrush, where I had no little difficulty in getting them together again into column.

Meanwhile the firing continued for fifteen or twenty minutes, until it gradually died away. As the Spaniards used smokeless powder, their artillery had an enormous advantage over ours, and, moreover, we did not have the best type of modern guns, our fire being slow.

As soon as the firing ceased, Wood formed his brigade, with my regiment in front, and gave me orders to follow behind the First Brigade, which was just moving off the ground. In column of fours we marched down the trail toward the ford of the San Juan River. We passed two or three regiments of infantry, and were several times halted before we came to the ford. The First Brigade, which was under Colonel Carroll— Lieutenant-Colonel Hamilton commanding the Ninth Regiment, Major Wessels the Third, and Captain Kerr the Sixth—had already crossed and was marching to the right, parallel to, but a little distance from, the river. The Spaniards in the trenches and block-houses on top of the hills in front were already firing at the brigade in desultory fashion. The extreme advance of the Ninth Cavalry was under Lieutenants McNamee and Hartwick. They were joined by General Hawkins, with his staff, who was looking over the ground and deciding on the route he should take his infantry brigade.

Our orders had been of the vaguest kind, being simply to march to the right and connect with Lawton—with whom, of course, there was no chance of our connecting. No reconnoissance had been made, and the exact position and strength of the Spaniards was not known. A captive balloon was up in the air at this moment, but it was worse than useless. A previous proper reconnoissance and proper look-out from the hills would have given us exact information. As it was, Generals Kent, Sumner, and

Hawkins had to be their own reconnoissance, and they fought their troops so well that we won anyhow.

I was now ordered to cross the ford, march half a mile or so to the right, and then halt and await further orders; and I promptly hurried my men across, for the fire was getting hot, and the captive balloon, to the horror of everybody, was coming down to the ford. Of course, it was a special target for the enemy's fire. I got my men across before it reached the ford. There it partly collapsed and remained, causing severe loss of life, as it indicated the exact position where the Tenth and the First Cavalry, and the infantry, were crossing.

As I led my column slowly along, under the intense heat, through the high grass of the open jungle, the First Brigade was to our left, and the firing between it and the Spaniards on the hills grew steadily hotter and hotter. After awhile I came to a sunken lane, and as by this time the First Brigade had stopped and was engaged in a stand-up fight, I halted my men and sent back word for orders. As we faced toward the Spanish hills my regiment was on the right with next to it and a little in advance the First Cavalry, and behind them the Tenth. In our front the Ninth held the right, the Sixth the centre, and the Third the left; but in the jungle the lines were already overlapping in places. Kent's infantry were coming up, farther to the left.

Captain Mills was with me. The sunken lane, which had a wire fence on either side, led straight up toward, and between, the two hills in our front, the hill on the left, which contained heavy blockhouses, being farther away from us than the hill on our right, which we afterward grew to call Kettle Hill, and which was surmounted merely by some large ranch buildings or haciendas, with sunken brick-lined walls and cellars. I got the men as well-sheltered as I could. Many of them lay close under the bank of the lane, others slipped into the San Juan River and crouched under its hither bank, while the rest lay down behind the patches of bushy jungle in the tall grass. The heat was intense, and many of the men were already showing signs of exhaustion. The sides of the hills in front were bare; but the country up to them was, for the most part, covered with such dense jungle that in charging through it no accuracy of formation could possibly be preserved.

The fight was now on in good earnest, and the Spaniards on the hills were engaged in heavy volley firing. The Mauser bullets drove in sheets through the trees and the tall jungle grass, making a peculiar whirring or rustling sound; some of the bullets seemed to pop in the air, so that we thought they were explosive; and, indeed, many of those which were coated with brass did explode, in the sense that the brass coat was ripped off, making a thick plate of hard metal with a jagged edge, which inflicted a ghastly wound. These bullets were shot from a 45-calibre rifle carrying smokeless powder, which was much used by the guerillas and irregular Spanish troops. The Mauser bullets themselves made a small clean hole, with the result that the wound healed in a most astonishing manner. One or two of our men who were shot in the head had the skull blown open, but elsewhere the wounds from the minute steel-coated bullet, with its very high velocity, were certainly nothing like as serious as those made by the old large-calibre, low-power rifle. If a man was shot through the heart, spine, or brain he was, of course, killed instantly; but very few of the wounded died—even under the appalling conditions which prevailed, owing to the lack of attendance and supplies in the field-hospitals with the army.

While we were lying in reserve we were suffering nearly as much as afterward when we charged. I think that the bulk of the Spanish fire was practically unaimed, or at least not aimed at any particular man, and only occasionally at a particular body of men; but they swept the whole field of battle up to the edge of the river, and man after man in our ranks fell dead or wounded, although I had the troopers scattered out far apart, taking advantage of every scrap of cover.

Devereux was dangerously shot while he lay with his men on the edge of the river. A young West Point cadet, Ernest Haskell, who had taken his holiday with us as an acting second lieutenant, was shot through the stomach. He had shown great coolness and gallantry, which he displayed to an even more marked degree after being wounded, shaking my hand and saying, "All right, Colonel, I'm going to get well. Don't bother about me, and don't let any man come away with me." When I shook hands with him, I thought he would surely die; yet he recovered.

The most serious loss that I and the regiment could have suffered befell just before we charged. Bucky O'Neill was strolling up and down in front of his men, smoking his cigarette, for he was inveterately addicted to the habit. He had a theory that an officer ought never to take cover—a theory which was, of course, wrong, though in a volunteer organization the officers should certainly expose themselves very fully, simply for the effect on the men; our regimental toast on the transport running, "The officers; may the war last until each is killed, wounded, or promoted." As O'Neill moved to and fro, his men begged him to lie down, and one of the sergeants said, "Captain, a bullet is sure to hit you." O'Neill took his cigarette out of his mouth, and blowing out a cloud of smoke laughed and said, "Sergeant, the Spanish bullet isn't made that will kill me." A little later he discussed for a moment with one of the regular officers the direction from which the Spanish fire was coming. As he turned on his heel a bullet struck him in the mouth and came out at the back of his head; so that even before he fell his wild and gallant soul had gone out into the darkness.

My orderly was a brave young Harvard boy, Sanders, from the quaint old Massachusetts town of Salem. The work of an orderly on foot, under the blazing sun, through the hot and matted jungle, was very severe, and finally the heat overcame him. He dropped; nor did he ever recover fully, and later he died from fever. In his place I summoned a trooper whose name I did not know. Shortly afterward, while sitting beside the bank, I directed him to go back and ask whatever general he came across if I could not advance, as my men were being much cut up. He stood up to salute and then pitched forward across my knees, a bullet having gone through his throat, cutting the carotid.

When O'Neill was shot, his troop, who were devoted to him, were for the moment at a loss whom to follow. One of their number, Henry Bardshar, a huge Arizona miner, immediately attached himself to me as my orderly, and from that moment he was closer to me, not only in the fight, but throughout the rest of the campaign, than any other man, not even excepting the color-sergeant, Wright.

Captain Mills was with me; gallant Ship had already been killed. Mills was an invaluable aide, absolutely cool, absolutely unmoved or flurried in any way.

I sent messenger after messenger to try to find General Sumner or General Wood and get permission to advance, and was just about making up my mind that in the absence of orders I had better "march toward the guns," when Lieutenant-Colonel Dorst came riding up through the storm of bullets with the welcome command "to move forward and support the regulars in the assault on the hills in front." General Sumner had obtained authority to advance from Lieutenant Miley, who was representing General Shafter at the front, and was in the thick of the fire. The General at once ordered the first brigade to advance on the hills, and the second to support it. He himself was riding his horse along the lines, superintending the fight. Later I overheard a couple of my men talking together about him. What they said illustrates the value of a display of courage among the officers in hardening their soldiers; for their theme was how, as they were lying down under a fire which they could not return, and were in consequence feeling rather nervous, General Sumner suddenly appeared on horseback, sauntering by quite unmoved; and, said one of the men, "That made us feel all right. If the General could stand it, we could."

The instant I received the order I sprang on my horse and then my "crowded hour" began. The guerillas had been shooting at us from the edges of the jungle and from their perches in the leafy trees, and as they used smokeless powder, it was almost impossible to see them, though a few of my men had from time to time responded. We had also suffered from the hill on our right front, which was held chiefly by guerillas, although there were also some Spanish regulars with them, for we found their dead. I formed my men in column of troops, each troop extended in open skirmishing order, the right resting on the wire fences which bordered the sunken lane. Captain Jenkins led the first squadron, his eyes literally dancing with joyous excitement.

I started in the rear of the regiment, the position in which the colonel should theoretically stay. Captain Mills and Captain McCormick were both with me as aides; but I speedily had to send them off on special duty in getting the different bodies of men forward. I had intended to go into action on foot as at Las Guasimas, but the heat was so oppressive that I found I should be quite unable to run up and down the line and superintend matters unless I was mounted; and, moreover, when on horseback, I could see the men better and they could see me better.

A curious incident happened as I was getting the men started forward. Always when men have been lying down under cover for some time, and are required to advance, there is a little hesitation, each looking to see whether the others are going forward. As I rode down the line, calling to the troopers to go forward, and rasping brief directions to the captains and lieutenants, I came upon a man lying behind a little bush, and I ordered him to jump up. I do not think he understood that we were making a forward move, and he looked up at me for a moment with hesitation, and I again bade him rise, jeering him and saying: "Are you afraid to stand up when I am on horseback?" As I spoke, he suddenly fell forward on his face, a bullet having struck him and gone through him lengthwise. I suppose the bullet had been aimed at me; at any rate, I, who was on horseback in the open, was unhurt, and the man lying flat on the ground in the cover beside me was killed. There were several pairs of brothers with us; of the two Nortons one was killed; of the two McCurdys one was wounded.

I soon found that I could get that line, behind which I personally was, faster forward than the one immediately in front of it, with the result that the two rearmost lines of the regiment began to crowd together; so I rode through them both, the better to move on the one in front. This happened with every line in succession, until I found myself at the head of the regiment.

Both lieutenants of B Troop from Arizona had been exerting themselves greatly, and both were overcome by the heat; but Sergeants Campbell and Davidson took it forward in splendid shape. Some of the men from this troop and from the other Arizona troop (Bucky O'Neill's) joined me as a kind of fighting tail.

The Ninth Regiment was immediately in front of me, and the First on my left, and these went up Kettle Hill with my regiment. The Third, Sixth, and Tenth went partly up Kettle Hill (following the Rough Riders and the Ninth and First), and partly between that and the block-house hill, which the infantry were assailing. General Sumner in person gave the Tenth the order to charge the hills; and it went forward at a rapid gait. The three regiments went forward more or less intermingled, advancing steadily and keeping up a heavy fire. Up Kettle Hill Sergeant George Berry, of the Tenth, bore not only his own regimental colors but those of the Third, the color sergeant of the Third having been shot down; he kept shouting "Dress on the colors, boys, dress on the colors!" as he followed Captain Ayres, who was running in advance of his men, shouting and waving his hat. The Tenth Cavalry lost a greater proportion of its officers than any other regiment in the battle—eleven out of twenty-two.

By the time I had come to the head of the regiment we ran into the left wing of the Ninth Regulars, and some of the First Regulars, who were lying down; that is, the troopers were lying down, while the officers were walking to and fro. The officers of the white and colored regiments alike took the greatest pride in seeing that the men more than did their duty; and the mortality among them was great.

I spoke to the captain in command of the rear platoons, saying that I had been ordered to support the regulars in the attack upon the hills, and that in my judgment we could not take these hills by firing at them, and that we must rush them. He answered that his orders were to keep his men lying where they were, and that he could not charge without orders. I asked where the Colonel was, and as he was not in sight, said, "Then I am the ranking officer here and I give the order to charge"—for I did not want to keep the men longer in the open suffering under a fire which they could not effectively return. Naturally the Captain hesitated to obey this order when no word had been received from his own Colonel. So I said, "Then let my men through, sir," and rode on through the lines, followed by the grinning Rough Riders, whose attention had been completely taken off the Spanish bullets, partly by my dialogue with the regulars, and partly by the language I had been using to themselves as I got the lines forward, for I had been joking with some and swearing at others, as the exigencies of the case seemed to demand. When we started to go through, however, it proved too much for the regulars, and they jumped up and and came along, their officers and troops mingling with mine, all being delighted at the chance. When I got to where the head of the left wing of the Ninth was lying, through the courtesy of Lieutenant Hartwick, two of whose colored troopers threw down the fence, I was enabled to get back into the lane, at the same time waving my hat, and giving the order to charge the hill on our right front. Out of my sight, over on the right, Captains McBlain and Taylor, of the Ninth, made up their minds independently to charge at just about this time; and at almost the same moment Colonels Carroll and Hamilton, who were off, I believe, to my left, where we could see neither them nor their men, gave the order to advance. But of all this I knew nothing at the time. The whole line, tired of waiting, and eager to close with the enemy, was straining to go forward; and it seems that different parts slipped the leash at almost the same moment. The First Cavalry came up the hill just behind, and partly mixed with my regiment and the Ninth. As already said, portions of the Third, Sixth, and Tenth followed, while the rest of the members of these three regiments kept more in touch with the infantry on our left.

By this time we were all in the spirit of the thing and greatly excited by the charge, the men cheering and running forward between shots, while the delighted faces of the foremost officers, like Captain C. J. Stevens, of the Ninth, as they ran at the head of their troops, will always stay in my mind. As soon as I was in the line I galloped forward a few yards until I saw that the men were well started, and then galloped back to help Goodrich, who was in command of his troop, get his men across the road so as to attack the hill from that side. Captain Mills had already thrown three of the other troops of the regiment across this road for the same purpose. Wheeling around, I then again galloped toward the hill passing the shouting, cheering, firing men, and went up the lane, splashing through a small stream; when I got abreast of the ranch buildings on the top of Kettle Hill, I turned and went up the slope. Being on horseback I was, of course, able to get ahead of the men on foot, excepting my orderly, Henry Bardshar, who had run ahead very fast in order to get better shots at the Spaniards, who were now running out of the ranch buildings. Sergeant Campbell and a number of the Arizona men, and Dudley Dean, among others, were very close behind. Stevens, with his platoon of the Ninth, was abreast of us; so were McNamee and Hartwick. Some forty yards from the top I ran into a wire fence and jumped off Little Texas, turning him loose. He had been scraped by a couple of bullets, one of which nicked my elbow, and I never expected to see him again. As I ran up to the hill, Bardshar stopped to shoot, and two Spaniards fell as he emptied his magazine. These were the only Spaniards I actually saw fall to aimed shots by any one of my men, with the exception of two guerillas in trees.

Almost immediately afterwards the hill was covered by the troops, both Rough Riders and the colored troopers of the Ninth, and some men of the First. There was the usual confusion, and afterward there was much discussion as to exactly who had been on the hill first. The first guidons planted there were those of the three New Mexican troops, G, E, and F, of my regiment, under their Captains, Llewellen, Luna, and Muller, but on the extreme right of the hill, at the opposite end from where we struck it, Captains Taylor and McBlain and their men of the Ninth were first up. Each of the five captains was firm in the belief that his troop was first up. As for the individual men, each of whom honestly thought he was first on the summit, their name was legion. One Spaniard was captured in the buildings, another was shot as he tried to hide himself, and a few others were killed as they ran.

Among the many deeds of conspicuous gallantry here performed, two, both to the credit of the First Cavalry, may be mentioned as examples of the others, not as exceptions. Sergeant Charles Karsten, while close beside Captain Tutherly, the squadron commander, was hit by a shrapnel bullet. He continued on the line, firing until his arm grew numb; and he then refused to go to the rear, and devoted himself to taking care of the wounded, utterly unmoved by the heavy fire. Trooper Hugo Brittain, when wounded, brought the regimental standard forward, waving it to and fro, to cheer the men.

No sooner were we on the crest than the Spaniards from the line of hills in our front, where they were strongly intrenched, opened a very heavy fire upon us with their rifles. They also opened upon us with one or two pieces of artillery, using time fuses which burned very accurately, the shells exploding right over our heads.

On the top of the hill was a huge iron kettle, or something of the kind, probably used for sugar refining. Several of our men took shelter behind this. We had a splendid view of the charge on the San Juan block-house to our left, where the infantry of Kent, led by Hawkins, were climbing the hill. Obviously the proper thing to do was to help them, and I got the men together and started them volley-firing against the Spaniards in the San Juan block-house and in the trenches around it. We could only see their heads; of course this was all we ever could see when we were firing at them in their trenches. Stevens was directing not only his own colored troopers, but a number of Rough Riders; for in a mêlée good soldiers are always prompt to recognize a good officer, and are eager to follow him.

We kept up a brisk fire for some five or ten minutes; meanwhile we were much cut up ourselves. Gallant Colonel Hamilton, than whom there was never a braver man, was killed, and equally gallant Colonel Carroll wounded. When near the summit Captain Mills had been shot through the head, the bullet destroying the sight of one eye permanently and of the other temporarily. He would not go back or let any man assist him, sitting down where he was and waiting until one of the men brought him word that the hill was stormed. Colonel Veile planted the standard of the First Cavalry on the hill, and General Sumner rode up. He was fighting his division in great form, and was always himself in the thick of the fire. As the men were much excited by the firing, they seemed to pay very little heed to their own losses.

Suddenly, above the cracking of the carbines, rose a peculiar drumming sound, and some of the men cried, "The Spanish machine-guns!" Listening, I made out that it came from the flat ground to the left, and jumped to my feet, smiting my hand on my thigh, and shouting aloud with exultation, "It's the Gatlings, men, our Gatlings!" Lieutenant Parker was bringing his four Gatlings into action, and shoving them nearer and nearer the front. Now and then the drumming ceased for a moment; then it would resound again, always closer to San Juan hill, which Parker, like ourselves, was hammering to assist the infantry attack. Our men cheered lustily. We saw much of Parker after that, and there was never a more welcome sound than his Gatlings as they opened. It was the only sound which I ever heard my men cheer in battle.

The infantry got nearer and nearer the crest of the hill. At last we could see the Spaniards running from the rifle-pits as the Americans came on in their final rush. Then I stopped my men for fear they should injure their comrades, and called to them to charge the next line of trenches, on the hills in our front, from which we had been undergoing a good deal of punishment. Thinking that the men would all come, I jumped over the wire fence in front of us and started at the double; but, as a matter of fact, the troopers were so excited, what with shooting and being shot, and shouting and cheering, that they did not hear, or did not heed me; and after running about a hundred yards I found I had only five men along with me. Bullets were ripping the grass all around us, and one of the men, Clay Green, was mortally wounded; another, Winslow Clark, a Harvard man, was shot first in the leg and then through the body. He made not the slightest murmur, only asking me to put his water canteen where he could get at it, which I did; he ultimately recovered. There was no use going on with the remaining three men, and I bade them stay where they were while I went back and brought up the rest of the brigade. This was a decidedly cool request, for there was really no possible point in letting them stay there while I went back; but at the moment it seemed perfectly natural to me, and apparently so to them, for they cheerfully nodded, and sat down in the grass, firing back at the line of trenches from which the Spaniards were shooting at them. Meanwhile, I ran back, jumped over the wire fence, and went over the crest of the hill, filled with anger against the troopers, and especially those of my own regiment, for not having accompanied me. They, of course, were quite innocent of wrong-doing;

and even while I taunted them bitterly for not having followed me, it was all I could do not to smile at the look of injury and surprise that came over their faces, while they cried out, "We didn't hear you, we didn't see you go, Colonel; lead on now, we'll sure follow you." I wanted the other regiments to come too, so I ran down to where General Sumner was and asked him if I might make the charge; and he told me to go and that he would see that the men followed. By this time everybody had his attention attracted, and when I leaped over the fence again, with Major Jenkins beside me, the men of the various regiments which were already on the hill came with a rush, and we started across the wide valley which lay between us and the Spanish intrenchments. Captain Dimmick, now in command of the Ninth, was bringing it forward; Captain McBlain had a number of Rough Riders mixed in with his troop, and led them all together; Captain Taylor had been severely wounded. The long-legged men like Greenway, Goodrich, sharp-shooter Proffit, and others outstripped the rest of us, as we had a considerable distance to go. Long before we got near them the Spaniards ran, save a few here and there, who either surrendered or were shot down. When we reached the trenches we found them filled with dead bodies in the light blue and white uniform of the Spanish regular army. There were very few wounded. Most of the fallen had little holes in their heads from which their brains were oozing; for they were covered from the neck down by the trenches.

It was at this place that Major Wessels, of the Third Cavalry, was shot in the back of the head. It was a severe wound, but after having it bound up he again came to the front in command of his regiment. Among the men who were foremost was Lieutenant Milton F. Davis, of the First Cavalry. He had been joined by three men of the Seventy-first New York, who ran up, and, saluting, said, "Lieutenant, we want to go with you, our officers won't lead us." One of the brave fellows was soon afterward shot in the face. Lieutenant Davis's first sergeant, Clarence Gould, killed a Spanish soldier with his revolver, just as the Spaniard was aiming at one of my Rough Riders. At about the same time I also shot one. I was with Henry Bardshar, running up at the double, and two Spaniards leaped from the trenches and fired at us, not ten yards away. As they turned to run I closed in and fired twice, missing the first and killing the second. My revolver was from the sunken battle-ship *Maine*, and had been given me by my brother-in-law, Captain W. S. Cowles, of the Navy. At the time I did not know of Gould's exploit, and supposed my feat to be unique; and although Gould had killed his Spaniard in the trenches, not very far from me, I never learned of it until weeks after. It is astonishing what a limited area of vision and experience one has in the hurly-burly of a battle.

There was very great confusion at this time, the different regiments being completely intermingled—white regulars, colored regulars, and Rough Riders. General Sumner had kept a considerable force in reserve on Kettle Hill, under Major Jackson, of the Third Cavalry. We were still under a heavy fire and I got together a mixed lot of men and pushed on from the trenches and ranch-houses which we had just taken, driving the Spaniards through a line of palm-trees, and over the crest of a chain of hills. When we reached these crests we found ourselves overlooking Santiago. Some of the men, including Jenkins, Greenway, and Goodrich, pushed on almost by themselves far ahead. Lieutenant Hugh Berkely, of the First, with a sergeant and two troopers, reached the extreme front. He was, at the time, ahead of everyone; the sergeant was killed and one trooper wounded; but the lieutenant and the remaining trooper stuck to their post for the rest of the afternoon until our line was gradually extended to include them.

While I was re-forming the troops on the chain of hills, one of General Sumner's aides, Captain Robert Howze—as dashing and gallant an officer as there was in the whole gallant cavalry division, by the way—came up with orders to me to halt where I was, not advancing farther, but to hold the hill at all hazards. Howze had his horse, and I had some difficulty in making him take proper shelter; he stayed with us for quite a time, unable to make up his mind to leave the extreme front, and meanwhile jumping at the chance to render any service, of risk or otherwise, which the moment developed.

I now had under me all the fragments of the six cavalry regiments which were at the extreme front, being the highest officer left there, and I was in immediate command of them for the remainder of the afternoon and that night. The Ninth was over to the right, and the Thirteenth Infantry afterward came up beside it. The rest of Kent's infantry was to our left. Of the Tenth, Lieutenants Anderson, Muller, and Fleming reported to me; Anderson was slightly wounded, but he paid no heed to this. All three, like every other officer, had troopers of various regiments under them; such mixing was inevitable in making repeated charges through thick jungle; it was essentially a troop commanders', indeed, almost a squad leaders', fight. The Spaniards, who had been holding the trenches and the line of hills, had fallen back upon their supports and we were under a very heavy fire both from rifles and great guns. At the point where we were, the grass-covered hill-crest was gently rounded, giving poor cover, and I made my men lie down on the hither slope.

On the extreme left Captain Beck, of the Tenth, with his own troop, and small bodies of the men of other regiments, was exercising a practically independent command, driving back the Spaniards whenever they showed any symptoms of advancing. He had received his orders to hold the line at all hazards from Lieutenant Andrews, one of General Sumner's aides, just as I had received mine from Captain Howze. Finally, he was relieved by some infantry, and then rejoined the rest of the Tenth, which was engaged heavily until dark, Major Wint being among the severely wounded. Lieutenant W. N. Smith was killed. Captain Biglow had been wounded three times.

Our artillery made one or two efforts to come into action on the firing-line of the infantry, but the black powder rendered each attempt fruitless. The Spanish guns used smokeless powder, so that it was difficult to place them. In this respect they were on a par with their own infantry and with our regular infantry and dismounted cavalry; but our only two volunteer infantry regiments, the Second Massachusetts and the Seventy-first New York, and our artillery, all had black powder. This rendered the two volunteer regiments, which were armed with the antiquated Springfield, almost useless in the battle, and did practically the same thing for the artillery wherever it was formed within rifle range. When one of the guns was discharged a thick cloud of smoke shot out and hung over the place, making an ideal target, and in a half minute every Spanish gun and rifle within range was directed at the particular spot thus indicated; the consequence was that after a more or less lengthy stand the gun was silenced or driven off. We got no appreciable help from our guns on July 1st. Our men were quick to realize the defects of our artillery, but they were entirely philosophic about it, not showing the least concern at its failure. On the contrary, whenever they heard our artillery open they would grin as they looked at one another and remark. "There go the guns again; wonder how soon they'll be shut up," and shut up they were sure to be. The light battery of Hotchkiss one-pounders, under Lieutenant J. B. Hughes, of the Tenth Cavalry, was handled with conspicuous gallantry.

On the hill-slope immediately around me I had a mixed force composed of members of most of the cavalry regiments, and a few infantrymen. There were about fifty of my Rough Riders with Lieutenants Goodrich and Carr. Among the rest were perhaps a score of colored infantrymen, but, as it happened, at this particular point without any of their officers. No troops could have behaved better than the colored soldiers had behaved so far; but they are, of course, peculiarly dependent upon their white officers. Occasionally they produce non-commissioned officers who can take the initiative and accept responsibility precisely like the best class of whites; but this cannot be expected normally, nor is it fair to expect it. With the colored troops there should always be some of their own officers; whereas, with the white regulars, as with my own Rough Riders, experience showed that the non-commissioned officers could usually carry on the fight by themselves if they were once started, no matter whether their officers were killed or not. . . .

None of the white regulars or Rough Riders showed the slightest sign of weakening; but under the strain the colored infantrymen (who had none of their officers) began to get a little uneasy and to drift to the rear, either helping wounded men, or saying that they wished to find their own regiments. This I could not allow, as it was depleting my line, so I jumped up, and walking a few yards to the rear, drew my revolver, halted the retreating soldiers, and called out to them that I appreciated the gallantry with which they had fought and would be sorry to hurt them, but that I should shoot the first man who, on any pretence whatever, went to the rear. My own men had all sat up and were watching my movements with the utmost interest; so was Captain Howze. I ended my statement to the colored soldiers by saying: "Now, I shall be very sorry to hurt you, and you don't know whether or not I will keep my word, but my men can tell you that I always do;" whereupon my cow-punchers, hunters, and miners solemnly nodded their heads and commented in chorus, exactly as if in a comic opera, "He always does; he always does!"

This was the end of the trouble, for the "smoked Yankees"—as the Spaniards called the colored soldiers—flashed their white teeth at one another, as they broke into broad grins, and I had no more trouble with them, they seeming to accept me as one of their own officers. The colored cavalrymen had already so accepted me; in return, the Rough Riders, although for the most part South-westerners, who have a strong color prejudice, grew to accept them with hearty good-will as comrades, and were entirely willing, in their own phrase, "to drink out of the same canteen." Where all the regular officers did so well, it is hard to draw any distinction; but in the cavalry division a peculiar meed of praise should be given to the officers of the Ninth and Tenth for their work, and under their leadership the colored troops did as well as any soldiers could possibly do. . . .

As night came on, the firing gradually died away. Before this happened, however, Captains Morton and Boughton, of the Third Cavalry, came over to tell me that a rumor had reached them to the effect that there had been some talk of retiring and that they wished to protest in the strongest manner. I had been watching them both, as they handled their troops with the cool confidence of the veteran regular officer, and had been congratulating myself that they were off toward the right flank, for as long as they were there, I knew I was perfectly safe in that direction. I had heard no rumor about retiring, and I cordially agreed with them that it would be far worse than a blunder to abandon our position.

To attack the Spaniards by rushing across open ground, or through wire entanglements and low, almost impassable jungle, without the help of artillery, and to force unbroken infantry, fighting behind earthworks and armed with the best repeating weapons, supported by cannon, was one thing; to repel such an attack ourselves, or to fight our foes on anything like even terms in the open, was quite another thing. No possible number of Spaniards coming at us from in front could have driven us from our position, and there was not a man on the crest who did not eagerly and devoutly hope that our opponents would make the attempt, for it would surely have been followed, not merely by a repulse, but by our immediately taking the city. There was not an officer or a man on the firing-line, so far as I saw them, who did not feel this way. . . .

Soon after dark, General Wheeler, who in the afternoon had resumed command of the cavalry division, came to the front. A very few words with General Wheeler reassured us about retiring. He had been through too much heavy fighting in the Civil War to regard the present fight as very serious, and he told us not to be under any apprehension, for he had sent word that there was no need whatever of retiring, and was sure we would stay where we were until the chance came to advance. He was second in command; and to him more than to any other one man was due the prompt abandonment of the proposal to fall back—a proposal which, if adopted, would have meant shame and disaster.

Shortly afterward General Wheeler sent us orders to entrench. The men of the different regiments were now getting in place again and sifting themselves out. All of our troops who had been kept at Kettle Hill came forward and rejoined us after nightfall. During the afternoon Greenway, apparently not having enough to do in the fighting, had taken advantage of a lull to explore the buildings himself, and had found a number of Spanish intrenching tools, picks, and shovels, and these we used in digging trenches along our line. The men were very tired indeed, but they went cheerfully to work, all the officers doing their part.

Crockett, the ex-Revenue officer from Georgia, was a slight man, not physically very strong. He came to me and told me he didn't think he would be much use in digging, but that he had found a lot of Spanish coffee and would spend his time making coffee for the men, if I approved. I did approve very heartily, and Crockett officiated as cook for the next three or four hours until the trench was dug, his coffee being much appreciated by all of us.

So many acts of gallantry were performed during the day that it is quite impossible to notice them all, and it seems unjust to single out any; yet I shall mention a few, which it must always be remembered are to stand, not as exceptions, but as instances of what very many men did. It happened that I saw these myself. There were innumerable others, which either were not seen at all, or were seen only by officers who happened not to mention them; and, of course, I know chiefly those that happened in my own regiment. . . .

We finished digging the trench soon after midnight, and then the worn-out men laid down in rows on their rifles and dropped heavily to sleep. About one in ten of them had blankets taken from the Spaniards. Henry Bardshar, my orderly, had procured one for me. He, Goodrich, and I slept together. If the men without blankets had not been so tired that they fell asleep anyhow, they would have been very cold, for, of course, we were all drenched with sweat, and above the waist had on nothing but our flannel shirts, while the night was cool, with a heavy dew. Before any one had time to wake from the cold, however, we were all awakened by the Spaniards, whose skirmishers suddenly opened fire on us. Of course, we could not tell whether or not this was the forerunner of a heavy attack, for our Cossack posts were responding briskly. It was about three o'clock in the morning, at which time men's courage is said to be at the lowest ebb; but the cavalry division was certainly free from any weakness in that direction. At the alarm everybody jumped to his feet and the stiff, shivering, haggard men, their eyes only half opened, all clutched their rifles and ran forward to the trench on the crest of the hill.

The sputtering shots died away and we went to sleep again. But in another hour dawn broke and the Spaniards opened fire in good earnest. There was a little tree only a few feet away, under which I made my headquarters, and while I was lying there, with Goodrich and Keyes, a shrapnel burst among us, not hurting us in the least, but with the sweep of its bullets killing or wounding five men in our rear, one of whom was a singularly gallant young Harvard fellow, Stanley Hollister. An equally gallant young fellow from Yale, Theodore Miller, had already been mortally wounded. Hollister also died.

The Second Brigade lost more heavily than the First; but neither its brigade commander nor any of its regimental commanders were touched, while the commander of the First Brigade and two of its three regimental commanders had been killed or wounded.

In this fight our regiment had numbered 490 men, as, in addition to the killed and wounded of the first fight, some had had to go to the hospital for sickness and some had been left behind with the baggage, or were detailed on other duty. Eighty-nine were killed and wounded: the heaviest loss suffered by any regiment in the cavalry division. The Spaniards made a stiff fight, standing firm until we charged home. They fought much more stubbornly than at Las Guasimas. We ought to have expected this, for they have always done well in holding intrenchments. On this day they showed themselves to be brave foes, worthy of honor for their gallantry.

In the attack on the San Juan hills our forces numbered about 6,600.[¶¶¶]

¶¶¶   According to the official reports, 5,104 officers and men of Kent's infantry, and 2,649 of the cavalry had been landed. My regiment is put down as 542 strong, instead of the real figure, 490, the difference being due to men who were in hospital and on guard at the sea-shore, etc. In other words, the total represents the total landed; the details, etc., are included. General Wheeler, in his report

There were about 4,500 Spaniards against us.**** Our total loss in killed and wounded was 1,071. Of the cavalry division there were, all told, some

---

of July 7th, puts these details as about fifteen per cent of the whole of the force which was on the transports; about eighty-five per cent got forward and was in the fight.

**** The total Spanish force in Santiago under General Linares was 6,000: 4,000 regulars, 1,000 volunteers, and 1,000 marines and sailors from the ships. (Diary of the British Consul, Frederick W. Ramsden, entry of July 1st.) Four thousand more troops entered next day. Of the 6,000 troops, 600 or thereabouts were at El Caney, and 900 in the forts at the mouth of the harbor. Lieutenant Tejeiro states that there were 520 men at El Caney, 970 in the forts at the mouth of the harbor, and 3,000 in the lines, not counting the cavalry and civil guard which were in reserve. He certainly very much understates the Spanish force; thus he nowhere accounts for the engineers mentioned on p. 135; and his figures would make the total number of Spanish artillerymen but 32. He excludes the cavalry, the civil guard, and the marines which had been stationed at the Plaza del Toros; yet he later mentions that these marines were brought up, and their commander, Bustamente, severely wounded; he states that the cavalry advanced to cover the retreat of the infantry, and I myself saw the cavalry come forward, for the most part dismounted, when the Spaniards attempted a forward movement late in the afternoon, and we shot many of their horses; while later I saw and conversed with officers and men of the civil guard who had been wounded at the same time—this in connection with returning them their wives and children, after the latter had fled from the city. Although the engineers are excluded, Lieutenant Tejeiro mentions that their colonel, as well as the colonel of the artillery, was wounded. Four thousand five hundred is surely an understatement of the forces which resisted the attack of the forces under Wheeler. Lieutenant Tejeiro is very careless in his figures. Thus in one place he states that the position of San Juan was held by two companies comprising 250 soldiers. Later he says it was held by three companies, whose strength he puts at 300—thus making them average 100 instead of 125 men apiece. He then mentions another echelon of two companies, so situated as to cross their fire with the others. Doubtless the block-house and trenches at Fort San Juan proper were only held by three or four hundred men; they were taken by the Sixth and Sixteenth Infantry under Hawkins's immediate command; and they formed but one point in the line of hills, trenches, ranch-houses, and block-houses which the Spaniards held, and from which we drove them. When the city capitulated later, over 8,000 unwounded troops and over 16,000 rifles and carbines were surrendered; by that time the marines and sailors had of course gone, and the volunteers had disbanded.

In all these figures I have taken merely the statements from the Spanish side. I am inclined to think the actual numbers were much greater than those here given. Lieutenant Wiley, in his book "In Cuba with Shafter," which is practically an official statement, states that nearly 11,000 Spanish troops were surrendered; and this is the number given by the Spaniards, themselves, in the remarkable letter the captured soldiers addressed to General Shafter, which Wiley quotes in full. Lieutenant Tejeiro, in his chap. xiv explains that the volunteers had disbanded before the end came, and the marines and sailors had of course gone, while nearly a thousand men had been killed or captured or had died of wounds and disease, so that there must have been at least 14,000 all told. Subtracting the reinforcements who arrived on the 2d, this would mean about 10,000 Spaniards present on the 1st: in which case Kent and Wheeler were opposed by at least equal numbers.

2,300 officers and men, of whom 375 were killed and wounded. In the division over a fourth of the officers were killed or wounded, their loss being relatively half as great again as that of the enlisted men—which was as it should be.

I think we suffered more heavily than the Spaniards did in killed and wounded (though we also captured some scores of prisoners). It would have been very extraordinary if the reverse was the case, for we did the charging; and to carry earthworks on foot with dismounted cavalry, when these earthworks are held by unbroken infantry armed with the best modern rifles, is a serious task.

In dealing with the Spanish losses, Lieutenant Tejeiro contradicts himself. He puts their total loss on this day at 593, including 94 killed, 121 missing, and 2 prisoners—217 in all. Yet he states that of the 520 men at Caney but 80 got back, the remaining 440 being killed, captured, or missing. When we captured the city we found in the hospitals over 2,000 seriously wounded and sick Spaniards; on making inquiries, I found that over a third were wounded. From these facts I feel that it is safe to put down the total Spanish loss in battle as at least 1,200, of whom over a thousand were killed and wounded.

Lieutenant Tejeiro, while rightly claiming credit for the courage shown by the Spaniards, also praises the courage and resolution of the Americans, saying that they fought, "con un arrojo y una decision verdaderamente admirables." He dwells repeatedly upon the determination with which our troops kept charging though themselves unprotected by cover. As for the Spanish troops, all who fought them that day will most freely admit the courage they showed. At El Caney, where they were nearly hemmed in, they made a most desperate defence; at San Juan the way to retreat was open, and so, though they were seven times as numerous, they fought with less desperation, but still very gallantly.

Arts
and
Letters

"History as Literature" (1912)

Originally a speech delivered to the American Historical Association soon after Roosevelt's unsuccessful 1912 presidential campaign, this address became the title essay of a 1913 collection. As he would when he later addressed the American Academy of Arts and Letters, Roosevelt seems to relish speaking to scholars and writers on equal terms. Here he situates himself amid the ongoing debates on the role of science in historical writing, a concern that was beginning to bedevil all the humanities about how they might stand on equal footing with science and technology, both in the academy and public culture. For historians the argument developed along the lines of how objective historiography can be. At what point does it make sense to concede some fundamental, even surpassing power of subjectivity, what Roosevelt calls the "imagination"? What are the privileged subjects of historical analysis? What is the function of the historian at the present time? All of these questions occupy Roosevelt as he ruminates on the need to do thorough, painstaking research. He exhorts historians to mind their objective work and that merely "literary imagery" cannot replace patient, extended study. But even as the work of great historians is "wide and lofty," it must also be "sane, clear, and based on full knowledge of the facts and their interrelations." Indeed, for Roosevelt, the binary—science or poetry—that historians think they face is essentially false: "steeped in science" as historians must be, they must also exert the imaginative power to "take the science of history and turn it into literature." Only then can historians live out their proper destiny, and their place in the "modern state rise level to the complex modern needs." And nowhere do those needs assert themselves more vigorously, says Roosevelt at the close, than in the project of writing for the Americans of the future what the Americans of the present and past have truly wrought.

History as Literature

There has been much discussion as to whether history should not henceforth be treated as a branch of science rather than of literature. As with most such discussions, much of the matter in dispute has referred merely to terminology. Moreover, as regards part of the discussion, the minds of the contestants have not met, the propositions advanced by the two sides being neither mutually incompatible nor mutually relevant. There is, however, a real basis for conflict in so far as science claims exclusive possession of the field.

There was a time—we see it in the marvellous dawn of Hellenic life— when history was distinguished neither from poetry, from mythology, nor from the first dim beginnings of science. There was a more recent time, at the opening of Rome's brief period of literary splendor, when poetry was accepted by a great scientific philosopher as the appropriate vehicle for teaching the lessons of science and philosophy. There was a more recent time still—the time of Holland's leadership in arms and arts—when one of the two or three greatest world painters put his genius at the service of anatomists.

In each case the steady growth of specialization has rendered such combination now impossible. Virgil left history to Livy; and when Tacitus had become possible Lucan was a rather absurd anachronism. The elder Darwin, when he endeavored to combine the functions of scientist and poet, may have thought of Lucretius as a model; but the great Darwin was incapable of such a mistake. The surgeons of today would prefer the services of a good photographer to those of Rembrandt—even were those of Rembrandt available. No one would now dream of combining the history of the Trojan War with a poem on the wrath of Achilles.

Beowulf's feats against the witch who dwelt under the water would not now be mentioned in the same matter-of-fact way that a Frisian or Frankish raid is mentioned. We are long past the stage when we would accept as parts of the same epic Siegfried's triumphs over dwarf and dragon, and even a distorted memory of the historic Hunnish king in whose feast-hall the Burgundian heroes held their last revel and made their death fight. We read of the loves of the Hound of Muirthemne and Emer the Fair without attributing to the chariot-riding heroes who "fought over the ears of their horses," and to their fierce ladyloves more than a symbolic reality. The Roland of the Norman trouvères, the Roland who blew the ivory horn at Roncesvalles, is to our minds wholly distinct from the actual Warden of the Marches who fell in a rear-guard skirmish with the Pyrenean Basques.

As regards philosophy, as distinguished from material science and from history, the specialization has been incomplete. Poetry is still used as a vehicle for the teaching of philosophy. Goethe was as profound a thinker as Kant. He has influenced the thought of mankind far more deeply than Kant because he was also a great poet. Robert Browning was a real philosopher, and his writings have had a hundredfold the circulation and the effect of those of any similar philosopher who wrote in prose, just because, and only because, what he wrote was not merely philosophy but literature. The form in which he wrote challenged attention and provoked admiration. That part of his work which some of us—which I myself, for instance—most care for is merely poetry. But in that part of his work which has exercised most attraction and has given him the widest reputation, the poetry, the form of expression, bears to the thought expressed much the same relation that the expression of Lucretius bears to the thought of Lucretius. As regards this, the great mass of his product, he is primarily a philosopher, whose writings surpass in value those of other similar philosophers precisely because they are not only philosophy but literature. In other words, Browning the philosopher is read by countless thousands to whom otherwise philosophy would be a sealed book, for exactly the same reason that Macaulay the historian is read by countless thousands to whom otherwise history would be a sealed book; because both Browning's works and Macaulay's works are material additions to the great sum of English literature. Philosophy is a science just as history is a science. There is need in one case as in the other for vivid and powerful presentation of scientific matter in literary form.

This does not mean that there is the like need in the two cases. History can never be truthfully presented if the presentation is purely emotional. It can never be truthfully or usefully presented unless profound research, patient, laborious, painstaking, has preceded the presentation. No amount of self-communion and of pondering on the soul of mankind, no gorgeousness of literary imagery, can take the place of cool, serious, widely extended study. The vision of the great historian must be both wide and lofty. But it must be sane, clear, and based on full knowledge of the facts and of their interrelations. Otherwise we get merely a splendid bit of serious romance-writing, like Carlyle's "French Revolution." Many hard-working students, alive to the deficiencies of this kind of romance-writing, have grown to distrust not only all historical writing that is romantic, but all historical writing that is vivid. They feel that complete truthfulness must never be sacrificed to color. In this they are right. They also feel that complete truthfulness is incompatible with color. In this they are wrong. The immense importance of full knowledge of a mass of dry facts and gray details has so impressed them as to make them feel that the dryness and the grayness are in themselves meritorious.

These students have rendered invaluable service to history. They are right in many of their contentions. They see how literature and science have specialized. They realize that scientific methods are as necessary to the proper study of history as to the proper study of astronomy or zoology. They know that in many, perhaps in most, of its forms, literary ability is divorced from the restrained devotion to the actual fact which is as essential to the historian as to the scientist. They know that nowadays science ostentatiously disclaims any connection with literature. They feel that if this is essential for science, it is no less essential for history.

There is much truth in all these contentions. Nevertheless, taking them all together, they do not indicate what these hard-working students believed that they indicate. Because history, science, and literature have all become specialized, the theory now is that science is definitely severed from literature and that history must follow suit. Not only do I refuse to accept this as true for history, but I do not even accept it as true for science.

Literature may be defined as that which has permanent interest because both of its substance and its form, aside from the mere technical value that inheres in a special treatise for specialists. For a great work of literature there is the same demand now that there always has been; and in any great work of literature the first element is great imaginative power. The imaginative power demanded for a great historian is different from that demanded for a great poet; but it is no less marked. Such imaginative power is in no sense incompatible with minute accuracy. On the contrary, very accurate, very real and vivid, presentation of the past can come only from one in whom the imaginative gift is strong. The industrious collector of dead facts bears to such a man precisely the relation that a photographer bears to Rembrandt. There are innumerable books, that is, innumerable volumes of printed matter between covers, which are excellent for their own purposes, but in which imagination would be as wholly out of place as in the blueprints of a sewer system or in the photographs taken to illustrate a work on comparative osteology. But the vitally necessary sewer system does not take the place of the cathedral of Rheims or of the Parthenon; no quantity of photographs will ever be equivalent to one Rembrandt; and the greatest mass of data, although indispensable to the work of a great historian, is in no shape or way a substitute for that work.

History, taught for a directly and immediately useful purpose to pupils and the teachers of pupils, is one of the necessary features of a sound education in democratic citizenship. A book containing such sound teaching, even if without any literary quality, may be as useful to the student and as creditable to the writer as a similar book on medicine. I am not slighting such a book when I say that once it has achieved its worthy purpose it can be permitted to lapse from human memory as a good book on medicine, which has outlived its usefulness, lapses from memory. But the historical work which does possess literary quality may be a permanent contribution to the sum of man's wisdom, enjoyment, and inspiration. The writer of such a book must add wisdom to knowledge, and the gift of expression to the gift of imagination.

It is a shallow criticism to assert that imagination tends to inaccuracy. Only a distorted imagination tends to inaccuracy. Vast and fundamental truths can be discerned and interpreted only by one whose imagination is as lofty as the soul of a Hebrew prophet. When we say that the great historian must be a man of imagination, we use the word as we use it when we say that the great statesman must be a man of imagination. Moreover, together with imagination must go the power of expression. The great speeches of statesmen and the great writings of historians can live only if they possess the deathless quality that inheres in all great literature. The greatest literary historian must of necessity be a master of the science of history, a man who has at his finger-tips all the accumulated facts from the treasure-houses of the dead past. But he must also possess the power to marshal what is dead so that before our eyes it lives again.

Many learned people seem to feel that the quality of readableness in a book is one which warrants suspicion. Indeed, not a few learned people seem to feel that the fact that a book is interesting is proof that it is shallow. This is particularly apt to be the attitude of scientific men. Very few great scientists have written interestingly, and these few have usually felt apologetic about it. Yet sooner or later the time will come when the mighty sweep of modern scientific discovery will be placed, by scientific men with the gift of expression, at the service of intelligent and cultivated laymen. Such service will be inestimable. Another writer of "Canterbury Tales," another singer of "Paradise Lost," could not add more to the sum of literary achievement than the man who may picture to us the phases of the age-long history of life on this globe, or make vivid before our eyes the tremendous march of the worlds through space.

Indeed, I believe that already science has owed more than it suspects to the unconscious literary power of some of its representatives. Scientific writers of note had grasped the fact of evolution long before Darwin and Huxley; and the theories advanced by these men to explain evolution were not much more unsatisfactory, as full explanations, than the theory of natural selection itself. Yet, where their predecessors had created hardly a ripple, Darwin and Huxley succeeded in effecting a complete revolution in the thought of the age, a revolution as great as that caused by the discovery of the truth about the solar system. I believe that the chief explanation of the difference was the very simple one that what Darwin and Huxley wrote was interesting to read. Every cultivated man soon had their volumes in his library, and they still keep their places on our bookshelves. But Lamarck and Cope are only to be found in the libraries of a few special students. If they had possessed a gift of expression akin to Darwin's, the doctrine of evolution would not in the popular mind have been confounded with the doctrine of natural selection and a juster estimate than at present would obtain as to the relative merits of the explanations of evolution championed by the different scientific schools.

Do not misunderstand me. In the field of historical research an immense amount can be done by men who have no literary power whatever. Moreover, the most painstaking and laborious research, covering long periods of years, is necessary in order to accumulate the material for any history worth writing at all. There are important bypaths of history, moreover, which hardly admit of treatment that would make them of interest to any but specialists. All this I fully admit. In particular I pay high honor to the patient and truthful investigator. He does an indispensable work. My claim is merely that such work should not exclude the work of the great master who can use the materials gathered, who has the gift of vision, the quality of the seer, the power himself to see what has happened and to make what he has seen clear to the vision of others. My only protest is against those who believe that the extension of the activities of the most competent mason and most energetic contractor will supply the lack of great architects. If, as in the Middle Ages, the journeymen builders are themselves artists, why this is the best possible solution of the problem. But if they are not artists, then their work, however much it represents of praiseworthy industry, and of positive usefulness, does not take the place of the work of a great artist. . . .

The great historian of the future will have easy access to innumerable facts patiently gathered by tens of thousands of investigators, whereas the great historian of the past had very few facts, and often had to gather most of these himself. The great historian of the future cannot be excused if he fails to draw on the vast storehouses of knowledge that have been accumulated, if he fails to profit by the wisdom and work of other men, which are now the common property of all intelligent men. He must use the instruments which the historians of the past did not have ready to hand. Yet even with these instruments he cannot do as good work as the best of the elder historians unless he has vision and imagination, the power to grasp what is essential and to reject the infinitely more numerous non-essentials, the power to embody ghosts, to put flesh and blood on dry bones, to make dead men living before our eyes. In short, he must have the power to take the science of history and turn it into literature.

Those who wish history to be treated as a purely utilitarian science often decry the recital of the mighty deeds of the past, the deeds which always have aroused, and for a long period to come are likely to arouse, most interest. These men say that we should study not the unusual but the usual. They say that we profit most by laborious research into the drab monotony of the ordinary, rather than by fixing our eyes on the purple patches that break it. Beyond all question the great historian of the future must keep ever in mind the relative importance of the usual and the unusual. If he is a really great historian, if he possesses the highest imaginative and literary quality, he will be able to interest us in the gray tints of the general landscape no less than in the flame hues of the jutting peaks. It is even more essential to have such quality in writing of the commonplace than in writing of the exceptional. Otherwise no profit will come from study of the ordinary; for writings are useless unless they are read, and they cannot be read unless they are readable. Furthermore, while doing full justice to the importance of the usual, of the commonplace, the great historian will not lose sight of the importance of the heroic.

It is hard to tell just what it is that is most important to know. The wisdom of one generation may seem the folly of the next. This is just as true of the wisdom of the dry-as-dusts as of the wisdom of those who write interestingly. Moreover, while the value of the by-products of knowledge does not readily yield itself to quantitative expression, it is none the less real. A utilitarian education should undoubtedly be the foundation of all education. But it is far from advisable, it is far from wise, to have it the end of all education. Technical training will more and more be accepted as the prime factor in our educational system, a factor as essential for the farmer, the blacksmith, the seamstress, and the cook, as for the lawyer, the doctor, the engineer, and the stenographer. For similar reasons the purely practical and technical lessons of history, the lessons that help us to grapple with our immediate social and industrial problems, will also receive greater emphasis than ever before. But if we are wise we will no more permit this practical training to exclude knowledge of that part of literature which is history than of that part of literature which is poetry. Side by side with the need for the perfection of the individual in the technic of his special calling goes the need of broad human sympathy, and the need of lofty and generous emotion in that individual. Only thus can the citizenship of the modern state rise level to the complex modern social needs.

No technical training, no narrowly utilitarian study of any kind will meet this second class of needs. In part they can best be met by a training that will fit men and women to appreciate, and therefore to profit by, great poetry and those great expressions of the historian and the statesman which rivet our interest and stir our souls. Great thoughts match and inspire heroic deeds. The same reasons that make the Gettysburg speech and the Second Inaugural impress themselves on men's minds far more deeply than technical treatises on the constitutional justification of slavery or of secession, apply to fitting descriptions of the great battle and the great contest which occasioned the two speeches. The tense epic of the Gettysburg fight, the larger epic of the whole Civil War, when truthfully and vividly portrayed, will always have, and ought always to have, an attraction, an interest, that cannot be roused by the description of the same number of hours or years of ordinary existence. There are supreme moments in which intensity and not duration is the all-important element. History which is not professedly utilitarian, history which is didactic only as great poetry is unconsciously didactic, may yet possess that highest form of usefulness, the power to thrill the souls of men with stories of strength and craft and daring, and to lift them out of their common selves to the heights of high endeavor.

The greatest historian should also be a great moralist. It is no proof of impartiality to treat wickedness and goodness as on the same level. But of course the obsession of purposeful moral teaching may utterly defeat its own aim. Moreover, unfortunately, the avowed teacher of morality, when he writes history, sometimes goes very far wrong indeed. It often happens that the man who can be of real help in inspiring others by his utterances on abstract principles is wholly unable to apply his own principles to concrete cases. Carlyle offers an instance in point. Very few men have ever been a greater source of inspiration to other ardent souls than was Carlyle when he confined himself to preaching morality in the abstract. Moreover, his theory bade him treat history as offering material to support that theory. But not only was he utterly unable to distinguish either great virtues or great vices when he looked abroad on contemporary life—as witness his attitude toward our own Civil War—but he was utterly unable to apply his own principles concretely in history. His "Frederick the Great" is literature of a high order. It may, with reservations, even be accepted as history. But the "morality" therein jubilantly upheld is shocking to any man who takes seriously Carlyle's other writings in which he lays down principles of conduct. In his "Frederick the Great" he was not content to tell the facts. He was not content to announce his admiration. He wished to square himself with his theories, and to reconcile what he admired, both with the actual fact and with his previously expressed convictions on morality. He could only do so by refusing to face the facts and by using words with meanings that shifted to meet his own mental emergencies. He pretended to discern morality where no vestige of it existed. He tortured the facts to support his views. The "morality" he praised had no connection with morality as understood in the New Testament. It was the kind of archaic morality observed by the Danites in their dealings with the people of Laish. The sermon of the Mormon bishop in Owen Wister's "Pilgrim on the Gila" sets forth the only moral lessons which it was possible for Carlyle truthfully to draw from the successes he described.

History must not be treated as something set off by itself. It should not be treated as a branch of learning bound to the past by the shackles of an iron conservatism. It is neither necessary rigidly to mark the limits of the province of history, nor to treat of all that is within that province, nor to exclude any subject within that province from treatment, nor yet to treat different methods of dealing with the same subject as mutually exclusive. Every writer and every reader has his own needs, to meet himself or to be met by others. Among a great multitude of thoughtful people there is room for the widest possible variety of appeals. Let each man fearlessly choose what is of real importance and interest to him personally, reverencing authority, but not in a superstitious spirit, because he must needs reverence liberty even more. . . .

The great historian must be able to paint for us the life of the plain people, the ordinary men and women, of the time of which he writes. He can do this only if he possesses the highest kind of imagination. Collections of figures no more give us a picture of the past than the reading of a tariff report on hides or woolens gives us an idea of the actual lives of the men and women who live on ranches or work in factories. The great historian will in as full measure as possible present to us the every-day life of the men and women of the age which he describes. Nothing that tells of this life will come amiss to him. The instruments of their labor and the weapons of their warfare, the wills that they wrote, the bargains that they made, and the songs that they sang when they feasted and made love: he must use them all. He must tell us of the toil of the ordinary times, and of the play by which that ordinary toil was broken. He must never forget that no event stands out entirely isolated. He must trace from its obscure and humble beginnings each of the movements that in its hour of triumph has shaken the world.

Yet he must not forget that the times that are extraordinary need especial portrayal. In the revolt against the old tendency of historians to deal exclusively with the spectacular and the exceptional, to treat only of war and oratory and government, many modern writers have gone to the opposite extreme. They fail to realize that in the lives of nations as in the lives of men there are hours so fraught with weighty achievement, with triumph or defeat, with joy or sorrow, that each such hour may determine all the years that are to come thereafter, or may outweigh all the years that have gone before. In the writings of our historians, as in the lives of our ordinary citizens, we can neither afford to forget that it is the ordinary every-day life which counts most; nor yet that seasons come when ordinary qualities count for but little in the face of great contending forces of good and of evil, the outcome of whose strife determines whether the nation shall walk in the glory of the morning or in the gloom of spiritual death.

The historian must deal with the days of common things, and deal with them so that they shall interest us in reading of them as our own common things interest us as we live among them. He must trace the changes that come almost unseen, the slow and gradual growth that transforms for good or for evil the children and grandchildren so that they stand high above or far below the level on which their forefathers stood. He must also trace the great cataclysms that interrupt and divert this gradual development. He can no more afford to be blind to one class of phenomena than to the other. He must ever remember that while the worst offense of which he can be guilty is to write vividly and inaccurately, yet that unless he writes vividly he cannot write truthfully; for no amount of dull, painstaking detail will sum up as the whole truth unless the genius is there to paint the truth. . . .

The true historian will bring the past before our eyes as if it were the present. He will make us see as living men the hard-faced archers of Agincourt, and the war-worn spearmen who followed Alexander down beyond the rim of the known world. We shall hear grate on the coast of Britain the keels of the Low-Dutch sea-thieves whose children's children were to inherit unknown continents. We shall thrill to the triumphs of Hannibal. Gorgeous in our sight will rise the splendor of dead cities, and the might of the elder empires of which the very ruins crumbled to dust ages ago. Along ancient trade-routes, across the world's waste spaces, the caravans shall move; and the admirals of uncharted seas shall furrow the oceans with their lonely prows. Beyond the dim centuries we shall see the banners float above armed hosts. We shall see conquerors riding forward to victories that have changed the course of time. We shall listen to the prophecies of forgotten seers. Ours shall be the dreams of dreamers who dreamed greatly, and who saw in their vision peaks so lofty that never yet have they been reached by the sons and daughters of men. Dead poets shall sing to us the deeds of men of might and the love and the beauty of women. We shall see the dancing girls of Memphis. The scent of the flowers in the Hanging Gardens of Babylon will be heavy to our senses. We shall sit at feast with the kings of Nineveh when they drink from ivory and gold. With Queen Meave in her sun-parlor we shall watch the nearing chariots of the champions. For us the war-horns of King Olaf shall wail across the flood, and the harps sound high at festivals in forgotten halls. The frowning strongholds of the barons of old shall rise before us, and the white palace-castles from whose windows Syrian princes once looked across the blue Ægean. We shall know the valor of the two-sworded Samurai. Ours shall be the hoary wisdom and the strange, crooked folly of the immemorial civilizations which tottered to a living death in India and in China. We shall see the terrible horsemen of Timour the Lame ride over the roof of the world; we shall hear the drums beat as the armies of Gustavus and Frederick and Napoleon drive forward to victory. Ours shall be the woe of burgher and peasant, and ours the stern joy when freemen triumph and justice comes to her own. The agony of the galley-slaves shall be ours, and the rejoicing when the wicked are brought low and the men of evil days have their reward. We shall see the glory of triumphant violence, and the revel of those who do wrong in high places; and the broken-hearted despair that lies beneath the glory and the revel. We shall also see the supreme righteousness of the wars for freedom and justice, and know that the men who fell in these wars made all mankind their debtors.

Some day the historians will tell us of these things. Some day, too, they will tell our children of the age and the land in which we now live.

They will portray the conquest of the continent. They will show the slow beginnings of settlement, the growth of the fishing and trading towns on the seacoast, the hesitating early ventures into the Indian-haunted forest. Then they will show the backwoodsmen, with their long rifles and their light axes, making their way with labor and peril through the wooded wilderness to the Mississippi; and then the endless march of the white-topped wagon-trains across plain and mountain to the coast of the greatest of the five great oceans. They will show how the land which the pioneers won slowly and with incredible hardship was filled in two generations by the overflow from the countries of western and central Europe. The portentous growth of the cities will be shown, and the change from a nation of farmers to a nation of business men and artisans, and all the far-reaching consequences of the rise of the new industrialism. The formation of a new ethnic type in this melting-pot of the nations will be told. The hard materialism of our age will appear, and also the strange capacity for lofty idealism which must be reckoned with by all who would understand the American character. A people whose heroes are Washington and Lincoln, a peaceful people who fought to a finish one of the bloodiest of wars, waged solely for the sake of a great principle and a noble idea, surely possess an emergency-standard far above mere money-getting.

Those who tell the Americans of the future what the Americans of today and of yesterday have done will perforce tell much that is unpleasant. This is but saying that they will describe the arch-typical civilization of this age. Nevertheless, when the tale is finally told, I believe that it will show that the forces working for good in our national life outweigh the forces working for evil, and that, with many blunders and shortcomings, with much halting and turning aside from the path, we shall yet in the end prove our faith by our works, and show in our lives our belief that righteousness exalteth a nation.

"An Introduction to American Literature"
(1896)

In this brief review of Brander Matthews's critical study on American writers, Roosevelt exhibits his interest in belles lettres, perhaps the least appreciated aspect of his career as a writer. While extolling his friend's felicitous style, he also praises the Columbia University professor's critical understanding. Similarly was Roosevelt pleased that Matthews's erudition was never couched in the language of the "small pedant." Here Roosevelt is explicitly expressing his distrust of the new academic industry of literary scholars whose interest in American writing was then burgeoning. But he is perhaps also venting his frustration with himself for having given up a career as a professional writer.

An Introduction to American Literature

A thoroughly good book for young people is almost invariably one of the best books that grown people can read. Similarly, an introduction to any study, if done as it should be, by a man capable of writing not merely the introduction, but also the study itself, is certain to be of interest to the most advanced student.

Mr. Brander Matthews's volume on American literature is a piece of work as good of its kind as any American scholar has ever had in his hands. It is just the kind of book which should be given to a beginner, because it will give him a clear idea of what to read, and of the relative importance of the authors he is to read; but it is much more than merely a book for beginners. Any student of the subject who wishes to do good work hereafter must not only read Mr. Matthews's book, but must largely adopt Mr. Matthews's way of looking at things; for these simply written, unpretentious chapters are worth many times as much as the ponderous tomes which contain what usually passes for criticism of our literary work; and the principles upon which Mr. Matthews insists with such quiet force and good taste are those which must be adopted, not only by every student of American writings, but by every American writer if he is going to do work that is really worth doing.

In his opening chapters Mr. Matthews very happily defines literature as "a written record so skilfully made as to give pleasure to the reader." It seems rather odd that it should be necessary to insist upon the fact that the essence of a book is to be readable; but most certainly the average scientific or historical writer needs to have this elementary proposition drilled into his brain. Perhaps if this drilling were once accomplished, we Americans would stand a greater chance of producing an occasional Darwin or Gibbon; though there would necessarily be some havoc in the ranks of those small pedants who with laborious industry produce works which are never read excepting by other small pedants, or else by the rare master who can take the myriad bricks of these myriad little workers and out of them erect one of the great buildings of thought.

Perhaps the best, because the most original, point made by Mr. Matthews is his insistence upon what American literature really is. He shows that it is a branch of English literature, but not a branch of that portion of English literature which is created contemporaneously in the British Isles, and which he very appropriately calls British literature. American literature of this century, like British literature of this century, is a branch of the great stock of English literature, the literature common to all the English-speaking peoples. In the past not only English, but also American authors have often seemed to take it for granted that the literature produced in Great Britain at the present day was in a peculiar sense the English literature of the present day, and the representative in the direct line of the English literature of the past. This is, of course, not true. A New York novelist is no more and no less the heir of the creator of "Moll Flanders" than is a London novelist. The Biglow papers contain as much of the broad humanity of Chaucer as any contemporary poem published in Great Britain, and their author was as much influenced, consciously or unconsciously, as his average British contemporary, by the man who five centuries before had written high thoughts in a homely tongue.

It seems extraordinary that it should have been left to Mr. Matthews to formulate what so many Americans had felt—namely, that the American has precisely the same right to the English speech as the Briton. He is not the Briton's younger brother, any more than he is his elder brother. Each has an equal claim to a common inheritance—the inheritance of the great language and literature which are the most precious possessions of the two nations. If the present-day literature of either America or Great Britain depart in any way from the standards of the past—as depart it must—the departure must be judged purely on its own merits, and without the least regard to what course literature is taking in the other country at the same time. England has no more right to set the standard for America than America has to set the standard for England. The standard is set partly by the great masters of the past, partly by the force and good taste of the masters of the present day; it has nothing to do with any artificial standard raised in the other country; and neither country has the slightest right to treat a variation from its own standard as being a variation from the true standard of English literature. These points have been successfully elaborated by Mr. Matthews in his "Americanisms and Briticisms," which is by far the most noteworthy critical or literary essay which has been published by any American writer for a score of years.

American literature must naturally develop on its own lines. Politically, Americans, unlike Canadians and Australians, are free from the colonial spirit which accepts, as a matter of course, the inferiority of the colonist as compared to the man who stays at home in the mother country. We are not entirely free as yet, however, from this colonial idea in matters social and literary. Sometimes it shows itself in an uneasy self-consciousness, whether of self-assertion or self-depreciation; but it always tacitly admits the assumption that American literature should in some way be tried by the standard of contemporary British literature. Mr. Matthews, with entire good temper, and with complete absence of literary Chauvinism, shows the folly of this view.

In dealing with the authors whom he has chosen as representatives of American literature, Mr. Matthews has sketched briefly the life and life-work of each. He has accomplished the difficult feat of writing so as to be "understanded of the multitude," without conveying any impression of writing *down* to the multitude. Each chapter is eminently readable and interesting; but it also always contains a singularly just estimate of the author's real worth. Mr. Matthews's wide and deep acquaintance not only with American literature, but with the literatures of other countries, enables him to place each author about where he belongs. Of course there must be individual differences of opinion. The present reviewer, for instance, is inclined to think that the relative importance given, on the one hand, to Halleck and Drake, and on the other, to Motley and Prescott and Walt Whitman could with advantage have been reversed, and that more stress might have been laid upon some of Longfellow's ballad-like poems, such as "The Discoverer of the North Cape," and, especially, the "Saga of King Olaf"; but these are matters of detail. There is very little room for division of opinion as to the excellence of Mr. Matthews's arrangement as a whole and as to the soundness of his judgments. He preserves always the difficult proper balance between sympathy and justice. He deserves especial credit for recognising in Parkman the greatest American historian. No better little sketch of Franklin has ever appeared than that which he gives; he is profoundly impressed by Franklin's greatness, and yet he shows, in a sentence in which he contrasts him with Abraham Lincoln, his appreciation of that side of Franklin's character wherein the philosopher fell short. His power of appreciating infinitely different qualities is shown by his capital sketches of Cooper and Hawthorne. Where all the work is so good it is difficult to choose, but the chapters on Lowell and Holmes are singularly appreciative and just.

In short, Mr. Matthews has produced an admirable book, both in manner and in matter, and has made a distinct addition to the very literature of which he writes.

"Nationalism in Literature and Art" (1916)

Near the end of his life, Roosevelt frequently turned to some of his earliest concerns, and this address to a joint meeting of the American Academy of Arts and Letters and the National Institute of Arts and Letters provided him with the occasion to revisit his ideas about the beaux arts and the expression of national genius, a question that had occupied various writers and thinkers for most of the nineteenth century and about which Roosevelt had very little original to say. What does distinguish the speech is the way Roosevelt relates the idea of a lively, substantive national artistic life with a country's ambition of attaining international prestige. Roosevelt believed that in order for a nation to be taken seriously, it ought to be able to point to a literature or aesthetic range of accomplishments to demonstrate the vitality of its national character and the viability of its national politics. The idea that a nation had such a combined *Volksgeist* and *Zeitgeist* dominated the preceding century's cultural historiographies, with each country asserting the uniqueness and legitimacy of its contribution to art as expressing some national temper. That challenge gives Roosevelt his chance to intervene in then-current debates about how American literature was losing its ties to its English antecedents. In Roosevelt's point of view, if America is reshaping itself along such lines, then its art must reflect this new diversity or it will be dishonest. Moreover, as much as he applauds the characteristically American artist (like Remington) and distrusts the cosmopolite (like Henry James) who absents himself from his country, he holds that it would be foolishly provincial and willfully ignorant to imagine that either one country had nothing to learn or another everything to teach. Thus it is wise to be internationally minded, even as it is foolish to imitate servilely, since appropriating a country's art without absorbing into its own genius, contributes nothing to a nation's cultural treasure.

Nationalism in Literature and Art

Mr. Chancellor, our distinguished guest, Monsieur Lanson, fellow members of the Academy and Institute: I am in the position of having had my speech made for me by Monsieur Lanson far better than I could make it. I do not mean that I am to speak about France; but that what I have to say on "Nationalism in Literature and Art" has been said by our guest with that clearness and fineness of expression which can perhaps be attained only by masters of the French language.

And let me at the outset say anent the tribute paid to William James as having familiarized France with the philosophy of pragmatism, that not a few of us admired William James without clearly understanding him until Monsieur Émile Boutroux translated him for us.

In speaking of the French genius, Monsieur Lanson has most clearly set forth the attitude that should be taken in every country as regards both the duty of seeking for everything good that can be contributed by outside nations and the further duty of refusing merely to reproduce or copy what is thus taken, but of adapting it and transmuting it until it becomes part of the national mind and expression.

There is only one thing worse than the stolid refusal to accept what is great and beautiful from outside, and that is servilely to copy it. Monsieur Lanson must permit me to say that even the greatest authors do not shine at their best when they are nearest to copying a foreign masterpiece. A great French dramatist has produced a play modelled on a great Spanish epic, and the great English dramatist in "Troilus and Cressida" adapted part of a mediævalized tradition of Homer. I think I prefer the Spanish epic to the French drama in that particular case, and I know that I prefer even a dozen lines of the Greek epic to all but half a dozen lines of the

English play—although in some of his other plays I believe that the dramatist in question rose above all the other poets of all time.

The greatest good that is done by the reception and the assimilation of a foreign culture is in the effect on the mind of the person who so assimilates it that he can use it in doing productive work in accordance with the genius of his own country.

I cannot forbear saying in the presence of Monsieur Lanson a word as to the debt we all owe France for the French example, and especially the French example at this moment. As one of our own beloved American writers who is present with us today has said—in speaking of what he will hardly pardon me for calling a warped, although a rugged, genius of American poetry, Walt Whitman—as John Burroughs has said, strength comes before beauty and valor before grace. If France had been only a literary and artistic country, we should not now have the feeling that we have as we rise to our feet when French heroism is mentioned.

The other day I was interested in certain paleontological and archæological studies at the point where the two sciences come together, and I happened to be reading the work of a great Frenchman. I made inquiries about him, and found that he is dead in the trenches, because, although he was a great archæologist, he put patriotism, love of country, and the duty to be a man ahead of the duty of being a scientific or literary man.

There is another example for us in France. Our guest has correctly said that the Frenchman is not bound by local ideas: he is national; he is not addicted merely to the cult of belfry patriotism; he is content to be a Frenchman and nothing else. It would be well for us here, when we grow a little melancholy as to the time taken by the melting-pot to turn out a purely American product, to remember that, vast though this country is, the racial differences are not one whit greater in our population than in the population of France. The Norman, the Breton, the Gascon, the man of Languedoc, the man of the centre of France, represent the extreme types of all the different races of central and western Europe; but they have all been assimilated into one coherent and distinctive French nationality, so that the man of Toulouse, the man of Rouen, the man of Marseilles, the man of Lyons or of Paris, are all essentially alike, despite the wide differences in blood and ancestry. This is something worth our while remembering, and it is something that is encouraging to remember.

And in what I am about to say it really would hardly be necessary for me to do more than to tell us to take example by the development of French art and literature from the days of the "Song of Roland" down to the present year.

French literature has changed much. Our guest will allow me to comment upon the fact that in the great epic which I have mentioned, a great, typical French poem, containing scores of thousands of lines, only one woman—at least only one Frenchwoman—is mentioned, and only three lines are devoted to her, and two of these lines describe her death. There has been development in French literature since that time!

France has helped humanity because France has remained French. There is no more hopeless creature from the point of view of humanity than the person who calls himself a cosmopolitan, who spreads himself out over the whole world, with the result that he spreads himself out so thin that he comes through in large spots. We can help humanity at large very much to the extent that we are national—in the proper sense, not in the chauvinistic sense—that we are devoted to our own country first. I prize the friendship of the man who cares for his family more than he cares for me; if he does not care for his family any more than he cares for me, I know that he cares for me very little. What is true in individual relations is no less true in the world at large.

So you see that the most important part of my paper had been given before I came to it!

One thing that the French can teach us is the need of leadership. There can be no greater mistake from the democratic point of view, nothing more ruinous can be imagined from the point of view of a true democracy, than to believe that democracy means absence of leadership. Of course it is hard to tell exactly how much can be done in any given case by the leadership that is differentiated from the mass work. That is true in producing a national art or national literature, just as it is true in other activities of national life. Something, of course, and in some cases much, can be accomplished. But the greatest literature, the greatest art, must spring from the soul of the people themselves. There must be leadership in the blossoming period, in any blossoming period, of any great artistic or literary nation. But if the art is genuinely national, the leadership must take advantage of the life of the people, and must follow the trend of its marked currents. Greek art, like Gothic architecture, owed more to the national spirit than to any conscious effort of any group of men; and this is likewise true of the Greek and English literatures. On the other hand, Latin literature was not really an expression of the soul of the Latin race at all, and this will seem strange only to the men who have not succeeded in freeing their thought from the narrow type of scholastic education prevalent in our universities and schools up to the present day. Latin literature was merely an elegant accomplishment developed by small groups of Latin-speaking men who self-consciously set themselves to the production of a literature and an art modelled on Greek lines. The result of the efforts of these men has had a profound effect upon the civilization of the last two thousand years throughout the world; but this effect has come merely because the race to which this artificial literature belonged was a race of conquerors, of administrators, of empire-builders. Greek literature and art, Greek philosophy, Greek thought, have profoundly shaped the after-destinies of the world, although the Greek was trampled under foot by the Roman. But Roman literature, Latin literature, would not be heard of at this day if it were not for the fact that the Latin stamped his character on all occidental and central Europe.

Normally there must be some relation between art and the national life if the art is to represent a real contribution to the sum of artistic world development. Nations have achieved greatness without this greatness representing any artistic side; other great nations have developed an artistic side only after a preliminary adoption of what has been supplied by the creative genius of some wholly alien people. But the national greatness which is wholly divorced from every form of artistic production, whether in literature, painting, sculpture, or architecture, unless it is marked by extraordinary achievements in war and government, is not merely a one-sided, but a malformed, greatness, as witness Tyre, Sidon, and Carthage.

It behooves us in the United States not to be content with repeating on a larger scale the history of commercial materialism of the great Phœnician commonwealths. This means that here in America, if we do not develop a serious art and literature of our own, we shall have a warped national life. Most certainly I do not mean that the art and literature are worth developing unless they are built on a national life which is strong and great in other ways, unless they are expressions of that valor of soul which must always come before beauty. If a nation is not proudly willing and able to fight for a just cause—for the lives of its citizens, for the honor of its flag, even for the rescue of some oppressed foreign nationality—then such a nation will always be an ignoble nation, and this whether it achieves the sordid prosperity of those who are merely successful hucksters, or whether it kills its virility by an exclusive appreciation of grace, ease, and beauty. Strength, courage, and justice must come first. When the beauty-loving, beauty-producing Greek grew corrupt and lost his hold upon the great arts of war and government, his proficiency in arts of a different kind did not avail him against the Roman. The glory of Greece culminated in those centuries when her statesmen and soldiers ranked as high as her sculptors and temple-builders, her poets, historians, and philosophers.

We of this nation are a people different from all of the peoples of Europe, but akin to all. Our language and literature are English, and the fundamentals of our inherited culture are predominantly English. But we have in our veins the blood of many different race-stocks, and we have taken toll of the thought of many different foreign nations. We have lived for three centuries, and are still living under totally new surroundings. These new surroundings and the new strains in our blood interact on one another in such fashion that our national type must certainly be new; and it will either develop no art and no literature, or else the art and literature must be distinctly our own.

In a recent number of *The Sewanee Review*—incidentally, *The Sewanee Review* represents the kind of work which Americans should welcome—it was pointed out how the names of our writers, painters, and poets of today show the growing divergence of our people from the English stock. This does not in the least mean that there should be any break with English scholarship and culture, any failure to take full advantage of their immense storehouse; but it does mean that this country is steadily evolving a new national type. This new national type can add to the sum of world achievement only if it develops its own forms of national expression, social, literary, and artistic.

Of course to make the type self-consciously anti-English shows as mean a sense of uneasy inferiority as to make it a mere imitation of the English. Take three widely different books which have dealt with vital conditions during the last two years, and consider the names of the authors. Two of them deal with conditions growing out of the World War and the failure of this nation to act in accordance with its loftiest traditions of the past. The other, the first one of which I speak, refers not to anything special to this nation, but to something of vital interest to all modern nations. I refer to Bade's "The Old Testament in the Light of Today," very much the ablest and most remarkable Biblical study produced anywhere in any country of recent years. Another is Owen Wister's "Pentecost of Calamity," which every American should read, and the third is Gustavus Ohlinger's "Their True Faith and Allegiance," which should be read by every man who claims to be an American, whether he is of old colonial stock or is a naturalized citizen or is the son of a naturalized citizen; and if any man fails with all his heart to stand for the doctrines therein set forth, this country is not the place for him to live. None of these three authors is English by blood, at least on his father's side. All are of mixed blood, and all are purely American, *through and through*—American in every sense which can possibly aid in making the term one of pride to us and one of usefulness to mankind at large.

Now, conditions in this country are such that from time to time a certain number of our people are lost to us. Some painters go to live in France, some writers in England, some musicians and even occasionally some scientists, elsewhere in Continental Europe. Occasionally these men may individually benefit themselves, in which case all I can say is, I trust they cease calling themselves Americans. I don't want to call them American-French or American-English. Let them be frankly English or French and stop being American. They represent nothing but loss from the point of view of national achievement and must be disregarded in any study of our development.

It is eminently necessary that we should draw on every hoard of gar-nered wisdom and ability anywhere in the world of art and of literature, whether it be in France or Japan, in Germany, England, Russia, or Scan-dinavia. But what we get we must adapt to our own uses. Largely we must treat it as an inspiration to do original productive work ourselves, so that we may develop naturally along our own lines. We need have scant patience with artificial development in nationalism or in anything else. I care little more for the Cubist school in patriotism than I care for it in art or in poetry. The effort to be original by being fantastic is always cheap. Second-rate work is second-rate work, even if it is not done badly. Nor does the possession of a national art mean in the least that the subjects treated shall be only domestic subjects. But the possession of a national art does mean that the training and habit of thought of the men of artistic and literary expression shall put them into sympathy with the nation to which they belong. Partly they must express the soul of a nation, partly they must lead and guide the soul of the nation; but only by being one with it can they become one with humanity at large. When the greatest men, the men whose appeal is to mankind at large, make their appeal, it will be found that it carries most weight when they speak in terms that are natural to them, when they speak with the soul of their own land. Normally the man who can do most for the nations of the world as a whole is the man the fibres of whose being are most closely intertwined with those of the people to which he himself belongs.

Merely to copy something already produced by another nation is probably useless. Cultivated Englishmen, for example, have added immensely to their scholarly productivity by their study of the Latin tongue and their familiarity with it. The study of Latin has helped them to do productive work. But when they themselves have tried to become Latin writers they have never done anything at all. One form of their effort to write Latin has represented, I suppose, in the aggregate, as large an amount of sheer waste as anything in all education, and that is the setting of boys and young men to writing Latin verses. Millions of Latin verses have been written by Englishmen, cultivated Englishmen; and there isn't one of them which any human being would put in a Latin anthology today. It has represented sheer waste of effort—a waste as sheer as learning the Koran by heart in a Moslem university, and the product is of no more permanent value than the verses scribbled at a weekend house-party.

There have been countless American artists who have spent their time painting French and Dutch subjects. Some have done good work—almost as good as if they were Frenchmen or Dutchmen. All of them put together have not added to the sum of American achievement or to the world's artistic development as much as Remington when he painted the soldier, the cowboy, and the Indian of the West. Now let me add for the benefit of the worthy persons who, having seen this statement, will write me the day after tomorrow, yearning for a commission, that the fact that they would like to paint Indians does not mean that they are going to do good work. If Remington's desire had not been equalled by his power of artistic achievement, what he did would have been worthless. Good

Joel Barlow found he had a new nation and no epic; and as he figured to himself that Homer had self-consciously written the epic of Greece, and as he knew about Milton, he sat down and wrote an epic of America conceived in the same spirit that made us put Washington naked to the waist and with a toga around him in front of the Capitol—the same spirit, if our guest will pardon me, which made the French seventeenth-century sculptors put Louis XIV in a Roman corselet. Well, poor Joel Barlow wrote his "Columbiad"; I have one of the copies of the original edition. I would not have it out of my library for any consideration unless I were required to read it; if I had to read it I would surrender it.

Many Americans of wealth have rendered real service by bringing to this country collections of pictures by the masters of painting. But all of these men of wealth who have brought over paintings to this country, put together, have not added to the sum of productive civilization in this country as much as that strange, imaginative genius, Marcius-Simons, who was utterly neglected in life, who isn't known in death, but who will assuredly be known to generations that come after us as perhaps the greatest imaginative colorist since Turner.

I was struck the other day by something that Lady Gregory mentioned to me. She is one of that knot of men and women who of recent years have made Ireland a genuine influence in the world of literature. She and her fellows have done this because their work has been essentially national. In this country she lectured upon the need that we Americans should develop our own drama and poetry along similar national lines. She has told with much humor (and in private conversation has elaborated with examples) how some of her auditors, like those victims of mediæval magic who were made to learn the Lord's Prayer backward, deliberately inverted her teachings, and proposed themselves to her to write not American, but Irish, prose or poems! She spoke in various cities of the need that we should develop local schools of literary activity, not antinational schools, but representative of all the local features of our composite nationality. She urged our people to realize the deep humor and interest in the new types developed in each new centre of American life. She asked the hearers in different centres to develop from each the local story, the local play, the local poem, exactly as she and those like her had done in Ireland. She described in some detail what they had done in Ireland; whereupon in each unit a considerable portion of her auditors thought they would like to imitate what she had done in Ireland, under the impression that they were following out her advice to be original!

For example, she told of one case where, having produced one of her plays in which a cowherd was concerned, one of her auditors sent her a few days afterward a play of his own on "Irish Cattle-keeping," where one of the features was the tinkling of the cow-bells. Now, they do not have cow-bells in Ireland. He knew how cow-bells sounded in the pasture lot at home, just as he knew how the rails sound when they clatter down on the ground as the hired man lets the cows out. And he might just as well have attributed the sound of the falling of rails to a region of stone walls as to have attributed cow-bells to Ireland. He and his kind are zealous, well-meaning, profoundly foolish persons, who thought that they were inspired by her teachings to undertake something for which they were exquisitely unfitted. They were not really inspired at all. They were simply filled with the desire to copy somebody else because they did not have in their own souls the capacity for original or productive work.

The easiest of all things is to copy. Ordinary writers do not write about what they themselves see, for they see very little. They merely repeat what has already been written in books about what somebody else has seen. You remember Oliver Wendell Holmes's statement that it took over a century to banish the lark from American literature, and I am bound to say that the lark occasionally survives here and there in American literature to this day. Yet no American has ever heard the skylark in America, because he is not here to be heard. But the average American writer has read Hogg or Shelley or Shakespeare; and so when he thinks of going out in the early morning in the country, and does not know anything about the country, he thinks he ought to feel inspired by the skylark, and writes accordingly.

Ordinary people, as they grow wealthy and become vaguely aware of new needs—or, if that is too strong an expression, grow vaguely to feel that they ought to show some evidence of growth in taste to parallel their growth in wealth—find it easier to import not only their own ideas, but their material surroundings. When our multimillionaires become wealthy enough, they are apt to copy Old World palaces and to fill these palaces with paintings brought from the Old World. If the millionaire is sufficiently primitive, he will explain to you with pride that the paintings are hand-made. Now, it is eminently right to try to add to our own development by the studies of great architecture and the great schools of painting of the Old World. If we do not study them, we shall never develop anything worth having on our own side of the water. But neither the mere reproduction of a specimen of a great architecture nor the mere purchase of the product of a great school of painting is of the slightest consequence in adding to the sum total of worthy national achievement. A minutely accurate reproduction of a beautiful and very expensive French château, popped down at the foot of some unkempt mountain range, or elbowing another imitation château of a totally different nationality and type in some summer capital of the wealthy, does not represent any advance in our taste or culture or art of living. It represents nothing but a personal inability to make wise use of acquired or inherited riches. The Raphaels in England reflect credit primarily on Italy, not on England. It is to the Turners in the National Gallery that we must turn when we desire to consider real achievements by England in the field of art. We neither know nor care whether the Spanish grandees and Dutch burgomasters of the seventeenth century accumulated masterpieces of Italian painters. Our concern is solely with the artistic genius that produced Velasquez and Murillo, with the artistic genius that produced Rembrandt and Franz Hals. Similarly, it means very little to have an Egyptian obelisk in Central Park. (In the effort to avoid overstatement, I have made this statement feebly.) But it means a great deal to have Saint Gaudens's Farragut and Sherman in New York, Saint Gaudens's Lincoln in Chicago, and MacMonnies's Kit Carson in Denver.

Of course an over-self-conscious straining after a nationalistic form of expression may defeat itself. But this is merely because self-consciousness is almost always a drawback. The self-conscious striving after originality also tends to defeat itself. Yet the fact remains that the greatest work must bear the stamp of originality. In exactly the same way the greatest work must bear the stamp of nationalism. American work must smack of our own soil, mental and moral, no less than physical, or it will have little of permanent value.

Let us profit by the scholarship, art, and literature of every other country and every other time; let us adapt to our own use whatever is of value in any other language, in any other literature, in any other art; but let us keep steadily in mind that in every field of endeavor the work best worth doing for Americans must in some degree express the distinctive characteristics of our own national soul.

NOTES

The American Boy (1900)

5 younger Pliny . . . correspondence with the Emperor Trajan: Gaius Plinius Cascilius Secundus, known as Pliny the Younger (61–ca. AD 112), an author and lawyer who served Emperor Trajan (AD 53–117), who was Roman emperor from AD 98 to 117.

5 Persian kings had to forbid polo: King Qabus ibn Wushmagir, who ruled Gurgan and Tabaristan in medieval Iran in 977–81 and 997–1012, found it necessary to set fixed rules for polo, specifically addressing the game's physical dangers.

6 a fox-hunter who . . . was discovered pursuing his favorite sport just before a great battle between the Cavaliers and the Puritans: A contrast between two factions in the English Civil War (1642–1651), the Cavaliers, who were considered gallant, ostentatious, and distractible, with the Puritans, who were considered focused, sober, and industrious.

6 "Work while you work; play while you play": A popular proverb, known from the oft-reprinted poem by M. A. Stodart, titled variously "One Thing At a Time," "Work and Play," and "Work While You Work," which begins "Work while you work, play while you play, / That is the way to be cheerful and gay; / All that you do, do with your might, / Things done by halves are never done right; / Work while you work, play while you play, / That is the way to be cheerful and gay."

7 Thomas Hughes's "Tom Brown at Rugby," and Aldrich's "Story of a Bad Boy": *Tom Brown's School Days* (1857), is a novel by Thomas Hughes (1822–1896), drawn from his school experiences at Rugby, a famous English public boys' school. *The Story of a Bad Boy* (1870), is a novel by Thomas Bailey Aldrich (1836–1907), based on his youth in Portsmouth, New Hampshire.

7 fagging: A term used in British schools, under which younger students act as servants for older ones.

8 Kipling's . . . "Captains Courageous" . . . "Stalky & Co.": J. Rudyard Kipling (1865–1936), English poet and prose writer, wrote *Captains Courageous*, a serialized novel published in collected form in 1897, about the coming of age of the son of a railroad tycoon. The title comes from the first line of the English ballad "Mary Ambree," which begins "When captains courageous, whom death could not daunt." *Stalky & Co.*, a series of linked short stories, first published in collected form in 1899, is about the students in a British boys' boarding school.

The Strenuous Life (1899)

12 **the doctrine of ignoble ease:** A reference to the Latin phrase *ignobilis oti*, which appears in Virgil's *Georgics* (29 BC).

13 **a cumberer of the earth's surface:** A paraphrase of a line from Constance Isabella Stuart Smith's novel *A Cumberer of the Ground* (1894), in which a character remarks "I don't care to feel myself a complete cumberer of the earth. No one likes to do that." Thus, one who hinders or obstructs.

13 **helpmeet:** A partner or spouse, probably derived from *Genesis* 2:18, which in the King James Version reads "And the Lord God said, It is not good that the man should be alone; I will make him an help meet for him."

13 **one of Daudet's powerful and melancholy books:** Alphonse Daudet (1840–1897), a French novelist and author of *L'Immortel* (1888), published in English as *The Immortal, or, One of the Forty*, which contains this passage.

13 **righteous war:** A reference to the theory of a just war, a system of (often theological) arguments for waging war as appropriate or justified.

14 **We cannot . . . play the part of China, and be content to rot by inches:** At the time, China was near the end of its final imperial dynastic phase, as the Qing Dynasty adopted a defensive stance toward European aggression (including two Opium Wars with Britain, 1839–1842 and 1856–1860), which, coupled with a series of internal rebellions (from 1851 to 1877) and the rise of the militarily-strong Meiji period in Japan (1868–1912), greatly diminished China's strength. The Qing Dynasty would fall in 1911, and the Republic of China emerged in 1912.

15 **the responsibilities that confront us in Hawaii, Cuba, Porto Rico, and the Philippines:** Each of these had come under limited or extended United States control throughout the late 1890s. Hawaii was annexed in 1898, and Cuba became controlled by the United States, with Puerto Rico and the Philippines ceded to the United States by the Treaty of Paris following the end of the Spanish-American War of 1898.

15 **"stern men with empires in their brains":** Found in James Russell Lowell's "Mason and Sidell: A Yankee Idyll," in *The Biglow Papers*, second series (1867).

16 **We must build the isthmian canal:** At the time, the Panama Canal had been begun by the French, but was abandoned in the 1890s. The United States, under Roosevelt's presidency, took over the completion of the canal in 1904.

17 **Congress most wisely made a series of appropriations to build up a new navy:** Following a decline after the American Civil War, the U.S. Navy entered a period in the 1880s–1890s known as the "New Navy," during which efforts were made to modernize the fleet, including the building of modern

armored cruise- and battleships, which elevated the Navy to the fifth-largest national navy in the world by the end of the century. The Spanish-American War was seen as a successful test of this "New Navy."

17 **Secretary Long and Admiral Dewey:** John Davis Long (1838–1915) was Governor of Massachusetts (1880–83) and Secretary of the Navy (1897–1902). George Dewey (1837–1917) was an admiral of the U.S. Navy, known for winning the Battle of Manila Bay (1 May 1898) during the Spanish-American War.

19 **those who so long delayed the adoption of the treaty of peace:** The Philippine Revolution against Spain had begun in August 1896, but was unsuccessful until backed by the United States. The Philippines declared independence in 1898, but the Treaty of Paris, which ended the Spanish-American War of 1898, ceded the Philippines to the United States. The First Philippine Republic did not recognize the treaty and declared war against the United States on 2 June 1899, beginning the bloody Philippine-American War, which officially ended in 1902, though hostilities continued through 1913.

19 **prattlers who sit at home in peace:** Roosevelt here, as elsewhere, condemns pacification solutions as lacking a practical or interventionist element.

20 **Porto Rico is not large enough to stand alone:** The United States had invaded Puerto Rico on 25 July 1898 during the Spanish-American War and the country was ceded to the United States by the Treaty of Paris. This led to a long-standing political and economic relationship, including later calls by figures such as Roosevelt for statehood or citizenship for Puerto Rico and its citizens.

20 **Cuba . . . shall be an independent state or an integral portion of the mightiest of republics:** Cuba had fought three liberation wars (1868–1878, 1879–1880, 1895–1898), the last of which became the Spanish-American War of 1898. At the time of this address, the United States had just taken over the country (on 1 January 1899), with General John R. Brooke (1838–1926) as governor.

20 **The Philippines offer a yet graver problem:** The Philippines had a more diverse mix of ethnic and religious groups, cross-cut by uneven economic prosperity and lacking a tradition of political autonomy, all of which combined to stoke revolutionary sentiments.

21 **England's rule in India:** England formally ruled India from 1858–1947, a period known as the British Raj, following nearly two centuries of rule by the British East India Company.

"Professionalism" in Sports (1890)

25 **growth of interest in and appreciation of healthy muscular amusements:** Baseball, American football, rowing, sailing, and soccer had all seen a growth in popularity in the mid- and late nineteenth century.

26 **self-reliance:** Perhaps an indirect reference to Ralph Waldo Emerson's influential essay, "Self-Reliance," first published in his 1841 collection, *Essays: First Series*, and containing the oft-quoted line: "A foolish consistency is the hobgoblin of little minds."

26 **the race:** Here, as elsewhere, Roosevelt uses "race" to connote cultural and national heritage.

29 **rat-pit and cock-pit:** Betting sports often regarded as disreputable. Rat-baiting involved filling a pit with rats and betting on how long it would take a terrier to kill them. Cockfighting involved fights, usually to the death, between two roosters.

At the Dedication Ceremonies of the Louisiana Purchase Exposition, St. Louis, April 30, 1903

33 **France and Castile:** The Louisiana Purchase encompassed land purchased from France that had previously been held by Spain, which was historically known as the Crown of Castile. Explorers and traders from both nations helped map these territories throughout the seventeenth and eighteenth centuries.

34 **the treaties of Jay and Pinckney:** The Treaty of Amity, Commerce, and Navigation, Between His Britannic Majesty and the United States of America, known as the Jay Treaty (for its negotiator, John Jay), signed in 1794, resolved lingering issues from the Treaty of Paris of 1783 (which concluded the American Revolution), and granted the removal of British forces from pre-Revolutionary forts in the Northwest Territory. Pinckney's Treaty, signed in 1795 between the United States and Spain, defined the boundaries of each nation's colonies and granted navigation rights on the Mississippi River.

35 **history of Rome and of Greece illustrates very well the two types of expansion:** Roosevelt uses the distinction between the empires of Greece and Rome elsewhere. Here he uses it to emphasize the balance between self-governance of states and the broad powers of the federal government afforded by the U.S. Constitution. Another portion has not been admitted to statehood, although a century has elapsed—although doubtless it soon will be. Oklahoma became a state in 1907 and New Mexico in 1912.

37 **The acquisition of the territory is a credit to . . . great statesmen:** Settled during the presidency of Thomas Jefferson (1743–1826) in 1803, the Louisiana Purchase had been negotiated by James Monroe (1758–1831) and Robert Livingston (1746–1813), and not only greatly increased the land area of the United States, but was regarded as a bold international move.

39 **in 1903, in the altered conditions:** Roosevelt presumably refers to the increasing hostile international scene, from the Spanish-American War of 1898 onward.

National Unity versus Class Cleavage

42 **class cleavage:** The purposeful division of voters into economic classes set against one another, rather than working (and voting) for a common purpose.

43 **speculative frenzy:** The financial practice of engaging in risky transactions hoping to profit from short-term market fluctuations, often resulting in economic bubbles and subsequent crashes.

44 **As soon as it becomes government by a class:** Roosevelt here gestures toward concerns over a growing class of professional politician, whose only occupation is the playing of politics and holding of offices.

48 **franchise-tax law in this State:** Ruling against corporate interests, the Court of Appeals in 1902 had upheld a franchise-tax law originally passed during Roosevelt's term as governor of New York, requiring companies to pay taxes in their respective localities. The U.S. Department of Commerce and Labor was formed in 1903 as a cabinet-level department, and was subsequently renamed the Department of Commerce in 1913, with some of its agencies becoming the newly created Department of Labor.

The Parasite Woman; the Only Indispensable Citizen (1917)

54 **"parasite woman":** The phrase "parasite woman" was in circulation in the 1910s, used both seriously, as in Olive Scheiner's *Woman and Labour* (1911), in which she writes that "if the parasite woman on the coach, loaded with gewgaws, the plaything and amusement of man, be the permanent and final manifestation of female human life on the globe, then that couch is also the deathbed of human evolution," and parodically, as in "The Parasite Woman Must Go!" by Don Marquis, in his collection of sketches *Hermione and Her Little Group of Serious Thinkers* (1916).

54 **professional feminists and so-called woman's-rights women:** One of their most prominent organizations was the National American Woman Suffrage Association (NAWSA), a group formed when two preexisting suffrage organizations merged in 1890, and was led from 1890 to 1900 by Susan B. Anthony (1820–1906), a leading suffragette.

55 **if the women of a country, and therefore if the country itself, expect any development:** After the Civil War, a number of overlapping women's rights and suffrage movements attempted to secure expanded civil liberties for women. The most prominent of these was the ratification of the Nineteenth Amendment, originally proposed in 1878 and enacted in 1920, which prohibited voting discrimination based on sex.

55 **scientific work has been done by women:** For example, Marie Skłodowska-Curie (1867–1934), a pioneer in researching radioactivity, and the first woman to win a Nobel Prize and only woman to win two, first in 1903 for physics with her husband, Pierre, and then in 1911 for chemistry.

56 **Julia Ward Howe or Harriet Beecher Stowe or Mrs. Homer:** American abolitionists Julia Ward Howe (1819–1910), who wrote "The Battle Hymn of the Republic," first published in *The Atlantic Monthly* in February 1862; Harriet Beecher Stowe (1811–1896), author of the influential *Uncle Tom's Cabin* (1852); and Henrietta Benson Homer (1809–1884), a member of Stowe's father's congregation, abolitionist, and mother of artist Winslow Homer (1836–1910).

56 **what they call "unwomanly" activities:** A number of writers engaged in distinguishing "womanly" from "unwomanly" activities. Miss C. S. Parrish, in "The Womanly Woman," published in *The Independent* (4 April 1901), reports: "An 'old Virginia gentlemen' once said in the presence of the writer that the higher education of women is unwomanly. Begged for reasons, he said that when a woman is well educated she is capable of supporting herself. As soon as she is able, she wishes to do it, and that is destructive if all true womanliness consists in being supported by a man."

58 **Mrs. Emmeline Pankhurst:** Emmeline Pankhurst (1858–1928), British political activist and advocate of women's suffrage, founded the Woman's Social and Political Union, dedicated to women's suffrage and "deeds, not words," and which published *The Suffrage*, and later, beginning in 1915, *Britannia*.

58 **strikes among workers in England:** Throughout World War I, pressures on productions and the importation of workers led to resentment and strikes in some sectors of British industry.

59 **appalling unfitness for world leadership:** An implicit criticism of Woodrow Wilson's presidency (1913–1921) and the delayed entry of the United States into World War I.

59 **We must . . . defend ourselves against outside aggression:** Roosevelt had been a strong supporter of increased American military strength, including the "New Navy" of the late nineteenth and early twentieth centuries.

The American Negro and the War (1918)

62 **Circle for Negro War Relief:** An organization for the support of black soldiers and their families during World War I. The Circle was formed in November 1917, led by Emily (Emilie) Bigelow Hapgood (unknown–1930), and quickly expanded to over sixty "units" throughout the country, providing material and social support for soldiers and local communities. After the war, the Circle established a theater company in New York, the Players' Guild, which put on productions starring performers like Paul Robeson. W. E. B. Du Bois (1868–1963) presided over the meeting at which Roosevelt spoke.

62 **divide the Nobel Peace Prize:** Roosevelt won the Nobel Peace Prize in 1906 for successfully mediating the end of the Russo-Japanese War, which ended in 1905. Roosevelt had waited until 1910 to receive the award and its

monetary prize, which he then divided in 1918 among a number of social, national, and international groups and causes.

62 **Mr. Scott:** Emmett Jay Scott (1873–1957) became Booker T. Washington's secretary in 1897 and helped him run the Tuskegee Institute. In 1917, Scott became special advisor on black affairs to Woodrow Wilson's Secretary of War, Newton Baker (1871–1937). Scott's *Official History of the American Negro in the World War* (1919) recounted much of the detail of the black experience of World War I, including meetings of the Circle for Negro War Relief.

62 **I tried by works to show the faith that is in me:** Similar phrasing to James 2:18 within the King James version, which reads, "Yea, a man may say, Thou hast faith, and I have works: shew me thy faith without thy works, and I will shew thee my faith by my works."

63 **Colonel Charles Young:** Charles Young (1864–1922), born into slavery, grew up a freeman and later became a decorated military officer. He was the third African American graduate of West Point, the first black military attaché, and the first black man to achieve the rank of colonel, and at the time of his death, remained the highest-ranking black officer.

64 **Hamilton Fish:** Hamilton (Stuyvesant) Fish III (1888–1991) was the grandson of Hamilton Fish (1808–1893), who had been governor of New York, a United States senator, and Secretary of State under President Ulysses S. Grant. Hamilton Fish III became captain of the 369th U.S. Infantry Regiment, composed of black enlisted men and known as the "Harlem Hellfighters." His troops spent 191 days on the front lines, the longest of any American regiment. Later, as a congressman, Fish opposed the United States' role in foreign affairs and was critical of President Franklin Roosevelt.

64 **sun-burned Yankees:** That is, the black enlisted men under his command; in *The Rough Riders*, Roosevelt notes that the Spanish called black soldiers "smoked Yankees."

64 **Mr. Cobb has spoken:** Irvin S. Cobb (1876–1944), author and columnist, originally from Kentucky, wrote more than sixty books and hundreds of short stories. At one time, Cobb was the highest-paid staff reporter in the United States and covered World War I for the *Saturday Evening Post*, publishing *Paths of Glory* (1915) about his experiences.

64 **our going in turned the scale:** The United States declared war on Germany on 6 April 1917, ultimately sending nearly four million servicemen, and after pushing Germany back during the Spring Offensive of 1918, was widely seen as having turned the tide of the war.

64 **the Germans and their vassal allies:** Germany's allies included Austria-Hungary, the Ottoman Empire, and Bulgaria.

65 **kaiserism and bolshevism:** Allegiance to German imperial rule, and particularly to the reign of Kaiser Wilhelm II (1859–1941), German Emperor

and King of Prussia from 1888 to 1918, led to the term *kaiserism*. The Bolsheviks were a primary faction of the Russian Social Democratic Labor Party (RSDLP), which split from the Menshevik faction in 1903, and, led by V. I. Lenin (1870–1924), became the Communist Party, which came to power during the October 1917 Russian Revolution.

65 **soldier we have with us tonight who won the cross of war:** Sergeant Henry Lincoln Johnson (1897–1929) was the first American to receive the Croix de Guerre with star and Gold Palm from the French government. Johnson served with the 369th Infantry Division, known as the Harlem Hellfighters or Black Rattlers, which was composed of entirely of African Americans. Roosevelt called him "one of the five bravest men who fought" in the war.

66 **Trotsky:** Leon Trotsky (1879–1940), a Russian Marxist revolutionary and theorist, joined the Bolsheviks just before the October 1917 Revolution, and became the first leader of the Red Army.

66 **square-deal:** The Square Deal, Roosevelt's term for his domestic program during his presidency, relied on the conservation of natural resources, control of corporations, and consumer protections.

The Control of Corporations (1902)

72 **period of great commercial prosperity:** Referring to the rise of major industrial corporations and trusts, such as Standard Oil, throughout the late nineteenth and early twentieth centuries.

72 **when the tower of Siloam fell upon all alike:** In Luke 13:1–5, Jesus refers to eighteen people who died when the tower in Siloam, in south Jerusalem, fell on them, though they were not at fault or to blame.

72 **If when people wax fat they kick, as they have kicked since the days of Jeshurun:** Jeshurun is a poetic name for Israel in the Hebrew Bible. Roosevelt paraphrases Deuteronomy 32:15, which in the King James version reads "But Jeshurun waxed fat, and kicked: thou art waxen fat, thou art grown thick, thou art covered with fatness; then he forsook God which made him, and lightly esteemed the Rock of his salvation."

75 **the States either can not or will not exercise a sufficient control:** An argument for the revival of the Sherman Antitrust Act of 1890, which allowed the federal government to sue for antitrust violations, thus working around individual states.

The Colonial Policy of the United States (1910)

80 **Christiania, Norway:** Roosevelt was in Norway to receive his 1906 Nobel Peace Prize for successfully mediating the end of the Russo-Japanese War (1904–5), having waited until after leaving his presidency and, on this date, following an African safari. Roosevelt was the first American Nobel Laureate.

80 **Mr. Bratlie:** Jens Kristian Meinich Bratlie (1856–1939), a Norwegian politician, who served as prime minister from 1912 to 1913.

80 **my own actions while I was President:** During Roosevelt's presidency, from 1901 to 1909, he oversaw the involvement of the United States in a number of international affairs, which he describes here.

80 **We appointed a day when we would leave Cuba:** Following the Spanish-American War of 1898 and the departure of Spanish troops, the United States took over Cuba on 1 January 1899, with General John R. Brooke (1838–1926) as governor. Congress passed an Army Appropriations Act in 1901, with an additional Platt Amendment that hobbled Cuban independence, though it allowed for the end of U.S. occupation on 20 May 1902. Tomás Estrada Palma (1832–1908) was elected president, but tried to extend his presidency beyond his four-year term, which led to a revolt in 1906. The U.S. representative William Howard Taft (1857–1930) negotiated an end to the revolt, and in the aftermath Charles Magoon (1861–1920) became Provisional Governor of Cuba until 1909.

81 **San Domingo, in the West Indies, had suffered from a good many revolutions:** Following the assassination of the despotic General Ulises Heureaux Lebert (1845–1899) in 1899, a series of short-lived governments ruled the Dominican Republic (still referred to in some circles as San Domingo).

81 **it became evident that certain European Powers would land and take possession of parts of the island:** In order to prevent European intervention and to protect trade routes to the newly acquired and under-construction Panama Canal, Roosevelt asserted the Roosevelt Corollary to the Monroe Doctrine to make a small military intervention into the Dominican Republic in 1905, securing an agreement for the U.S. administration of Dominican customs.

The New Nationalism (1910)

88 **the name of John Brown:** The speech was given at the dedication of the John Brown Memorial State Park in Osawatomie, Kansas. John Brown (1800–1859) was an American abolitionist notable for his use of violence, including the raid or civil insurrection he led in 1859 at Harpers Ferry, Virginia, which led to his execution for treason and contributed to the onset of the American Civil War.

88 **the struggle in Kansas:** A series of violent altercations between the anti-slavery "Free-Staters" and pro-slavery "Border Ruffians" known as Bleeding Kansas took place within the Kansas Territory and Missouri from 1854 to 1861. Seen as a direct precursor to the American Civil War, the central conflict was whether Kansas would become a free or slave-holding state. On the eve of the Civil War, Kansas entered the Union as a free state in 1861.

88 **through a glass, darkly:** In the King James Version, 1 Corinthians 13:12 reads: "For now we see through a glass, darkly; but then face to face: now I know in part; but then shall I know even as also I am known."

89 **"I hold that while man exists it is his duty":** From Lincoln's speech to Germans at Cincinnati, Ohio, 12 February 1861.

89 **"Labor is prior to, and independent of, capital":** From Lincoln's annual message to Congress, 3 December 1861.

90 **"Capital has its rights":** From Lincoln's annual message to Congress, 3 December 1861.

90 **"Nor should this lead to a war upon the owners of property":** Lincoln's reply to the New York Workingmen's Democratic Republican Association, delivered from the White House, 21 March 1864.

90 **"Let not him who is houseless pull down the house of another":** Lincoln's reply to the New York Workingmen's Democratic Republican Association, delivered from the White House, 21 March 1864.

92 **does not give the right of suffrage to any corporation:** Here, as elsewhere, Roosevelt attempts to limit the personification of corporations, namely trying to deny their right to vote or influence elections as voters do.

93 **Federal Bureau of Corporations:** Created in 1903 during Roosevelt's presidency, the Bureau of Corporations studied and produced a series of reports that led directly to regulatory legislation, including a 1906 report on petroleum transportation that led to the Hepburn Act and the Bureau's investigation of the petroleum industry, which led to the breakup of Standard Oil. The Bureau was replaced by the Federal Trade Commission in 1915.

93 **Interstate Commerce Commission:** Created by the Interstate Commerce Act of 1887, the Interstate Commerce Commission originally regulated railroad rates and rate discrimination. Its powers were expanded to cover trucking, bus lines, and telephone service. The Commission was disbanded in 1995.

93 **Hepburn Act:** Signed by Roosevelt on 29 June 1906, the Hepburn Act gave the Interstate Commerce Commission power to regulate railroad rates.

94 **expert tariff commission:** The United States Trade Commission would be established by Congress in 1916. Its powers were expanded through a series of acts throughout the twentieth century; its name was changed to the United States International Trade Commission in 1974.

95 **our currency will no longer fail at critical times:** The Federal Reserve Act was enacted in 1913, creating the Federal Reserve System, a central banking system, and provided the authority to issue Federal Reserve notes (that is, the U.S. dollar).

95 **Conservation means development as much as it does protection:** The National Park Service, created in 1916, is the federal agency charged with the maintenance of all national parks and some national monuments.

96 **great organizations of the farmers:** The National Farmers Union, formally the Farmers' Educational and Cooperative Union of America, was founded in 1902 to protect the interests of family farmers and ranchers.

96 **Departments of Agriculture of the various states:** Most states have a Department of Agriculture, and most were founded in the nineteenth century. The U.S. Department of Agriculture became an independent agency in 1862. The Hatch Act of 1887 authorized the establishment of agricultural experiment stations (or research centers), tied to each state's land grant college of agriculture.

97 **We need comprehensive workmen's compensation acts:** These policies regarding the regulation of labor for women and children, the emphasis on practice education, as well as improved sanitary conditions, constitute the "New Nationalism" platform Roosevelt would support throughout the 1910–12 period.

99 **executive power as the steward of the public welfare:** Part of the Progressive platform that Roosevelt would espouse in 1912.

100 **moneys received or expended for campaign purposes should be publicly accounted for:** An early version of campaign and party finance reform. Attempts to legislate finances did not take hold until the later part of the twentieth century.

100 **a good commissary—the cracker line:** A supply line for delivering food to troops and animals.

National Preparedness— Military—Industrial—Social (1916)

104 **copperhead pacifists:** A term for Northern Democrats who opposed the American Civil War and advocated for peace with the Confederates. Originally termed "copperheads" for the metaphorical connection to the venomous snake, some Democrats used the term "copper head" for the figure of Liberty that appeared on copper pennies.

107 **words of old Sir Thomas Browne:** "For since we cannot be wise by teachings . . . there is an unhappy necessity that we must smart in our own skins." Sir Thomas Browne (1605–1682) was an English author who wrote on a variety of subjects, including religion, medicine, and science. Roosevelt loosely quotes from a book of Browne's advice to his children, published posthumously, *Christian Morals* (1716), Part the Second, Sect. XI: "And since we cannot be wise by warnings; since plagues are insignificant, except we be personally plagued; since also we cannot be punished unto amendment by proxy or commutation, nor by vicinity, but contraction; there is an unhappy necessity that we must smart in our own skins, and the provoked arm of the Almighty must fall upon ourselves."

107 **the revolution in Mexico:** The Mexican Revolution began in 1910 with a rebellion led by Francisco I. Madero (1873–1913) against then-president

Porfirio Díaz (1830–1915). This two-sided conflict escalated to a multi-sided civil war, involving figures such as Pancho Villa (1878–1923) and Emiliano Zapata (1879–1919) and his Zapatistas, and spilled over onto contested U.S. land as well, through the conclusion of the revolution in 1920.

109 **outrages committed on well-behaved nations, particularly on Belgium:** Roosevelt addresses the Belgian situation in a section titled "The Belgian Tragedy" in his *America and the World War* (1915). Belgium had remained neutral but was overrun (along with Luxembourg) by Germany as part of the Schlieffen Plan to reach Paris quickly. The invasion of Belgium meant that Britain was obligated (by treaty) to enter the war.

113 **My sons have gone and are going to these camps:** Roosevelt had four sons, Theodore (1887–1944), Kermit (1889–1943), Archie (1893–1979), and Quentin (1897–1918), each of whom received military training and served in a branch of the armed services.

114 **I spoke on universal service in Detroit:** Address delivered 19 May 1916 in Detroit, Michigan, titled "Righteous Peace and National Unity."

115 **it was my good fortune to give, first to Sam Young, and afterwards to Adna Chaffee:** Samuel Baldwin Marks Young (1840–1924), was a U.S. Army general, veteran of the Civil War, Acting Superintendent of Yellowstone National Park in 1897, first president of Army War College from 1902 to 1903, and first Chief of Staff of the General Staff of the U.S. Department of War from 1903 to 1904. Roosevelt promoted him to lieutenant general on 8 August 1903. Adna Romanza Chaffee (1842–1914) was U.S. Army general, veteran of the Civil War, Indian Wars, and the Spanish-American War of 1898. Chaffee also ended the Boxer Rebellion in China (1900), and was Chief of Staff of the Army from 1904 to 1906. Roosevelt promoted him to lieutenant general on 9 January 1904.

119 **we must try to abolish child labor:** Throughout the 1900s and 1910s, a number of efforts attempted to reduce or restrict child labor. In 1916, the National Child Labor Committee and the National Consumers League pressured Congress to pass the Keating-Owen Act, which prohibited the interstate sale of goods produced by factories that employed children. The bill was declared unconstitutional by the Supreme Court in *Hammer v. Dagenhart* (1918).

121 **Lowell wrote to the pacifists:** James Russell Lowell (1819–1891) was one of the Fireside Poets, New England writers who rivaled the popularity of British poets. Roosevelt is quoting from *The Biglow Papers*.

The League of Nations (1919)

124 **Peace Conference:** The Paris Peace Conference was an ongoing series of meetings between the leaders of the Allied Powers (President Woodrow

Wilson of the United States, prime minister David Lloyd George of Great Britain, George Clemenceau of France, and Italian prime minister Vittorio Orlando) to set peace conditions for the Central Powers following the armistices of 1918, which concluded World War I. The Conference opened on 18 January 1919 and came to an end on 21 January 1920, with the inaugural General Assembly of the League of Nations.

124 **League of Nations:** The first permanent international organization devoted to maintaining world peace sprang from the Paris Peace Conference, at which the Covenant of the League of Nations was drafted, and the League established by the Treaty of Versailles (28 June 1919). Its stated purposes included the prevention of wars through collective security and disarmament, as well as the settlement of international disputes through negotiation and arbitration.

124 **There is not a young man in this country who has fought:** The United States entered World War I on 6 April 1917 and participated until the end of the war on 11 November 1918. Over four million American soldiers participated, with about 110,000 dying, including 43,000 due to the 1918 Spanish flu pandemic.

125 **the "fourteen points":** A speech by Woodrow Wilson to a joint session of Congress on 8 January 1918, outlining a series of optimistic outcomes for the then-ongoing world war. Many of the terms of Wilson's speech guided Germany's surrender after the Armistice on 11 November 1918 and were extensions of progressive domestic policy into the arena of foreign policy.

125 **the fourteen points . . . construed as having a mischievous significance:** Though well-received in Europe, Wilson's points were received with skepticism by Allied leaders, with whom Wilson met at the Paris Peace Conference.

125 **Russia—with which, incidentally, we are still waging war:** Russia had pulled out of the World War late in 1917 after the October Revolution, led by Vladimir Lenin and the Bolshevik Party. Allied forces invaded Russia in 1918, entering into their then-ongoing civil war, hoping to prevent Germany from taking Russian territory and to secure their own supplies which were being kept in Russian ports.

125 **the sinking of the *Lusitania*:** The Cunard ocean liner RMS *Lusitania*, carrying civilian passengers and rifle ammunition, was sunk on 7 May 1915 by a German U-boat off the coast of Ireland, killing 1,198 of its 1,959 passengers. The event turned public opinion firmly against Germany and was used to urge the United States to enter the war.

125 **military training modeled on the Swiss plan:** In 1874, the Swiss constitution was revised to extend the federal army to include every able-bodied citizen, which led the still-neutral Switzerland to have a well-trained militarized populace.

125 **Meddlesome Matty:** A character type derived from a children's poem of the same name by English writer Ann Taylor (1782–1866). The poem featured a child, Matilda, who could not help herself from meddling in dangerous situations.

125 **obscure fights in the Balkans or in Central Europe:** The First Balkan War, October 1912 to May 1913, pitted the Balkan League (Serbia, Greece, Montenegro, and Bulgaria) against the Ottoman Empire, and led directly to the Second Balkan War, in which Bulgaria attacked Serbia and Greece (16 June 1913), leading to even more fighting between the Balkan states. These conflicts led to the July Crisis of 1914 and the assassination of Archduke Franz Ferdinand of Austria in Sarajevo, which sparked the First World War.

125 **Monroe Doctrine:** The policy introduced by President James Monroe on 2 December 1823, asserting that any further attempts by European nations to further colonize lands in North or South America would be viewed as acts of aggression by the United States.

126 **let the United States treat Mexico as our Balkan Peninsula:** That is, follow the Monroe Doctrine, refusing outside interference.

The Enforcement of Law (1895)

130 **Sunday excise law:** Prohibition against selling alcohol on Sundays unless in a restaurant served with food.

130 **Our opponents:** Presumably supporters of the established, corrupt Tammany Hall system.

131 **Tammany:** Tammany Hall was a political organization that dominated New York City and New York State politics from the 1790s through the middle of the twentieth century. In the 1860s and 1870s, the Tammany Hall system became known for graft and corruption, particularly under the leadership of William Magear Tweed (1823–1878), known as "Boss" Tweed, who came to power in 1858 and influenced New York politics until his conviction in 1877 for stealing millions of dollars from city taxpayers. After Tweed's conviction, reformers attempted to clean up the system, including the Republicans who ran Roosevelt in the 1886 mayoral election against Henry George (1839–1897) of the United Labor Party and Abram Hewitt (1822–1903) of the Democrats. Hewitt, the Tammany-sponsored candidate, won. David B. Hill (1843–1910) was lieutenant governor of New York (1883–85), governor (1885–91), and a U.S. Senator (1892–97).

131 **jeopardize the success of the Republican party:** Roosevelt here counters the arguments that Republicans should play politics within the existing system, rather than enact principled policy.

132 **their god is their belly:** Drawn from Philippians 3:18–19, which in the King James Version reads: "For many walk, of whom I have told you often, and now tell you even weeping, that they are the enemies of the cross of Christ:

Whose end is destruction, whose God is their belly, and whose glory is in their shame, who mind earthly things."

132 **present Board of Police Commissioners in New York:** Roosevelt was appointed police commissioner by Republican mayor William Strong (1827–1900) on 17 April 1895 and took office on 27 May.

136 **Mayor Hewitt:** Abram Stevens Hewitt (1822–1903), U.S. Representative (1875–79), chairman of the Democratic National Committee (1876–77), and mayor of New York City (1887–88). With his father-in-law Peter Cooper (1791–1883), Hewitt also helped plan and finance the construction of New York City's subway system, for which he is now considered the "Father of the New York City Subway System."

136 **Superintendent Byrnes:** Thomas F. Byrnes (1842–1910) was head of the New York City Police Department detective department from 1880 to 1895.

137 **income-tax law was passed through Congress:** The Wilson-Gorman tariff of 1894 imposed the first peacetime income tax. In 1895, the U.S. Supreme Court ruling *Pollock v. Farmers' Loan & Trust Co.* invalidated parts of the new tax code (particularly the taxes on property) but allowed that Congress could levy future taxes.

137 **Whitecap outrages:** The Whitecapping movement, which began in Indiana in 1873, consisted of a vigilante group known as the "White Caps," composed of white men. Their actions became increasingly violent and racialized as the movement reached the South in the 1880s and 1890s.

137 **Mr. Jacob A. Riis:** Jacob August Riis (1849–1914) was a Danish-American social reformer, documentary photographer, and journalist, primarily known for his work of social criticism, *How the Other Half Lives: Studies Among the Tenements of New York* (appearing first in 1889 in *Scribner's Magazine*, expanded to book length in 1890), which, along with his prose articles, set the standard for "muckraking" journalism. Riis later wrote a biography, *Theodore Roosevelt, The Citizen* (1904).

At Laying of Cornerstone of Gateway to Yellowstone National Park, Gardiner, Montana (1903)

142 **Mr. Mayor, Mr. Superintendent:** Gardiner, Montana, named for a fur trapper, Johnson Gardner, is a main entrance to Yellowstone National Park. The Superintendent of the ark at the time was Major John Pitcher (1854–1926), who served from 1901 to 1907.

142 **the Park:** Yellowstone National Park, the first American national park, was established in 1872, at the intersection of Wyoming, Montana, and Idaho.

142 **preservation is noteworthy in its essential democracy:** Part of Roosevelt's argument for conservation and the national parks was their accessibility and use by all citizens, as opposed to game reserves or private shooting clubs.

143 **carriage roads throughout the Park:** Carriage roads were initially built for

the use of horses and carriages (and later automobiles), as opposed to more mechanized transportation systems.

143 **a liberal education to any man of the East to come West:** As demonstrated by Roosevelt's repeated trips through the Midwest and West, including building a ranch, Elkhorn, in North Dakota.

144 **passing the irrigation bill:** The Newlands Reclamation Act of 1902 was a federal law that funded irrigation projects in twenty Western states.

Natural Resources—Their Wise Use or Their Waste (1908)

148 **Inland Waterways Commission:** Created in 1907, the Inland Waterways Commission was a temporary commission created to study transportation issues related to produce and industrial production and offer suggestions about more efficient waterway use.

151 **an interstate waterways commission was appointed by Virginia and Maryland:** George Washington held a conference on the navigation of interstate waterways in 1786 at Mount Vernon, his home.

152 **Gifford Pinchot:** This American forester and politician (1865–1946) reformed the management and development of forests and coined the term "conservation ethic." Pinchot served as the first Chief of the U.S. Forest Service from 1905 to 1910, and as governor of Pennsylvania, 1923–27 and 1931–35.

How I Became a Progressive (1912)

154 **in the legislature at Albany:** Roosevelt served three terms in the New York State Assembly beginning in 1882, writing more bills than any other legislator.

154 **social and industrial injustice:**Roosevelt revisits the topics of social, civil, and workers' rights in *An Autobiography* (1913), chap. 13, "Social and Industrial Justice."

155 **machinery for getting adequate and genuine popular rule:** Roosevelt is referring to the effort to ratify the Seventeenth Amendment to the U.S. Constitution, which provided for direct election of United States senators as opposed to leaving their appointment to state legislatures. A version of the amendment had been introduced as early as the 1820s, but had finally become a prominent issue in the 1900s, and was ratified by a majority of states in 1912–13.

155 **short ballot:** Features only the most important executive and legislative positions to be filled.

155 **manufacture of cigars in tenement-houses:** Jacob Riis, in *How the Other Half Lives* (1890), devoted an entire chapter to the dangerous conditions generated by the cigar-making industry operating out of urban tenements.

155 **workmen's compensation act:** Legislation to provide compensatory wages

and/or benefits for injured workers. The first federal workmen's compensation act was passed in 1906.

155 **Liebig's statement:** Justus Freiherr von Liebig (1803–1873) was a German chemist who discovered that nitrogen was essential for plant growth; he became known as "father of the fertilizer industry." His "Law of the Minimum" states that growth is primarily controlled by the scarcest resource available—known as a limiting factor.

156 **Mr. Newell:** Frederick Haynes Newell (1862–1932) helped prepare various congressional bills for conservation, including the Reclamation Act, which was signed by Roosevelt in 1902. Newell served as a member of the Inland Waterways Commission and was the first director of the U.S. Reclamation Service, which oversees water resource management.

156 **country-life movement:** Reacting to the forces of industrialization and urbanization, it had deep ties to the concurrent conservation moment. One of the primary leaders of the country life movement, Liberty Hyde Bailey (1858–1954), was a horticulturist and botanist, and was appointed chairman of the National Commission on Country Life by Roosevelt. The commission issued a report in 1909 that called for America to rebuild itself as an agricultural society.

156 **Mary E. Wilkins to Sarah O. Jewett:** Mary Eleanor Wilkins Freeman (1852–1930), an American writer of short stories and novels, was primarily known for the collections *A Humble Romance and Other Stories* (1887) and *A New England Nun and Other Stories* (1891) and her novel *Pembroke* (1894), which deal primarily with New England life. Sarah Orne Jewett (1849–1909), also a American novelist and short story writer, wrote *A Country Doctor* (1884), *A White Heron* (1886), and *The Country of the Pointed Firs* (1896), which are known for their local color and set primarily in Maine.

157 **fortify and protect the Panama Canal:** The United States, under Roosevelt's presidency, in 1904 took over the completion of the Panama Canal, which was protected by the U.S. Navy during its construction until its completion in 1914.

157 **China . . . a nation which cannot defend itself against aggression:** After years of internal strife, the Wuchang Uprising of 10 October 1911 ended the Qing Dynasty and nearly two thousand years of imperial rule in China, leading to the establishment of the Republic of China on 1 January 1912.

The Case Against the Reactionaries (1912)

161 **fellow Republicans:** At the time, Roosevelt and William Howard Taft (1857–1930) were competing for the Republican nomination at the Republican National Convention held in Chicago, 18–22 June 1912. Taft became the Republican nominee and Roosevelt formed the Progressive Party, becoming its candidate.

161 **The actions of the Taft leaders in the national committee:** Roosevelt here accuses Taft, who held the power to make decisions on contested delegates—awarding himself 235 of the contested delegates and Roosevelt 19—thus allowing him to unfairly steal the nomination.

162 **Mr. Taft . . . surrendered himself wholly to the biddings of the professional political bosses:** Roosevelt's claim here echoes his description of the Tammany Hall system of the late nineteenth century.

163 **Messrs. Crane, Barnes, Brooker, Penrose, Murphy, Guggenheim, Mulvane, Smoot, New, and their associates:** Various Republican National Committee members.

164 **Judge Ben B. Lindsey . . . Mr. Stevenson's political activities in Denver:** A. M. Stevenson was a local Colorado party official. Benjamin Barr Lindsey (1869–1943), an American judge and social reformer, wrote a series of autobiographical sketches on him titled *The Beast and the Jungle*, serialized in *Everybody's Magazine* and published in collected form as *The Beast* (1910).

168 **supported Mr. Parker against me in 1904:** Alton Brooks Parker (1852–1926) was a lawyer and judge who was the Democratic nominee for president in 1904.

170 **words which Lincoln used fifty-four years ago:** Roosevelt is quoting Lincoln from his final debate with Senator Stephen A. Douglas (1813–1861) during their final debate at Alton, Illinois, 15 October 1858.

172 **We fight in honorable fashion for the good of mankind:** Roosevelt would reuse this phrasing at the conclusion of his Progressive Party Convention speech, "A Confession of Faith," 6 August 1912. It became one of his most celebrated constructions.

The Leader and the Cause (1912)

174 **I have just been shot:** Just before this speech, Roosevelt was shot by a saloon-keeper, John Schrank (1876–1943), who opposed Roosevelt's political leanings. The bullet penetrated Roosevelt's eyeglass case and the copy of his speech, lodging in his chest. Roosevelt went on to speak for ninety minutes and the bullet was never removed from his chest, leading to later health complications.

174 **Bull Moose:** Roosevelt's phrasing here led to the Progressive Party being popularly termed the "Bull Moose Party."

177 **Arthur von Briesen, who was born in Germany:** Arthur von Briesen (1843–1920) was a German American who served in the American Civil War, and went on to help found the German Legal Aid Society in 1876, which provided free legal services to poor German immigrants in New York.

178 **what Mr. Wilson did not do while he was governor:** Woodrow Wilson was governor of New Jersey from 1911 to 1913.

179 **the antitrust law was practically a dead letter:** The Sherman Antitrust Act was much criticized after its passage in 1890, as was the Interstate Commerce Act of 1887. Roosevelt, via the Department of Justice, put both to use in a prominent series of cases against large corporations, including a suit in 1902 against the railroad trust Northern Securities Company, Standard Oil (which was broken up in 1911), the American Sugar Refining Company (a suit in 1910), and the American Tobacco Company (a suit in 1908).

180 **"There are no snakes in Ireland":** That is, claiming credit for solving a problem, when you have really done nothing.

181 **Senator Beveridge's bill to abolish child labor:** Albert J. Beveridge (1862–1927) was an Indiana senator who introduced a bill to restrict child labor in 1906, the first attempt to do so.

181 **bill to prohibit women from working more than eight hours a day:** This policy, along with a minimum wage law, were among Roosevelt's platform known as the "New Nationalism," which he described in 1910.

Hunting the Grisly (1893)

186 **killed a grisly:** The proper name "grizzly" refers to the bears' grizzled, gray hairs. "Grisly" is sometimes used to connote the creature's gruesome nature. Its scientific name, *Ursus arctos horribilis*, comes from this semantic confusion.

186 **head-waters of the Salmon and Clarke's Fork:** The headwaters of the Salmon River are in the mountains of central and eastern Idaho, which Clark Fork runs through in northern Idaho and Montana.

186 **lea of a windbreak:** The lee (or lea) is the sheltered side of a barrier.

187 **still-hunter:** Hunting by slow pursuit or stalking.

187 **toll it to baits:** To draw out or lead prey with bait.

188 **whisky-jacks:** Another name for the gray jay or Canada jay, a member of the crow and jay family.

189 **head-waters of the Madison:** A headwater tributary of the Missouri River, running through Wyoming and Montana.

189 **chickadees and nut-hatches . . . a Clarke's crow:** All passerine birds, sometimes known as perching birds or songbirds. The Clark's nutcracker, also called the Clark's-crow, is named for William Clark (1770–1838), who, along with Meriwether Lewis (1774–1809) led the Lewis and Clark Expedition of 1803–6 through the Louisiana Purchase to the Pacific.

189 **cross-bills:** The crossbill is a type of finch, with mandibles that cross at their tips.

190 **head coulies:** Coulee, or coulée (from the French *couler*, "to flow"), refers to a variety of types of land that contain valleys or drainage zones.

190 **kinnikinnic berries:** A colloquial name for bearberries (genus *Arctostaphylos*), an edible fruit often eaten by bears.

191 **He was quartering to me:** Approach at or near head-on, not offering a flank or rear shot.

A Chilean Rondeo (1913)

196 *rondeo:* As Roosevelt defines it, similar to an American rodeo, that is, "round-up and sports."

196 **Andes into Chile by rail:** Roosevelt was in South America in 1913–14, a planned trip to Argentina and Brazil that was extended into a joint effort with Brazilian explorer Cândido Rondon (1865–1958) to explore the Brazilian "River of Doubt," which was later renamed the Roosevelt River.

196 **Spanish successors:** The first European to arrive in Argentina was Amerigo Vespucci in 1502, with the Spaniard Juan Díaz de Solís arriving in 1516. A series of Spanish settlements were established throughout the 1500s and much of the region came under Spanish rule over the subsequent centuries.

196 **the army of San Martin:** José Francisco de San Martín (1778–1850) was an Argentine general who led the southern part of South America to independence from the Spanish Empire. On 9 July 1816, the Congress of Tucumán met in San Miguel de Tucumán and declared the independence of the United Provinces of South America.

196 **peak of Aconquija:** A 17,740-foot mountain peak in northwestern Argentina, just west of San Miguel de Tucumán.

196 **Santiago:** The capital of Chile, located just west of the Andes Mountains.

197 **known as *huasos* . . . kin to the Argentine *gauchos*:** National terms for skilled horsemen, primarily trained in the herding of livestock.

197 **men wore the light *manta,* less heavy than the *serapi*:** Types of ponchos with fine, colorful woven patterns.

197 **sugar-loaf cones:** Before granulated and cube forms of sugar, a rounded cone was a standard form of refined sugar.

197 **rowels:** The spiked disc on the end of spurs that are attached to riding boots.

198 **graded stock:** Evaluated or graded for market purposes.

198 **the Little Missouri:** A tributary of the Missouri River that runs from Wyoming to North Dakota. Roosevelt's ranch, Elkhorn, was located near the Little Missouri in North Dakota.

201 **galleries and colonnades:** Hallmarks of a traditional Spanish ranch style, as adapted in various South American countries.

The Struggle with the Nullifiers (1887)

206 **Jacksonian Democrats:** During the Second Party System of the 1820s and 1830s, which saw the demise of the Federalists and the rise of newer political parties (like the Whigs), Andrew Jackson (1767–1845) led the split of the Democratic Party from the then-existing Democratic-Republican Party, which had been organized by Thomas Jefferson and James Madison. With his

election as president in 1828, he ushered in a period of "Jacksonian democracy."

206 **Nullifiers:** Begun by then–vice president John C. Calhoun in the early 1830s, the Nullifier Party, based in South Carolina, was a states' rights party that had members in both houses of Congress, and held that states could nullify federal laws within their borders.

206 **very high tariff:** The Tariff of 1828, called the Tariff of Abominations by its southern opponents, protected northern industries and imposed higher taxes on southerners purchasing goods not produced in the South. These taxes were somewhat reduced by the Tariff of 1832.

206 **South Carolina's original complaint:** The Ordinance of Nullification, passed by the South Carolina state convention on 24 November 1832, declared the Tariffs of 1828 and 1832 null and void within the state's borders.

206 **Calhoun:** John Caldwell Calhoun (1782–1850), a political thinker and Democratic politician from South Carolina, served as a United States Representative (1811–17), Secretary of War (1817–25), Vice President (1825–32), Senator (1832–43, 1845–50), and Secretary of State (1844–45). Calhoun was known as one of the "Great Triumvirate" or the "Immortal Trio" of congressmen, along with Daniel Webster and Henry Clay.

206 **series of nullification resolutions:** Beginning with the "South Carolina Exposition and Protest" essay, which became known as "Calhoun's Exposition," in December 1828, Calhoun both wrote and attempted to legislate against the Tariff of 1828, with others following suit.

206 **Webster:** Daniel Webster (1782–1852), an American statesman, primarily representing the Whig party, from Massachusetts, served as U.S. Representative (1813, 1817, 1823–27), Senator (1827–41, 1845–50), and Secretary of State (1841–43, 1850–52).

207 **"higher than Haman":** Haman, the main antagonist in the Book of Esther, plotted to kill all the Jews of ancient Persia and their leader Mordecai. The plot was foiled by Queen Esther, and Haman was hanged from the gallows he had constructed to execute Mordecai.

207 **Henry Clay:** Henry Clay Sr. (1777–1852), a lawyer and politician from Kentucky, served as U.S. Senator (1806–7, 1810–11, 1831–42, 1849–52), U.S. Representative and Speaker of the House (1811–14, 1815–21, 1823–25), and Secretary of State (1825–29). He ran unsuccessfully for president in 1824, 1832, and 1844.

207 **the so-called "Force bill":** On 16 January 1833, President Jackson sent a Force Bill message to Congress, authorizing actions to enforce the Tariffs of 1828 and 1832, including the use of militias and the regular United States military.

207 **Tyler of Virginia:** John Tyler (1790–1862), Virginia politician, served as U.S. Representative (1816–21), Governor of Virginia (1825–27), U.S. Sen-

ator (1827–36), President pro tempore of the Senate (1835), Vice President (1841), President (1841–45), and later became Chancellor of the College of William and Mary (1859–62).

208 **Clay and Calhoun met and agreed on a curious bill:** Following the Force Bill, the Compromise Tariff of 1833 was quickly drafted and approved, which avoided open warfare between the federal government and South Carolina.

208 **Silas Wright:** Silas Wright Jr. (1795–1847), a Democratic politician, served as U.S. Senator (1833–44) and Governor of New York (1845–46). "Dough-face," a disparaging term applied to him by Roosevelt, was used for politicians perceived to be pliable or of weak will, particularly Northern Democrats who allied with Southern Democrats.

211 **[Webster's] reply to Hayne:** The debate over the issue of protectionist tariffs between Daniel Webster and Senator Robert Y. Hayne (1791–1839) of South Carolina took place 19–27 January 1830. Webster's "Second Reply to Hayne," delivered 26–27 January, has come to be regarded as a high point of nineteenth-century political rhetoric, and describes government as "made for the people, made by the people, and answerable to the people," which was paraphrased by Lincoln in his Gettysburg Address of 1863.

211 **his own state was against him:** Thomas Hart Benton (1782–1858), who had served as a U.S. Senator from 1821 to 1851, was denied a sixth term by the Missouri legislature, who considered his position on slavery too moderate. He ran successfully for the U.S. House of Representatives in 1852, but was defeated in 1854 over his opposition to the repeal of the Missouri Compromise. He unsuccessfully ran for Missouri governor in 1856.

212 **"he took up the rod of correction and shook it over her":** Roosevelt is paraphrasing Davy Crockett (1786–1836), frontiersman from Tennessee who served as a U.S. Representative (1827–31, 1833–35). Crockett originally wrote that South Carolina "had a right to expect that the President was favorable to the principle [of nullification]: but he took up the rod of correction, and shook it over South Carolina." The "rod of correction" appears in some translations of Proverbs 29:15.

Minister to France (1888)

214 **two years' history as minister:** Gouverneur Morris (1752–1816) traveled to France on business in 1789 and served as Minister Plenipotentiary to France from 1792 to 1794.

214 **factions of the revolutionists:** The French Revolution, a turbulent period, lasted from 1789 to 1799 during which the monarchy was overthrown. It began with the convocation of the Estates-General in 1789, followed by the founding of a republic in 1792, the deposition and execution of King Louis XVI (1754–1793) and Marie Antoinette (1755–1793) in 1793, the rise of Maximilien

Robespierre (1758–1794) and the Jacobins, who imposed a Reign of Terror, and the Directory, which took control of France from 1795 to 1799, when it was replaced by the Consulate under Napoleon Bonaparte (1769–1821).

214 **payment of our obligations to France:** France had aided America during the Revolutionary War, contributing monetary, military, and diplomatic support. The debt France incurred was one of the major causes of the French Revolution, and the United States flag, in particular, was seen by some as symbolizing misplaced French allegiances.

214 **Mr. Washburne, in the time of the commune:** Elihu Benjamin Washburne (1816–1887), a Maine politician, helped found the Republican Party, served as Secretary of State for eleven days in March 1869 and as minister to France (1869–77). He remained in Paris through the Franco-Prussian War (1870–71), the Siege of Paris (1870–1871), and the Paris Commune. The Paris Commune, or Fourth French Revolution, ruled Paris from 18 March to 28 May 1871, and was seen as the first acquisition of power by the working class during the Industrial Revolution.

215 **effort to save the king's life:** Morris supported Louis XVI's unsuccessful attempt in 1791 to escape from the country, which put him at odds with the Republican government, leading to his recall to the United States.

215 **forty thousand sovereignties:** During one phase of the French Revolution, each district was given authority independent of all others.

215 **the address he had drawn up for Louis:** Louis XVI was forced to accept the constitution of 1791, and speak on its behalf.

215 **fractional sovereignties . . . same sovereignties rise up in successful rebellion:** A direct parallel with the American Revolution.

215 **Lafayette:** The Marquis de La Fayette (1757–1834), a French aristocrat and military officer, was a general in the American Revolutionary War and head of the Garde nationale during the French Revolution. Suspected of being a constitutional monarchist, Lafayette was forced to flee to Austria in 1792 when his soldiers refused to follow his orders.

216 **the maddened mob:** Following the Jacobin Insurrection of 20 June 1792, a series of mob actions commenced, culminating in the storming of Tuileries Palace on 10 August 1792, during which the Swiss Guard were killed and after which Louis XVI fled to the Legislative Assembly.

217 **Count d'Estaing:** Jean Baptiste Charles Henri Hector, comte d'Estaing (1729–1794), a French general and admiral who fought in the War of the Austrian Succession (1740–1748), was a prisoner of the British during the Seven Years' War (1754–63) and led a fleet in 1778 to aid American forces, fighting with them until 1780, when he returned to France. Though sympathetic to the French revolutionaries, he was loyal to the royal family, and was executed during the Reign of Terror.

Champlain (1882)

224 **Champlain:** Lake Champlain, a freshwater lake primarily situated in New York and Vermont, stretching into southern Quebec, was named for French explorer Samuel de Champlain (1574–1635), who encountered it in 1609. It is the site of the port towns of Burlington, Vermont; Port Henry, New York; and Plattsburgh, New York.

224 **greatest naval battle of the war:** Fought on 11 September 1814, the Battle of Plattsburgh (sometimes called the Battle of Lake Champlain) ended the British invasion of the northern states, and was one of the major battles that helped bring the War of 1812 to a close.

224 **Macdonough and Downie:** Thomas Macdonough Jr. (1783–1825), son of a Revolutionary War officer, was an American naval officer who participated in the first Barbary War (1801–5) and the War of 1812. George Downie was the British Royal Navy officer who led the attack on the American fleet at the Battle of Plattsburgh, at which he was killed.

224 **General Macomb:** Alexander Macomb (1782–1841), field commander at the Battle of Plattsburgh, became known as "The Hero of Plattsburgh." Subsequently promoted to Major General, he served as the Commanding General of the U.S. Army from 1828 to 1841.

225 **Lossing says 882 in all:** Benson John Lossing (1813–1891), a popular American historian, published illustrated histories of the American Revolution and Civil War and was featured in popular magazines such as *Harper's*.

225 **prize-money list:** Money paid for captures during or after the battle.

226 **The *Confiance* . . . the *Constellation*, *Congress*, and *Macedonian*:** HMS *Confiance*, a Royal Navy frigate, constructed at the Île aux Noix Naval Shipyards and launched 25 August 1814, was the largest ship at the Battle of Plattsburgh. The U.S. Congress approved the construction of six frigates in 1794, designed to compete with French and British models. Two of those original six frigates, the USS *Constellation*, the first naval vessel put to sea, and the USS *Congress*, were launched in 1797 and 1799, respectively. The USS *Macedonian* was launched in 1810.

226 **spar-deck; on her poop:** The spar deck is another term for the upper deck. The poop deck, on which most of the navigation and steering is done, sits atop the poop cabin at the aft of the ship. The forecastle is a forward elevated deck near the prow of the ship.

226 **Lieutenant E. A. F. Lavallette:** Elie Augustus Frederick La Vallette (1790–1862), a naval officer and historian, was one of the first rear admirals appointed to the rank after its creation in 1862.

227 **Commander Ward:** James Harmon Ward (1806–1861), commander of the *Jamestown* in the 1850s, which hunted slave ships off the coast of Africa, published *A Manual of Naval Tactics* (1859) and was the first officer of the U.S. Navy killed during the American Civil War.

227 **Sir George Prevost:** Sir George Prévost, 1st Baronet (1767–1816), a British soldier and colonial administrator, served in the West Indies and North America. He was commander of St. Vincent (1794–96); lieutenant governor of St. Lucia (1798–1802); and governor of Dominica (1802–5). During the War of 1812, he served as the civilian Governor General and military Commander in Chief in British North America, which is now part of Canada. Following the Plattsburgh loss, Prévost was relieved of his command.

228 **kedge . . . with a hawser:** A kedge is a light anchor; a hawser, a cable or rope used for mooring or towing a ship.

229 **laid athwart the hawse:** Athwart, from side to side of a ship; hawse, the opening through which an anchor chain or rope passes.

231 **bow-gun:** One of the forwardmost guns on the deck.

231 **quoin:** A wedge used to elevate a gun.

235 **the victory had a very great effect on the negotiations for peace:** The American victory at Plattsburgh stopped the British advances, which, in combination with British failure at the Battle of Baltimore (12–15 September 1814), kept the British from gaining territory via the Treaty of Ghent (signed on 24 December 1814, ratified by the United Kingdom on 30 December 1814). Before news of the treaty's signing reached North America, the Battle of New Orleans was fought (8 January 1815). The treaty was ratified by the U.S. Congress in February 1815.

The Spread of the English-Speaking Peoples (1889)

239 **world's waste spaces:** An expansionist descriptive phrase for largely unoccupied lands, or lands claimed by indigenous peoples.

239 **Bacon:** Francis Bacon (1561–1626), an English philosopher, statesman, and author, served as Attorney General and Lord Chancellor of England. His education was in Latin, as were many of his published works, including *Novum Organum Scientiarum* (1620), from which the "Baconian method" of inductive scientific reasoning derives.

239 **Common Law which Coke jealously upheld:** Sir Edward Coke (1552–1634), an English barrister and judge considered to be the greatest jurist of the Elizabethan era, was known for defending the role of common law, rather than drawing only on established statutes and royal decree.

239 **other races . . . race expansion:** Roosevelt uses "race" throughout as a substitute for national and cultural heritages and peoples.

240 **Teutoburger Wald, when the legions of Varus were broken by the rush of Hermann's wild warriors:** In the Battle of the Teutoburg Forest in AD 9 a group of Germanic tribes led by Arminius (18/17 BC–AD 21), also known as Hermann, of the Cheruscia destroyed three Roman legions and their auxiliaries, led by Publius Quinctilius Varus (46 BC–AD 9).

240 **woodland east of the Rhine:** Primarily, the Black Forest region of southeast Germany.

240 **Volga to the Pillars of Hercules:** The Volga is the longest river in Europe, and runs through central Russia to empty into the Caspian Sea. The Pillars of Hercules is the classical term for the promontories on either side of the Strait of Gibraltar at the entrance to the Mediterranean Sea.

240 **sons of Odin:** In traditional Eddic poems, Thor, Baldur, and Váil are identified as sons of Odin; here, the god of war and death as well as poetry and wisdom refers to peoples of Germanic origin.

240 **Rome and Novgorod:** The respective capitals of the much-contested lands that would become parts of modern Italy and Russia.

240 **descendants of Alaric, as well as to the children of Rurik:** Alaric I (370–410), King of the Visigoths (395–410), sacked Rome in 410. Rurik (ca. 830–ca. 879), a Varangian chieftain, founded the Rurik Dynasty, which ruled Russia until the seventeenth century.

240 **The Dane in Ireland became a Celt:** A broad overview of European cultural lines, from the era of scattered tribes into the Middle Ages.

241 **Theodoric, and Clovis:** Theodoric the Great (454–526) was king of the Ostrogoths (471–526), conqueror and ruler of Italy (493–526), as well as regent of the Visigoths (511–26) and a viceroy of the Eastern Roman Empire. Clovis I (ca. 466–511), or Chlodowech, was the first king to unite all of the Frankish tribes under one ruler (509–11), and the first Christian king, having been baptized in 496, to rule Gaul, now modern France.

241 **the race of Goth, Frank, and Burgund:** The Goths became Italians and Spaniards; the Franks were later French; the Burgundians, a Germanic people, largely became French (in the Burgundy region).

241 **Saxon, Anglian, and Friesic warriors:** The northern and western European tribes of Germany, the Netherlands, and France, who spread to the British Isles and over northern Europe.

242 **Alfred reigned:** Alfred the Great (849–899), King of Wessex from 871 to 899, defended his kingdom from Vikings and was the first to appear as King of the Anglo-Saxons.

242 **Charlemagne reigned:** Charlemagne (ca. 742–814), also known as Charles the Great or Charles I, founded the Carolingian Empire, over which he reigned from 768 to 814, expanding the Frankish kingdom to include Italy and parts of Spain, making him the first emperor in western Europe since the end of the Roman Empire.

242 **dynasty of the Capets:** The House of Capet ruled the Kingdom of France from 987 to 1328, succeeding the Carolingian dynasty.

242 **people across the Channel then showed little trace of Celtic or Romance influence:** Roosevelt here argues for an English distinctiveness, after the

time of Alfred, derived from Anglo-Saxon roots, and thus not directly influenced by later continental changes.

242 **Vercingetorix or Cæsar, Clovis or Syagrius:** Vercingetorix (ca. 82–46 BC) was the chieftain who united the Gauls in an unsuccessful revolt against Roman forces during the Gallic Wars (58–50 BC), which took place during the reign of Julius Caesar (100–44 BC). Vercingetorix was paraded through Rome before his execution. Clovis I (c. 466–511) of the Franks defeated Syagrius (430–486/7), the last Roman official in Gaul, marking the end of Western Roman rule.

242 **half-mythical glories of Hengist and Horsa:** Recorded as Germanic brothers, these fifth-century figures of Anglo-Saxon legend led the Angle, Saxon, and Jutish armies to conquer territories in Britain.

243 **Civilis the Batavian:** Gaius Julius Civilis led the Batavian rebellion in 69–70 that led to a series of Roman defeats. The Roman army ultimately defeated the rebels.

243 **Silurian chief Caractacus . . . Emperor Vespasian:** The Silures were an ancient Welsh tribe. Caratacus, a first-century British chieftain, led the resistance to Roman forces. Vespasian (9–79) was the founder of the Flavian dynasty, a successful military commander continuing the Roman invasion of Britain, and Roman Emperor from 69 to 79.

245 **rivals waged many a long war:** The French, Dutch, and English.

245 **fleets of Holland:** The Dutch Navy became the most powerful in the world in the seventeenth century, destroying a large component of the Spanish fleet and fighting a series of naval battles with the English throughout the latter half of the century.

248 **Greek colonists in the Tauric Chersonese:** The Tauric Chersonese was the name by which the Crimean Peninsula was known by the Greeks and Romans. Roosevelt here predicts the twentieth-century racial tensions in South Africa by drawing an analogy with the failure of the Greek colonizing presence in the Crimean.

248 **wars of Rome and Carthage:** Namely, the Punic Wars, a series of three wars between Rome and Carthage from 264 to 146 BC.

249 **voyageurs and coureurs des bois:** Fur traders and their companies were primarily responsible for the exploration and expansion through Canada from the 1500s through 1800s. *Voyageurs* were those engaged in the transport of furs by canoe. *Coureurs des bois*, or "runners of the woods," were French-Canadian woodsmen, fur trappers, and traders.

249 **Red River and the Saskatchewan a singular race of half-breeds:** The Red River flows north through Minnesota, North Dakota, and Manitoba into Lake Winnipeg. The Saskatchewan River flows eastward across Saskatchewan and Manitoba into Lake Winnipeg. Roosevelt here refers loosely to what were called the "half-breed" or *métis* peoples of Canada.

250 **de Soto would have repeated the work of Cortes:** Spanish explorer Hernando de Soto (ca.1496/7–1542) led the first European expedition into what is now the United States, becoming the first European to cross the Mississippi River and encounter the native populations living nearby. Hernán Cortés de Monroy y Pizarro (1485–1547), a Spanish conquistador, led an expedition that led to the fall of the Aztec Empire and the colonization of Mexico.

251 **territory between the Ohio and the Great Lakes:** Britain relinquished most of this land after the American Revolutionary War.

251 **By a purchase:** The Louisiana Purchase of 1803, by which the United States acquired a large swath of land from France.

253 **Celt of Cornwall and the Saxon of Wessex:** The peoples of southwest England, now unified by geography and a common culture.

253 **Hollander and Huguenot, whether in New York or South Carolina:** The Huguenots, fleeing religious persecution, settled in the American colonies. "Hollander" is the informal term for someone from the Netherlands and can be used derogatorily.

253 **followed Cromwell or charged behind Rupert:** Oliver Cromwell (1599–1658), an English military and political figure, served as a military commander during the English Civil War (1642–1646) and later became Lord Protector of England, Wales, Scotland, and Ireland in 1653 after dismissing the Rump Parliament by force. Prince Rupert of the Rhine (1619–1682), a soldier, admiral, and colonial governor, fought the Spanish during the Eighty Years' War (1568–1648) and was commander of the Royalist cavalry during the English Civil War.

The Cavalry at Santiago (1899)

259 **toward Santiago:** The main fighting of the decisive battle of the Spanish-American War (1898), the Battle of San Juan Hill, took place on 1 July 1898, on what American forces termed San Juan Hill and Kettle Hill, just outside Santiago, Cuba.

259 **Lawton's infantry division:** Henry Lawton (1843–1899), a U.S. Army officer, served in the Civil War, Apache Wars, and Spanish-American War, and was killed in the Philippine-American War. A borough of Havana, Cuba, takes its name from Lawton.

259 **El Caney:** A Spanish stronghold outside Santiago.

259 **Wood:** Leonard Wood (1860–1927) was a physician who served presidents Grover Cleveland and William McKinley. With Roosevelt, Wood helped organize the 1st Volunteer Cavalry regiment, known as the Rough Riders, to fight in the Spanish-American War. After the Battle of San Juan, Wood led the 2nd Cavalry Brigade, and then remained in Cuba, where he served as military governor of Santiago in 1898 and of Cuba from 1899 to 1902. Wood was later named U.S. Army Chief of Staff in 1910.

260 **Mason Mitchell:** A New York stage actor who joined the Rough Riders.

261 **Kent's infantry:** Jacob Ford Kent (1835–1918) was a U.S. Army general who served in the Civil War and Spanish-American War. Kent was in command of the 1st Division, encompassing the 1st Brigade (6th U.S. Infantry, 16th U.S. Infantry, 71st New York Volunteer Infantry), the 2nd Brigade (2nd U.S. Infantry, 10th U.S. Infantry, 21st U.S. Infantry), and the 3rd Brigade (9th U.S. Infantry, 13th U.S. Infantry, 24th U.S. Infantry).

262 **Bucky O'Neill:** William Owen "Buckey" O'Neill (1860–1898), American soldier, sheriff, newspaper editor, politician, and lawyer, was killed at the Battle of San Juan Hill.

263 **General Sumner:** Samuel Storrow Sumner (1842–1937), a U.S. Army general during the Spanish-American War, Boxer Rebellion (1899–1901), and Philippine-American War (1899–1902), was in command, along with Major General Wheeler, of the Cavalry Division, encompassing the 1st Brigade (3rd U.S. Volunteer Cavalry, 6th U.S. Cavalry, 9th U.S. Cavalry) and the 2nd Brigade (1st U.S. Cavalry, 10th U.S. Cavalry, 1st U.S. Volunteer Cavalry, the "Rough Riders").

264 **my "crowded hour" began:** The term Roosevelt would often invoke to describe his heroism at the Battle of San Juan Hill.

267 **guidons planted:** Guidons are military flags specific to a company or platoon.

269 **carbines . . . Gatlings:** A carbine is a firearm shorter than a rifle or musket. The Gatling gun, an early rapid-fire weapon, invented by Richard Gatling (1818–1903), was first introduced during the American Civil War.

270 **battle-ship *Maine* . . . my brother-in-law, Captain W. S. Cowles:** The USS *Maine* was the Navy's second battleship, launched in 1890. It was sunk by an explosion in the Havana harbor, 15 February 1898, which was blamed on Spain (without much evidence), leading to the call to action "Remember the Maine, to Hell with Spain!" that helped precipitate the Spanish-American War. William Sheffield Cowles (1846–1923) was a rear admiral in the U.S. Navy, commanded a gunboat during the Spanish-American War, and served as naval aide to William McKinley (1843–1901). Cowles married Anna Roosevelt (1855–1931), Roosevelt's eldest sister, in 1895.

272 **the antiquated Springfield:** A reference to older Springfield muskets and breech-loading rifles, which were inferior to their cartridge-loaded replacements.

274 **General Wheeler:** Joseph Wheeler (1836–1906), an American military officer and later politician, served as a general in the Confederate States Army during the Civil War, and later in the U.S. Army in the Spanish-American and Philippine-American Wars. Between wars, Wheeler served as U.S. representative from Alabama from 1882 to 1900.

History as Literature (1912)

282 **science claims exclusive possession of the field:** In the early twentieth century, the academic study of history was shifting from epic narratives that glorified nations or great men to objective analyses of social, economic, and intellectual forces.

282 **Virgil left history to Livy:** Publius Vergilius Maro (70–19 BC), known as Virgil, was a Roman poet and author of the *Aeneid*, the *Eclogues*, and the *Georgics*. Titus Livius Patavinus (59 BC–AD 17), known as Livy, was a Roman historian and author of *Ab Urbe Condita Libri*, "Books from the Foundation of the City."

282 **when Tacitus had become possible Lucan was a rather absurd anachronism:** Publius (or Gaius) Cornelius Tacitus (56–117), a Roman senator and historian, was author of the *Annals* and the *Histories*. Marcus Annaeus Lucanus (39–65), known as Lucan, a Roman poet, was known for his youth and quick compositions.

283 **the witch who dwelt under the water:** One of the main antagonists of the Old English epic *Beowulf*, Grendel's mother dwells in a lake and is often referred to as a "water witch."

283 **Hound of Murithemne and Emer the Fair:** Variously known as the Hound of Ulster, or Cuchulain of Muirthemnem, all are versions of the Cú Chulainn, an Irish legend. Emer the Fair is Cuchulain's lover.

283 **Roland who blew the ivory horn at Roncesvalles:** The oldest surviving major work in French, *La Chanson de Roland* is a heroic poem about the Battle of Roncesvalles (a pass in the Pyrenees) in 778 during which Roland, a prefect of the Breton March and commander of the rear guard of Charlemagne's army, fell to the Basques.

285 **comparative osteology:** The comparative study of bones, skeletons, teeth, etc.

286 **Darwin and Huxley:** Thomas Henry Huxley (1825–1895), an English biologist, advocated Darwin's theory of evolution and was known as "Darwin's Bulldog."

286 **Lamarck and Cope:** Jean-Baptiste Pierre Antoine de Monet, Chevalier de Lamarck (1744–1829), a French naturalist, formulated a Theory of Inheritance that was surpassed by Darwin's theory of evolution. Edward Drinker Cope (1840–1897) was an American paleontologist and founder of the Neo-Lamarckism school of thought.

288 **Technical training will more and more be accepted:** In the early twentieth century, efforts by figures such as Holmes Beckwith (1884–1921) were made to introduce new vocational, apprenticeship, and continuation schools based on German models.

289 **his theory:** Carlyle popularized the Great Man Theory of history, by which historical turns are largely explained by the impact of singularly influential figures.

290 **the Danites in their dealings with the people of Laish . . . Owen Wister's "Pilgrim on the Gila":** Recounted in the *Book of Judges*, the Tribe of Dan, one of the Tribes of Israel, conquered Laish, which they burned to the ground and rebuilt, naming the town Dan. Owen Wister (1860–1938), a novelist famous for his tales of the West, wrote "A Pilgrim on the Gila," a short story in *Red Men and White* (1895).

291 **archers of Agincourt, and the war-worn spearmen who followed Alexander:** The Battle of Agincourt (25 October 1415, Saint Crispin's Day) was a major English victory during the Hundred Years' War, during which Henry V's army, supported by large numbers of longbowmen, defeated the superior French army. Alexander III of Macedon (356–323 BC), known as Alexander the Great, never lost a battle and introduced new tactics, including the Macedonian phalanx, armed with long spears (the six-meter *sarissa*).

292 **Timour the Lame ride over the roof of the world:** Timur, Tarmashirin Khan, Emir Timur (known as Tamerlane, 1336–1405) was a Turco-Mongolian ruler who conquered West, South, and Central Asia and founded the Timurid dynasty (1370–1526). The "roof of the world" is a metaphoric description of the mountainous interior of Asia, including the Himalayas, Tibet, and Mount Everest.

292 **drums beat as the armies of Gustavus and Frederick and Napoleon drive forward to victory:** Roosevelt is referring to Gustav II Adolf (1594–1632), known as Gustavus Adolphus, who was widely regarded as one of the greatest military commanders. King of Sweden from 1611 to 1632, he led Sweden to supremacy through the Thirty Years' War (1618–48) and was known for his victory at the battle of Breitenfeld (1631). Frederick II (1712–1786), known as Frederick the Great, and King of Prussia (1740–86) from the Hohenzollern family succession, was known for his military prowess and organization of Prussian armies.

An Introduction to American Literature (1896)

296 **Mr. Brander Matthews's volume on American literature:** *An Introduction to the Study of American Literature* (New York: American Book Co., 1896) was one of the first textbooks solely devoted to American authors and their works.

296 **Darwin or Gibbon:** Charles Robert Darwin (1809–1882), English naturalist, whose *On the Origin of Species* (1859) established a theory of evolution based on descent from common ancestors and natural selection. Edward Gibbon (1737–1794), an English historian and Member of Parliament, whose six-volume *The History of the Decline and Fall of the Roman Empire* was published between 1776 and 1788.

297 **Biglow papers:** An 1848 collection of poetry by James Russell Lowell (1819–1891), one of the Fireside Poets, New England writers who rivaled the popu-

larity of British poets. *The Biglow Papers* featured three characters, speaking in regional American dialects.

297 **homely tongue:** That is, vernacular.

298 **Mr. Matthews in his "Americanisms and Briticisms":** The initial essay in Matthews's collection *Americanisms and Briticisms, With Other Essays on Other Isms* (1892) deals with notions of national literature and criticism.

298 **Halleck and Drake:** Fitz-Greene Halleck (1790–1867), an American poet sometimes called "the American Byron" and one of the Knickerbocker Group, wrote and published the anonymous *Croaker Papers* in 1819, satires of New York society, with his friend Joseph Rodman Drake (1795–1820).

298 **Motley and Prescott:** John Lothrop Motley (1814–1877), historian and diplomat, wrote epic histories: *The Rise of the Dutch Republic* (3 vols., 1856) and the *History of the United Netherlands* (4 vols., 1860–67). William Hickling Prescott (1796–1859), historian and Hispanist, wrote histories of Spain as well as of Peru and, most famously, *The Conquest of Mexico* (1843).

298 **Longfellow's ballad-like poems:** Henry Wadsworth Longfellow (1807–1882), the American poet known for the epic works *Evangeline, A Tale of Acadie* (1847), and *The Song of Hiawatha* (1855), as well as the popular poem "Paul Revere's Ride" (1860), was one of the five Fireside Poets. "The Saga of King Olaf" appeared in *Tales of a Wayside Inn* (1863), "The Discoverer of the North Cape" appeared in *Birds of Passage* (1858).

299 **he shows . . . his appreciation of that side of Franklin's character:** In *American Literature*, Matthews's passage reads: "Like Lincoln, he knew the world well and accepted it for what it was, and made the best of it, expecting no more. But Franklin lacked the spirituality, the faith in the ideal, which was at the core of Lincoln's character. And here was Franklin's limitation: what lay outside of the bounds of common sense he did not see—probably he did not greatly care to see; but common sense he had in a most uncommon degree."

Nationalism in Literature and Art (1916)

302 **Mr. Chancellor . . . Monsieur Lanson:** The meeting of the American Academy of Arts and Letters, presided over by Chancellor William M. Sloane, was held at the Ritz-Carlton Hotel, New York City, 16–17 November 1916. Monsieur Gustave Lanson (1857–1934), French historian and literary critic, who helped reform the French university system in the twentieth century, spoke before Roosevelt, delivering an address titled "La Fonction des Influences Étrangères dans le Développement de la Littérature Française."

303 **as John Burroughs has said:** John Burroughs (1837–1921), naturalist and essayist, was known for his nature essays and support of the conservation movement. Burroughs published a memoir of his camping trip in Yellowstone National Park with Roosevelt, *Camping and Tramping with Roosevelt* (1906).

303 **cult of belfry patriotism:** That is, patriotism limited to provincial or local interests.

306 **the names of our writers, painters, and poets of today show the growing divergence:** Roosevelt is referring to "Is Our Literature Still English?" by H. Houston Peckham, in *The Sewanee Review* 24/3 (July 1916): 331–39.

307 **Bade's "The Old Testament in the Light of Today":** A 1915 book by William Frederic Badè (1871–1936), a religious scholar who also worked with conservation groups, including the Sierra Club.

307 **Gustavus Ohlinger's "Their True Faith and Allegiance":** A 1917 book by Gustavus Ohlinger (1877–1972), a Toledo lawyer who incited strong anti-German sentiments during the first World War.

308 **Remington when he painted the soldier, the cowboy, and the Indian:** Frederic S. Remington (1861–1909), an American painter, illustrator, and sculptor, was known for his depictions of the American West.

309 **Joel Barlow:** Joel Barlow (1754–1812), poet, diplomat, and politician, helped draft the Treaty of Tripoli in 1796 and was best known in his time for the epic *Vision of Columbus* (1787), which he extended and elaborated into the *Columbiad* (1807).

309 **Marcius-Simons:** Pinckney Marcius-Simons (1865–1909), an American painter who lived and worked in Europe, had important one-man shows in New York, Boston, and Chicago in the 1890s and 1900s. Roosevelt was one of Marcius-Simons's patrons.

309 **Lady Gregory:** Isabella Augusta, Lady Gregory (1852–1932), an Irish playwright and folklorist, cofounded the Irish Literary Theatre and the Abbey Theatre with William Butler Yeats (1865–1939) and Edward Martyn (1859–1923), and was a leading figure of the Irish Literary Revival.

310 **no American has ever heard the skylark in America:** Oliver Wendell Holmes (1809–1894), physician and poet, claimed it took a century to banish the lark from American literature. The only lark species native to North America is the horned lark. Somewhat figuratively, Holmes was calling for an honest American literary imagery; Roosevelt is making the case rather literally.

310 **average American writer has read Hogg:** James Hogg (1770–1835), a Scottish poet and novelist and contemporary of Sir Walter Scott (1771–1832), known as "Ettrick Shepherd," and author of *The Private Memoirs and Confessions of a Justified Sinner* (1824).

311 **Velasquez and Murillo . . . Rembrandt:** Diego Rodríguez de Silva y Velázquez (1599–1660), a Spanish Baroque painter in the court of King Philip IV, is known for his masterpiece *Las Meninas* (1656). Bartolomé Esteban Murillo (1617–1682), a Spanish Baroque painter, is known for his religious subjects and paintings of everyday woman and children. Rembrandt Harmenszoon van Rijn (1606–1669) helped inaugurate the Dutch Golden Age of painting.

311 **an Egyptian obelisk in Central Park . . . Saint Gaudens's Farragut . . . MacMonnies's Kit Carson:** Known as "Cleopatra's Needle," an Egyptian obelisk whose American site was arranged in 1877 (along with a twin transported to London), was erected in New York City's Central Park in 1881. The major commissions of Augustus Saint-Gaudens (1848–1907), an Irish-born American sculptor in the Beaux-Arts tradition, included a monument to Civil War Admiral David Farragut (1801–1870), unveiled in 1881; an equestrian monument to Civil War General William Tecumseh Sherman finished in 1903; and a large standing Abraham Lincoln in Lincoln Park, Chicago, finished in 1887. Frederick William MacMonnies (1863–1937), an expatriate American sculptor of the Beaux-Arts school, and known for his *Columbian Fountain* at the 1893 World's Columbian Exposition, sculpted a monument in Denver at the end of the Smoky Hill Trail of frontiersman Kit Carson (1809–1868), unveiled in 1911.

BIBLIOGRAPHY

Aaron, Daniel. "Theodore Roosevelt as Cultural Artifact." In *Raritan: A Quarterly Review* 9/3 (1990): 109–26.

Brinkley, Douglas. *The Wilderness Warrior: Theodore Roosevelt and the Crusade for America*. New York: HarperCollins, 2009.

Burton, David H. "Theodore Roosevelt: Learned Style." In *The Learned Presidency: Theodore Roosevelt, William Howard Taft, Woodrow Wilson*. Rutherford, NJ: Fairleigh Dickinson University Press, 1988, 38–88.

Dalton, Kathleen. *Theodore Roosevelt: A Strenuous Life*. New York: Random House, 2002.

Dinunzio, Mario R., ed. *Theodore Roosevelt: An American Mind*. New York: St. Martin's, 1994.

Horne, Philip. "Henry James and 'the forces of violence': On the Track of 'big game' in 'The Jolly Corner.'" In *Henry James Review* 27/3 (2006): 237–47.

Kaplan, Amy. "Black and Blue on San Juan Hill." In *Cultures of United States Imperialism*. Edited by Donald Pease and Amy Kaplan. Durham, NC: Duke University Press, 1993, 219–36.

Mathews, Brander. "Theodore Roosevelt as a Man of Letters." In *The Tocsin of Revolt and Other Essays*. New York: Scribner's, 1922, 229–50.

McCullough, David. *Mornings on Horseback: The Story of an Extraordinary Family, a Vanished Way of Life and the Unique Child Who Became Theodore Roosevelt*. New York: Simon and Schuster, 1982.

Moers, Ellen. "Teddy Roosevelt: Literary Feller." In *Columbia University Forum* 6/3 (Summer 1963): 10–16.

Morris, Edmund. "Theodore Roosevelt the Writer." In *This Living Hand*. New York: Random House, 2012, 95–125.

——. *The Rise of Theodore Roosevelt*. New York: Coward, McGann & Geoghegan, 1979.

——. *Theodore Rex*. New York: Random House, 2001.

——. *Colonel Roosevelt*. New York: Random House, 2011.

Oliver, Lawrence. *Brander Matthews, Theodore Roosevelt, and the Politics of American Literature: 1880–1920*. Knoxville: University of Tennessee Press, 1992.

——, ed. *The Letters of Theodore Roosevelt and Brander Matthews*. Knoxville: University of Tennessee Press, 1995.

Schlesinger, Arthur Jr. "The Pragmatic Hero." In *Partisan Review* 18/4 (July–August 1951): 466–71.

Taubenfield, Aviva F. "Making American Homes and America Home: Theodore Roosevelt and Elizabeth Stern in the Pages of the *Ladies' Home Journal.*" In *Rough Writing: Ethnic Authorship in Theodore Roosevelt's America.* New York: New York University Press, 2008, 41–76.

Wald, Priscilla. *Constituting Americans: Cultural Anxiety and Narrative Form.* Durham, NC: Duke University Press, 1995.

INDEX

Page numbers from 313–346 refer to endnotes.